365 GODDESS

365
Goddess

A Daily Guide to
the Magic and Inspiration
of the Goddess

PATRICIA TELESCO

HarperSanFrancisco
A Division of HarperCollins*Publishers*

HarperCollins Web Site: http://www.harpercollins.com

HarperCollins®, ▲ ®, and HarperSanFrancisco™ are trademarks of Harper-Collins Publishers, Inc.

HarperCollins books may be purchased for educational, business, or sales promotional use. For information please write: Special Markets Department, HarperCollins Publishers, Inc., 10 East 53rd Street, New York, NY 10022.

FIRST EDITION

Designed by Laura Lindgren

Library of Congress Cataloging-in-Publication Data
Telesco, Patricia.
     365 goddess : a daily guide to the magic and inspiration of the goddess /
Patricia. — 1st ed.
         p. cm.
     Includes bibliographical references.
     ISBN 0–06–251568–3
     1. Goddess religion—Prayer-books and devotions—English. 2. Devo-
tional calendars. I. Title.
BL325.F4T45 1998
291.1'4—dc21   98–7447

     99 00 01 02 ❖RRD(H) 10 9 8 7 6 5 4 3

For all those walking the Paths of Beauty:
May the Goddess unify us to revel in our diversity
and teach us that we are all truly children
of one Creator and one home: the earth.
And, no matter where you may be,
May the Goddess bless and keep you
and fill every moment of your life
with her very special magic

Acknowledgments

The author gratefully thanks the excellent efforts of the customer service department at Amazon Books (www.amazon.com) and the marketing department at ABC-Clio (www.abc-clio.com) in obtaining reference materials for this book. She also extends heartfelt appreciation to everyone at Harper for their hospitality, support, and patience.

Introduction

Our ancient ancestors the world over looked to nature and the force behind all creation, the Goddess, to provide insights into the way the world works. They did this recognizing that a truly healthy and happy existence wasn't forged solely in the temporal fires of earthly life. It depended on blending, balancing, and tempering everyday reality with spiritual principles.

Careful scrutiny of nature and its cycles led our forebears to associate every season with the Goddess in one of her forms. Come spring, she was a youthful dawn goddess full of blossoming enthusiasm. In summer, the Goddess was a fertile maiden. Autumn finds the Goddess just past her child-bearing years, reaping the rewards of hard labors. Finally, in winter she became the midnight crone, wise, weary, and ready to rest with the earth.

This goddess cycle became part of worldwide annual observances, festivals, and holidays. I wrote this book to introduce you to as many of these observances as I could, as well as others that somehow accented goddess energy. No matter the era or culture, people everywhere could be found celebrating her throughout the year in ways suited to the unique energies of a setting, date, or cycle. I hope you will join that celebration by dipping into this book each day, using the Goddess's magic to guide and enrich your life.

Unfortunately, not all systems of marking time's passage were the same, especially when East met West. Consequently, the timing for some festivals changes a great deal from year to year, or region to region, but this deviation won't spoil your daily efforts to honor the

Goddess in any way. You see, the heart of your celebration—the Goddess—is changeless and eternal. Her magic works outside of time and outside human convention, which is exactly why miracles are miracles! What's most important here isn't the exact date or holiday. It's taking the time to look at, appreciate, honor, and internalize the sacred energies of the Goddess in truly meaningful ways.

But which goddess is best suited to help with this personal recreation? The world's nations depict the Goddess with many different names, faces, and characteristics—but these are really all part of the same potent lady. As with a crystal that has distinct facets and angles, what one sees depends much on where one stands. These pages allow you to figuratively stand in a different cultural location every day and look at 365 different faces of the Goddess. From this vantage point, using the season's or holiday's themes and the activities provided, you can accent a particular goddess's attributes within to positively transform your reality, one day at a time.

So when you find the apathy bug biting at your heels, when you feel like your daily routine has become drab, when you yearn for a spiritual anchor to hold you firm in life's hectic storm, or when you want some real soul food, look to the Goddess and her scintillating magic for help and sustenance. She stands ready and waiting to become a partner with you in remodeling every corner of your life. By adorning yourself with her power, you can effectively apply the potential each day offers for exciting, empowering magic.

Like any great adventure, the process of personal change begins with just one step. So turn the page and begin. Ponder the day's goddess and how her special attributes might be significant for you right now. Allow her to become a new friend and an ally in achieving your hopes and dreams. Then apply the symbols and activities, adding heaping quantities of originality and personal vision, to rediscover the Goddess's magic that is already part of your spirit, the world, and every moment of living.

Helpful Hints for Using This Book

1. Peek ahead a day and scan the activities. If there's anything special you need to find or get, do so while you're out and about. This way you won't have to scramble for items at the last minute.
2. Before trying any activity, consider if you want to change, adapt, or personalize it in any way. Remember, if a magical procedure doesn't hold meaning for you, it probably won't work.
3. As you undertake each activity, recognize that you already have the Goddess's potential inside you. The exercises only augment and activate that potential. So, even if you don't have the exact components suggested, you have the most important ingredient for successful magic—*you*.
4. Repeat the activities that prove successful and personally pleasing anytime you wish. The dates provided in this book are only a sample construct for keeping your year filled with goddess energy. But really, anytime is the right time to call on the Goddess's power and work her magic.
5. If you have a pressing need in your life, look in the index under that topic (such as love, health, or wealth). Review the spells, charms, and other activities in the dates listed to see if any might help you *now!*
6. Follow this book day by day, or just open it randomly and see what the Goddess has to say to your heart. The pages here are dated only for convenience. Let your inner voice guide you in determining which approach to this book will be the most life-affirming and helpful for you.

365 GODDESS

January

J anuary starts the year with a plethora of fun, frolicsome festivity. The new year in particular is celebrated by at least 170 nations. The month gets its name from Jana, a moon goddess, which explains the abundance of water-related observances this month (in esoteric traditions, the moon represents the water element). It's also named after Janus (Jana's husband), the gatekeeper of heaven, who sees the past and future (see January 9). This couple oversees the year's beginning by offering you refreshed perspective and hope for a better tomorrow.

In terms of energy, January focuses on beginnings. It's a time for personal renewal, starting any beloved project, and sustaining those things already in progress. Magic for health, protection, and prosperity is particularly augmented by working during this month.

January 1

New Year's Day (Europe/United States)

GAMELIA

Themes: Luck; Health; Prosperity; New Beginnings

Symbols: Two-sided Items, Representing the Old and New (like coins and hourglasses)

About Gamelia: Gamelia is a lucky aspect of the Greek goddess Hera, who brings good fortune (especially in love). On this day of new beginnings, Gamelia extends a helping hand by teaching about the cycles in your life and how to cope with them more effectively, adding a little luck to make things easier. In ancient times, people would wash Gamelia's statues on this day, symbolically wiping winter away. They would also hang bay, palm, dates, and figs around the house to inspire a year filled with Gamelia's blessings.

To Do Today: Remember Gamelia today to manifest her luck and joy in your life. Eat dates or figs (raisins are a handy substitute), leaving a little outside as an offering to her.

To encourage a fresh start, consider turning over an hourglass (or egg timer) as midnight tolls. As you turn the hourglass, recite this incantation:

> *The sands of time turn again; with them new life begins.*
> *The old now departs; Gamelia, refresh my heart.*

For prosperity in the new year, carry any silver-colored coin in your pocket the entire day, then use it to make a wish at any nearby fountain or water source. To foster Gamelia's help with the wish, burn a little myrrh incense.

January 2

Shigoto Hajime (Japan)

BENTEN

Themes: Luck; Wealth; Beauty

Symbols: Boats; Dragons; Guitars; Snakes; Saltwater

About Benten: As the Japanese goddess steering the New Year's Treasure Ship, Benten is a perfect figure to call on for financial improvements this year. She is the only goddess of luck in Japan and is referred to as queen of the seas and patroness of gamblers. Japanese women invoke her to bring beauty and fortune into their lives. Benten is depicted as riding a gold dragon, playing a *biwa* (guitar), and sending out white snakes with her missives. Her robe bears a jewel that grants wishes.

To Do Today: To welcome Benten's prosperity into your home, sprinkle a little saltwater on the threshold today. Or, to generate beauty within and without, soak in a bath of Epsom salts while listening to guitar music.

The Shigoto Hajime festival honors the beginning of the work week in Japan, where it is believed that good omens for work begin today. If you want to get a peek at how your employment will fare this year, try divination by dice (a traditional gambler's tool). Hold one die in your hand, ask for Benten to provide a sign, then roll it. The results can be interpreted as follows: (1) a negative omen; (2) feeling torn between two good options; (3) a good omen; (4) financial security; (5) not much material change, but improvements in interoffice relationships; (6) an excellent omen; roll again. If you get two more sixes, Benten's treasures will be yours!

January 3
☾

Third Day of the First Moon (China)

CHIN MU

Themes: Health; Longevity; Femininity; Magic

Symbols: Peach; Mulberry; Cats; Gold-toned Objects

About Chin Mu: Chin Mu is the Queen of the West in China, dispensing peaches that cure disease and grant eternal life to all who eat them. Chinese art depicts her as an ageless, beautiful woman living in a golden castle (a solar symbol), thereby getting her translated name of "golden mother." She is also sometimes shown as a cat-woman, which represents her *yin* energy and connection with sorcery.

To Do Today: Honoring Chin Mu today brings health, long life, and a year filled with magic. One simple way to do this is by wearing a piece of gold jewelry or gold clothing.

Traditionally, Chinese women carry a bowl of hot vinegar into each room of the house today to protect those who live there from sickness all year. To try this yourself, slice up a peach (frozen if necessary) and add it to the heated vinegar (peach tea bags work, too, and release a nice fragrance). The peach invokes Chin Mu's blessing. Walk clockwise around the home, visualizing it filled with golden light (you can pray or chant as you go, if you wish). If you're pressed for time, eat a peach or drink some mulberry wine instead and internalize Chin Mu's hearty energies just the same!

Finally, meditate on the feminine aspects of yourself and the divine (a good time to do this is during your morning shower, or while driving to work). Honor the women who have influenced your life, even if you do this just by saying thanks.

January 4

☾

Chilseong-je (Korea)

CALLISTO

Themes: Instinct; Protection; Flexibility

Symbols: A Bear; a Willow Branch; the Constellation Ursa Major

About Callisto: Appearing sometimes as a she-bear guarding her cubs, the Greek goddess Callisto reinspires the natural instincts with which we have lost touch and illustrates the intensity of maternal love. Her other name is Helic, which means "to turn" or "willow branch"; she thus has the power to help with personal transformations. In mythology, Callisto became Ursa Major while pregnant with Zeus's child. Artemis changed her into a bear, along with her son, who became Ursa Minor.

To Do Today: In Korea, the festival of Chilseong-je begins at midnight with an offering of white rice and water to the seven stars (Ursa Major). This gift ensures Callisto's assistance when needed throughout the coming months. If you can't stay up till midnight, just leave the rice and water in a special spot before you go to bed.

From her celestial home, Callisto stands ready to protect us in the new year and provide us with adaptability as a coping mechanism. To encourage this, carry a silver or white stone bear, or a piece of dried willow wood. Bless this token, saying,

> Callisto, release in me the power of flexibility.
> Where'er I carry this little charm, keep me ever safe from harm.

If these tokens aren't handy, you can substitute any white or silver item, or a hand-drawn picture of Ursa Major (the Big Dipper).

January 5

Befana Fair (Italy)

BEFANA

Themes: Overcoming Evil; Wisdom

Symbols: Broom; Horns; Hag Poppets

About Befana: Befana is the Italian crone goddess. Call on her for wisdom and guidance through the other eleven months of the year. Because she has lived a long life, her astute insight will serve you well. Today is her festival day in Italy, celebrated with horns, noise makers, songs, and music. These loud sounds drive out evil and mark the passage of winter's darkness out of the region.

To Do Today: Have any children in your life follow the Italian tra-dition of leaving Befana a broom to fly on and a gift basket. Accord-ing to legend, Befana rewards this kindness with little gifts in stockings, much like Santa Claus.

Find a "kitchen witch" at a gift shop and hang it up near the hearth to welcome Befana's wisdom into your home. Or, take a broom clockwise around your house, sweeping inward toward a central spot to gather her beneficent energies.

To protect your home for the rest of the year, use a kazoo or other noise maker (pots with wooden spoons work well). Go into each room and make a loud racket, saying,

All evil, fear! Befana is here! Away, away, only goodness may stay.

If your schedule allows, make a poppet that looks like an old woman. Fill it with dried garlic, pearl onions, and any other herbs you associate with safety. Keep this near the stove or hearth to invoke Befana's ongoing protection.

January 6

Festival of Kore (*Greece*)

KORE

Themes: Luck; Cycles; Youthful Energy

Symbols: Coins; Corn; the Number Seven; Flower Buds; Pomegranate

About Kore: An aspect of Persephone before her marriage to Hades, this youthful goddess motivates good fortune, zeal, and a closer affinity to earth's cycles during the coming months.

Kore, whose name means "maiden," is the youngest aspect of the triune goddess. She was the daughter of Zeus and Demeter, as beautiful as spring's blossoms and as fragrant as its breezes. It was this beauty that inspired Hades to tempt her with a pomegranate, a symbol of eternal marriage. Because she ate the fruit, Persephone spends winter with Hades as his wife and returns to the earth in spring.

To Do Today: Traditionally, on this day the Greeks carried an image of Kore around the temple seven times for victory, protection, and good fortune. Since your home is your sacred space, consider walking clockwise around it seven times with any goddess symbol you have (a round stone, vase, or bowl will suffice). As you go, visualize every nook and cranny being filled with the yellow-white light of dawn, neatly chasing away any lingering winter blues.

This is also Twelfth Night. Customarily, all holiday decorations should be down by now. This day marks winter's passage and perpetuates Kore's gusto and luck in your home year-round. Also consider carrying a little unpopped popcorn in your pocket to keep Kore's zeal and vigor close by for when you need it.

January 7
Saint Distaff's Day (Europe)

ARACHNE

Themes: Work; Weaving Destiny

Symbols: Web; Spinning Wheel; Needle

About Arachne: Arachne, the Greek spider goddess, inspires positive changes in your destiny for the new year. Legend tells us that Arachne challenged Athena to a weaving contest and won. In anger, Athena destroyed the girl's tapestry. Arachne, grief-stricken, took her destiny in hand and turned herself into a spider, but she continues to use her weaving talents to spin and pattern the lives of mortals.

To Do Today: According to lore, Saint Distaff, the patroness of weaving, was a fictional persona made up to mark the resumption of normal activity after the holidays. Instead of this imaginary figure, we turn to Arachne to help us take the strands of our fate in hand and begin weaving a year filled with goddess energy.

To direct your spiritual focus toward the goddess, wear something woven today, or display it proudly. If you have no such items, braid together three strands of thread or yarn, saying,

Arachne, bless this magic braid, so on you my mind is staid.

Carry this as a charm to keep your thoughts and actions goddess-centered

Finally, mend any work clothes in need of repairs to improve your job standing. As you make the final knot in a button or hem, bind the magic by saying,

This thread I wind, the magic bind.

Visualize your professional goals as you work.

Midwives' Day (Greek Macedonia)

ELEITHYIA

Themes: Birth; Children; Creativity; Fertility

Symbols: A Torch; White Flowers

About Eleithyia: As the Aegean goddess of birth, Eleithyia acts as the midwife to your new year, filling it with creative power. Eleithyia's name translates as "Fluid of Generation," giving her strong fertile aspects, and she also has a hand in personal fate.

According to myth, Eleithyia was the midwife of the gods and even birthed Eos, the creative force behind all things. When Eleithyia's hands were closed, birth was delayed. When Eleithyia opened her body, a child arrived effortlessly.

To Do Today: The ancients honored their midwives today as the goddess's assistants by giving them gifts. In modern times, this might equate to sending a thank-you note to your physician or pediatrician.

If you want to bring Eleithyia's fertility to any area of your life this year, try this spell: Gather a handful of white flower petals. Work in an area that somehow represents your goal. If you want a fertile garden, for example, cast this spell in your garden; for fertile ideas, perform it in your study. Visualize your goal as you release all but one petal, turning clockwise to the winds, saying,

> The wish of my heart, Eleithyia see,
> and bring back to me fertility.

Carry the last petal to help the magic manifest.

January 9

Festival of Jana and Janus (Rome)

JANA

Themes: Lunar Energy; Perception

Symbols: The Moon; Silver or Shiny Items

About Jana: This Roman goddess, whose name means "luminous sky," shines her light on the new year, extending improved insight and awareness as we move ahead. She is strongly associated with Juno and Diana and was often invoked before any other goddess in important undertakings. Traditional offerings to Jana included wine, incense, and barley.

To Do Today: To get Jana's attention and assistance in any magic you have planned today, wear a piece of silver-toned jewelry or clothing (silver is the color of the moon).

For increased discernment to guide your actions in the months ahead, go outside with a silver-toned coin. Hold this to the moon, saying,

> Jana, through the darkness and through the day,
> Light my path and guide my way.

Carry this token with you. Touch it and recite the incantation anytime you feel your judgment wavering.

To improve your awareness of personal lunar attributes (sensitivity, intuition, and the like), burn a stick of jasmine incense or any sweet scent and meditate. Get comfortable, visualizing a full moon pouring its light into the area of your third eye. If it helps your focus, chant

> Jana, Juno, Diana, awake in me.

Make notes of the experience and any insights that come.

League of Nations Day (United States)

IRENE

Themes: Peace; Cooperation, Reconciliation

Symbols: A Peace Sign; White; Gates and Entryways

About Irene: Look to this Greek goddess of peace to get the year off harmoniously with your neighbor and with all those you meet. Irene is Zeus's daughter and one of three Horae who together preside over matters of peace, order, and justice. They guarded the gates of Mount Olympus to ensure that all who passed had good-intentioned hearts. Offerings to Irene were always bloodless, in honor of her amicable energy.

To Do Today: In 1920, the League of Nations was founded on this date to encourage harmony between nations. To commemorate this and honor Irene, extend the hand of truce to someone with whom you've been bickering. Let the energy of this day pour through you to begin healing that situation.

Peace is something that really begins in our own backyards. To generate harmony at home and in your heart, make this simple Irene charm. On a piece of white paper draw a peace sign. Fold this three times, saying,

> Order—never cease, justice—release, let there be peace.

Put this somewhere safe in your home so Irene's gentle warmth can fill your words and actions all year. Better still, make two charms and carry one with you to keep the peace in all your interactions!

Wear a white piece of clothing today as a reminder to approach life with peaceful intentions, words, and actions.

January 11

Burning of the Clavie (*Scotland*)

BANBA

Theme: Protection

Symbol: Soil

About Banba: A Celtic war goddess, Banba extends safety to those who follow her, wielding magic in their support. In Irish tradition, she protected the land from invaders. As a reward for her sorcery's assistance, Banba's name became linked with ancient poetic designations for parts of Ireland. Interestingly enough, Banba translates as "unplowed land," meaning it is left safe and untouched to grow fertile.

To Do Today: Considering crime and other societal problems, a little extra protection from Banba seems like something we could all use year-round. Think of your home and possessions as the "land" she guards. Gather a pinch of dirt from near your residence, take it inside, and keep it in a special spot. Light a candle (white is good) near this anytime you feel you need Banba's diligent sheltering.

On this day the Scots burn a pole attached to a barrel of tar (a Clavie) and take it around town to banish evil influences, especially magical ones. The Clavie's remaining ashes are gathered by people as an anticurse amulet. In keeping with this custom, burn a small bit of wood (perhaps oak) on a safe fire source. As it burns, recite this incantation:

> Banba, burn away negativity, burn away malintent.
> Let the energy return from where it was sent.

Keep the ashes as an anti-negativity talisman.

January 12

Hindu Solstice (India)

GANGA

Themes: Cleansing; Health; Mercy

Symbols: Water; Yellow-colored Items

About Ganga: As the Hindu goddess of the river Ganges, Ganga represents purification, wellness, and benevolence in the new year. Legend has it Ganga came to earth upon hearing the cries of people who were dying from drought. Shiva divided Ganga into seven streams so she would not flood the earth upon her arrival. Part of this stream remained in the heavens as the Milky Way, and the rest flows through India as the river Ganges, where the goddess lives.

Art depicts Ganga as beautiful, controlling the *makara* (a sea monster on which she stands), with water flowing all around her.

To Do Today: In India, people gather on the river Ganges on this day and bathe in the waters for health, protection, and forgiveness from ten sins. They welcome spring's approach during this festival by wearing yellow clothing and coloring food, like rice, with saffron. To adapt this tradition and prompt Ganga's blessings, wear any yellow-toned clothing or jewelry today, light a yellow candle, carry a yellow-toned stone (like citrine), and/or eat rice as part of any meal. Adapt your shower, tap, bath, hose, or lawn sprinkler to substitute for the river Ganges. As you stand beneath the water, visualize any figurative dirt being washed away down the drain.

January 13

Tyvendedagen (Norway)

MIELIKKI

Themes: Change; Providence

Symbols: Bear; Grain; Woodland Plants

About Mielikki: The Finnish goddess of game, hunting, and the forest, Mielikki protects our resources during the remaining cold season by keeping the pantry filled. As the goddess of abundant grain, she also encourages the return of fertility to the earth.

To Do Today: Go into your kitchen and get a small handful of any grain-based cereal. Take this outside and release a pinch of it to the earth, saying,

> Mielikki, see this grain and bless, return to earth in fruitfulness.
> Hear the prayer that fills my heart; to my home, providence
> impart.

Take the remaining pinch back in the house and store it in an airtight container, symbolically preserving your resources.

Tyvendedagen means "twentieth day after Christmas." In Norway, today marks the official end of the Yule season. It's celebrated with races, sleigh rides, and the storage of ornaments and by burning the Christmas tree to drive away winter. So, when you dismantle your Yule tree, keep a jar full of its needles handy. Burn these throughout the year to banish frosty feelings or to warm up a chilly relationship. The pine smoke, being from a woodland tree, also draws Mielikki's attention to any pressing needs you may have.

January 14

Carmentalia (Rome)

CARMENTA

Themes: Children; Fertility; Foresight; Birth

Symbols: Music; Babies

About Carmenta: Carmenta, the Roman goddess of prophecy and birth, joins in our new year festivities by teaching us the value of preparedness and productivity. The only offerings acceptable to Carmenta are vegetable matter—as a birth goddess, taking life is abhorrent to her.

Her magical, prophetic nature can be seen in Carmenta's name, specifically the root word *carmen*, meaning a spell or charm in the form of a song.

To Do Today: Put on some uplifting music while you get dressed this morning. Let it motivate the resourceful aspect of Carmenta within you for the entire day.

In ancient Rome, today was the second to last day of a five-day-long festival honoring Carmenta. Pregnant women offered her rice for a safe delivery, while those wishing to have children ate raspberries to internalize her fertility. Try either of these to prompt the successful completion of a project or to improve your physical, emotional, or spiritual fertility.

Romans considered this an excellent day to make predictions for a child. If you know someone who's expecting, take a ring on a long string and hold it still over the mother's belly. If the ring swings back and forth it indicates a boy; circular movements indicate a girl.

January 15

Feast of Vesta (Rome)

VESTA

Themes: Home; Love; Fertility; Peace

Symbols: Fire; Donkey; Veils

About Vesta: In Roman mythology, Vesta was part of every fire. As such, Vesta commands the sacred fires of the hearth, the heart of spiritual and emotional stability in your home. Today was one of her festival days, Christianized as the Feast of the Ass, which is a sacred animal to her. Traditional offerings for Vesta include homemade bread and salt cakes.

In works of art, Vesta was never shown directly but always depicted her in veils, possibly to honor her importance in Roman society. The vestal priestess was one of the few people considered suited to negotiating peace during war threats.

To Do Today: The first month of the year is a good time to think about the spiritual warmth in your living space. Ask Vesta to kindle those fires anew. Do this by lighting any fire source you have handy—a match, a candle, the oven, a pilot light—or, alternatively, just turn on a light as a symbolic fire. Be sure to keep this lit all day. When a fire goes out on Vesta's day, it's considered a bad omen, indicative of love being lost.

To encourage peace on any battleground you're facing this year, light a white candle (the color of truce) and put it in a window to invite Vesta's presence (being sure it's safe to do so, of course). Then take a piece of bread outside, breaking it into small bits so the birds can carry your wish of harmony across the earth.

January 16

☾

Mount Fuji Climbing Season (*Japan*)

SENGEN SANA

Theme: Growth; Maturity

Symbols: Flower Buds

About Sengen Sana: Sengen Sana, a Japanese growth goddess, lives high on Fujiyama, giving her unique perspectives about each person's path in life. When you need to see yourself more clearly or inspire development in your spirit, call on her for aid. According to Japanese tradition, this goddess makes the flowers blossom today, just as she can make our lives blossom into maturity. She also governs cherry blossoms, which represent the beauty and fragility of life.

To Do Today: Put a nosegay of new blossoms on your altar or in a special place to remember Sengen Sana today. Use one as a boutonniere to liven up your clothing and inspire progress in any situation that seems to be stagnating. After the day is done, dry the petals of the blossom and burn them on a day when you want a little extra motivation.

In Japan, this day is a time to honor those who have come of age (on turning twenty) in the last year. These people dress in new clothing to mark the transition and go to community centers to celebrate. In keeping with this theme, consider having a rite of passage for any children in your life who have shown unique maturity (no matter their age). Bring them into the magic circle, present them with ritual tools, let them choose a magical name, and then give them permission to participate as a full adult in all your rituals to come.

Wassail Day (England)

GUNNLOED

Themes: Creativity; Wisdom; Health; Protection; Fertility

Symbols: Mead; Poetry; Cauldron or Cup; Apples

About Gunnloed: This Teutonic goddess guards the mead (a honey wine often made with apples) of sagacity and the muse—a refreshment most welcome at the outset of a new year. In art, Gunnloed is depicted as a giantess; according to stories about her, she stood vigilantly by the magic cauldron of Odherie until Odin wooed her and stole much of the elixir away.

To Do Today: For inspiration and insight, pick out a cup that's special to you and fill it with apple tea and a teaspoon of honey (a mock mead). Stir it clockwise, saying,

Gunnloed, come to me, put ingenuity in this tea!

Drink the tea to internalize the magic. If possible, sip it quietly while enjoying a good book of heartening poetry.

Alternatively, sip some mead, quaff some apple juice, or eat an apple today for health, and give a little of the leftover liquid to nearby trees. In Anglo-Saxon tradition, this festival marked a time to enjoy wassail, a spiced apple cider or mead with herbs. Farmers shared this beverage with the apple groves to keep them fertile. Wassail literally means "be well" or "be whole." Drink of the wassail cup to ensure yourself of Gunnloed's gifts of well-being, creativity, and happiness all year.

January 18

Festival of Perth (Australia)

NUNGEENA

Themes: Restoration; Creativity; Beauty

Symbols: Birds or Feathers; All Artistic Creations

About Nungeena: This Aborigine mother goddess took on the task of restoring beauty to the world after an evil spirit destroyed it with insects. Call on her for assistance when you feel that a cherished project or goal has been ravaged similarly by malintent or negativity.

According to the legend, Nungeena made birds to eat all the insects Marmoo (an evil spirit) let loose on the world. But these were not just any birds: they were the most attractive of all—the lyre birds. In turn, the lyre birds made assistants like magpies to help with their sacred task. Together they renewed the world's beauty.

To Do Today: Dust off any home crafts or arts that have been neglected on a back shelf and work on them for a while today. If time doesn't allow for this, find some way to bring a little extra beauty to the world—toss some flowering seeds in an open field, deliver food or clothing to a charitable organization, or just smile at a stranger.

In Australia this is the Festival of Perth, a huge arts festival that features local talent including dancers, mimes, opera, musicians, and some sports competitions. If there are any art galleries in your neck of the woods, go to them today to honor Nungeena and enjoy the creative works.

January 19

☽

Water Blessing Festival (Bulgaria)

KUPALA

Themes: Joy; Health; Cleansing

Symbols: Water; Flowers; Fern; Birchwood

About Kupala: The Slavic goddess of springs and water, Kupala, whose name literally means "to bathe," washes us with happiness and longevity. Oddly enough, she has a fire aspect too, which likely alludes to purification, protection, and transformation. Wildflowers, birch trees, and ferns were sacred to her.

To Do Today: To bring a year filled with joy, contentment, and health, leave a natural-fiber cloth outside today to gather dew. Use it tomorrow to bathe in Kupala's magic!

Take some flower petals to any moving water source (even a hose) and toss them on the stream. As you do, make a wish for something that will make you really happy. Let Kupala, in the form of the water, carry your wish toward manifestation.

To rid yourself of sickness, negativity, or a bad habit before the year really gets rolling, find a safe fire source (such as a candle that's self-contained in glass). Put this on the floor and jump over it. As you do, say,

> Old burns away; only the good, the good shall stay.
> Old to new, old to new, Kupala, my heart renew.

This symbolically leaves the old behind and invokes Kupala's aid in your efforts for positive change.

January 20

Aquarius Begins (Various Locations)

OYA

Themes: Justice; Tradition; Zeal; Femininity

Symbols: Fire; Water; the Number Nine

About Oya: A Yoruban mother goddess and spirit of the river Niger, Oya flows with us through the last day of January, strengthening our passion for and appreciation of life. She is wild and irrepressible, like the fire she's said to have created, yet Oya presides over matters of fairness and custom, using that fire as the light of truth. Artistic depictions of Oya show a nine-headed woman whose bosom speaks of fertile femininity.

To Do Today: Enjoy a glass of water when you get up to begin generating Oya's zest for life in your body and soul. This is also very suited to the energies of the day. Aquarius represents the Water Bearer who continually pours inspiring, creative waters from celestial spheres into our lives.

Get out and do something daring today. Invoke Oya through your pleasure and pure excitement. Dare to dream; then try to make that dream come true somehow.

If there's some area of your life that needs more equity, try making this Oya charm: Take any small candle and carve Oya's name into it. Have a glass of water nearby. Light the candle to invoke the goddess. Hold the water over the candle, saying,

> *What injustice consumes, Oya's waters quell.*

Drop a little water on the candle, then trim off the taper, carrying it with you to draw justice to you.

January 21

Saint Agnes's Day (*Various Locations*)

OSHUN

Themes: Divination; Love

Symbols: Flowing Water; Seashells; Amber Beads

About Oshun: Oshun is a beautiful, oracular goddess of love. Generous and beneficent, she opens her eyes to let us peek into what the future holds for relationships. According to legends, Oshun didn't always know how to tell the future. She was taught by Obatala, one skilled in divination, in return for retrieving his stolen clothing from Elegba. But Elegba exacted his price too. Once Oshun learned to divine, she had to teach all the other orishas the fortune-telling secrets.

To Do Today: Traditionally, Saint Agnes's Day is spent divining information about love's path and relationships in the coming year. Following Oshun's example, make a fortune-telling tool from three shells, each of which has a "top" and "bottom." If shells aren't handy, use three coins. Think of a "yes" or "no" question related to love. Three tops (or heads) mean "yes." Two tops mean things are generally positive, but uncertain. One top indicates a "wait" or a negative response, and three bottoms is a definite "no." Put the shells under your pillow before you go to bed to dream of future loves.

Or, to encourage Oshun's problem-solving skills in a relationship, carry a small piece of amber or wear a piece of amber-colored clothing when you meet your loved one to talk things over.

January 22

Bonfim Festival (Brazil)

AUCHIMALGEN

Themes: Protection; Blessing

Symbols: Silver or Lunar Items; Water; White Flowers

About Auchimalgen: A Chilean goddess of the moon, Auchimalgen protects us from all evils and disasters that lie in wait in the months ahead. Her husband is the sun, who blesses the land with light, while she shines through the darkness to keep her followers safe and inspired.

To Do Today: Count your blessings today, and give thanks for them. In our rushed society, this is something that often gets overlooked, and life is far more pleasant when we appreciate the little things.

Wear any silver-colored clothing or jewelry to honor Auchimalgen, and burn some lunar incense (coconut, jasmine, lemon, or myrrh) to fill the sacred space of your home with her protection.

The Bonfim Festival takes place in Brazil today in a church known as the "church of happy endings" because it was built by a ship's captain in gratitude for a safe return to land. The priests of the area wash the steps of the church with flower water to cleanse and bless the sacred place anew, and as a way of thanking the gods for their ongoing kindness. In keeping with this tradition, sprinkle the doorway to your home with any floral-scented water (or personal cologne or perfume) to draw Auchimalgen's beneficent energies to you.

January 23

New Year of the Trees (Israel)

THE EARTHLY MOTHER

Themes: Nature; Earth Awareness

Symbols: Trees

About the Earthly Mother: This Essene goddess embodies nature and teaches us how to live in harmony with the earth. The Essenes portray her with the elements personified as four angels (earth, air, fire, water) plus two companions named Joy and Life, all helping the Earthly Mother in her work. What a magical blend to bless and energize this first month!

To Do Today: In the spirit of making every day Earth Day, why not launch the new year by giving something back to the earth in the tradition of the Israelites? Today (the fifteenth day of Shebat on the Hebrew calendar), plant a tree to rejuvenate the land. If you wish, name the tree after a deceased loved one, as the Israelites do. According to lore, doing so brings that person peace in the afterlife.

If your location or finances don't allow for tree plantings, just water a tree. By so doing you symbolically feed the whole earth. Sit down for a moment or two afterward and meditate. Feel the rich soil beneath you, and feel how it nourishes and enriches all living things, including you.

Finally, as you're walking around, pick up any stone that catches your eye. Put it in your pocket to carry a piece of the Earthly Mother with you as a gentle reminder that the earth is a sacred, living thing that blesses us daily.

January 24

Gold Rush Day (California)

NOKOMIS

Themes: Prosperity; Luck; Providence

Symbols: Golden Items; Corn

About Nokomis: In Algonquin tradition, Nokomis is the "grandmother" who supplies us with the earth's riches and gives nourishment to humankind in times of need. When people are hungry, Nokomis provides food. When there is no food to be found, she offers to let us consume her spirit, thereby continuing the cycle of life.

To Do Today: Today marks the anniversary of the discovery of gold in California and the resulting expansion westward in the United States. In keeping with this prosperous, fortunate theme, wear or carry something gold today to bring a little more of Nokomis's abundance your way.

For financial improvements, especially if you have any pressing bills, eat corn (any type) today. Before consuming it pray to Nokomis, saying,

> Grandmother, see the sincerity of my need. Go to
> your storehouse and dispense _____ [fill in the
> minimum amount you need to get by] so that I
> might meet my obligations.

Eating the corn internalizes the energy of the prayer so opportunities to make money start manifesting.

If you're pressed for time, grab a kernel of unpopped popcorn and put it in your wallet or purse to keep Nokomis's prosperity (and your cash) where it's needed most.

January 25

Vietnamese New Year

MOTHER OF TEN THOUSAND THINGS

Theme: Luck

Symbol: Any Lucky Token

About the Mother: This goddess represents the unknowable and uncontrollable things we face daily. In Indo-Chinese tradition, she is part of the Universe's ebb and flow, ever changing and ever the same. Turn to her when you feel as if ten thousand things in your life were up in the air.

To Do Today: Take out any item that you associate with good fortune. Name it after the one area of your life in which you need more luck (naming something designates its purpose and powers). Hold the token to the night sky (symbolic of the Universe's vastness), saying,

> *Mother, see this symbol of my need. Empower it*
> *with your fortunate influence to fill my year with*
> _____ [*fill in with the name of your token*].

Carry this with you as often as possible to manifest that energy in your life.

In Vietnam, this holiday, known as Tet, is filled with ceremonies for luck over several days, including an offering to the goddess and ancestors to give good fortune a boost. Eating rice today invokes the spirit of prosperity. Or you can try a traditional divinatory activity instead. Make note of the name of the first person you meet today. If the name has an auspicious meaning (check a baby-name book), your meeting presages a wonderful year filled with the Mother's serendipity.

January 26

Chinese New Year (China)

JUN TI

Themes: Long Life; Luck; Fertility; Wisdom; Tradition

Symbols: Dragons; Sun and Moon Symbols; the Numbers Three and Eighteen

About Jun Ti: This Chinese Buddhist goddess oversees all matters of life generously. In works of art she is depicted as living on Polaris, the star around which all things revolve, including each individual's fate. She has three eyes for wise discernment, eighteen arms holding weapons with which to protect her people, and a dragon's head that symbolizes her power and wisdom.

To Do Today: Jun Ti can help you live a more fulfilled life this year by overseeing your fortune and well-being. To encourage her assistance, think silver and gold (or white and yellow)—the colors of the moon and the sun. Wear items in these hues, or perhaps have a glass of milk followed by pineapple juice in the morning to drink fully of her attributes!

On or around this day, the Chinese take to the streets with new year festivities that last two weeks. Eating various rice-based dishes today encourages fertility, respect, and long life, while wearing new shoes brings Jun Ti's luck. It is also customary to be on one's best behavior and honor the ancestors throughout the day for good fortune. The climax of festivities is a dragon parade, the beast, Jun Ti's sacred animal, being associated with ancient knowledge and tradition. So, find a way to commemorate your personal or family customs today to draw Jun Ti's attention and blessing.

January 27

☾

Roman Planting Festival (*Rome*)

CERES

Themes: Fertility; Earth; Harvest; Growth

Symbols: Grains (especially Corn); Poppies; Bread

About Ceres: Ceres, the Roman goddess of corn, returns our attention to the land today to begin preparing for spring's crop plantings. At the same time, Ceres reminds us to plant some figurative seeds of character now so they will mature throughout this year. Ceres's name translates as "create." Ceres is truly the creator and mistress of our morning feast table, having lent her name to modern breakfast cereals, which shows her affiliation with essential food crops.

To Do Today: For growing energy and earth awareness, eat any grain-based food today. Ideal choices include corn bread, corn flakes, puffed wheat, buttered corn, or corn chowder.

If you're a gardener, or even if you just enjoy a few houseplants, today is the perfect time to tend the soil. The Romans took time out from their other duties and spent an entire week around this date blessing the land. They invoked Ceres as the essential vegetable spirit for aid after the seeds were laid into the ground.

While we may not be able to spend a week doing likewise, a few minutes of caring for the earth is well worth the time. Put any seeds you plan to plant on an altar or in another special spot. Visualize a yellow-golden light filling and fertilizing them. Leave them here to absorb Ceres's energy until your traditional planting season begins.

January 28

☾✲

Up-Helly-Aa (Shetland Islands)

FULLA

Themes: Abundance; Protection; Cycles; Magic

Symbols: Gold-colored Items; Hair

About Fulla: The Teutonic sister of Frigg, Fulla visits us with fulfillment this year, just as her name—which means "full-ness"—implies. In legends, Fulla had long golden hair bound by a golden band. She guarded her sister's enchanted casket of slippers, giving her an additional association as a protectress of magical tools.

To Do Today: In metaphysical traditions, hair is sometimes used in spells to empower them. In this case, to evoke Fulla's protection over your magical tools, use a piece of your own hair. Pull one strand and adhere it in some manner to any tool that you want guarded from undesired energies. As you attach the hair, say,

> *Fulla, safeguard this _____, even as you mind-*
> *fully guarded Frigg's treasures.*

If the hair ever falls off, re-create the spell.

The festival of Up-Helly-Aa has ancient origins and closely resembles Viking funeral rites, except that it's meant for the season of winter! People on the Shetland Islands gather to watch the burning of a longship. The fire's golden flame lights the way for spring's and Fulla's abundance. It also expels evil spirits. In keeping with this custom, light as many lamps or candles as you can in your home, ideally yellow ones, and leave them on for a while to cast out any lingering darkness.

January 29

Hikuli Dance (*Mexico*)

SPIDER WOMAN

Themes: Magical Charms; Growth

Symbols: Spiders; Woven items

About Spider Woman: Spider Woman appears in the myths of the southwestern Native Americans as a resourceful helper who spins magical charms and each person's fate. No matter what problems or obstacles you face, Spider Woman creates the right network of energy to put you on the road toward accomplishment.

To Do Today: In metaphysical traditions, all life is seen as a network within which each individual is one strand. Spider Woman reveals the power and purpose of each strand psychically and keeps you aware of those important connections in your life. To augment this, get a Native American dream catcher, which looks like a web, and hang it over your bed so Spider Woman can reveal her lessons while you sleep. Or, carry a woven item with you today. It will strengthen your relationship with this ancient helpmate and extend positive energy for success in all you do.

In Mexico, the Native Americans perform the Hikuli dance today, searching out peyote for their religious rites. As part of this ceremony, worshipers dance to reach altered states of awareness, honor the ancestors, and help crops to grow. So, if your schedule allows, put on some music and boogie! Visualize a web as you move, and empower your future path with the sacred energies of Spider Woman's dance.

January 30
☾

Festival of Pax (Rome)

PAX

Theme: Peace

Symbols: White Items; Corn; Cornucopia; Olive Branch

About Pax: Pax is the Roman goddess of peace; she urges us to keep harmony among one another as a sacred commodity throughout the year. On coins, Pax appears youthful and often bears an olive branch to extend the hand of truce or a cornucopia, indicating that there is an abundance of peace for those who truly seek it.

To Do Today: Remember Pax by wearing or carrying something white today and offering to make amends with someone with whom you've had an argument.

Alternatively, make a funnel from a piece of white paper (like a cornucopia). Leave this somewhere predominant. Each time you have an angry or discordant thought, toss a coin into the funnel. At the end of the day donate these coins (plus a few dollars) to a charity that promotes peace.

Roman custom dictated that the images of all leaders were to be placed at Pax's feet on this day, as if to invoke her amicable energy in their interactions. This isn't a bad idea for modern leaders, either! Take any pictures you have of world leaders (check newspapers and magazines). If you can't find pictures, write their names on white paper instead. Put these in a pile before a white candle. As you light the candle, say,

> Pax, let peace fill their hearts.
> Let all hatred depart.
> Peace be between me and thee, and all those I meet.

January 31

Festival of Sarasvati (India)

SARASVATI

Themes: Learning; Wisdom; Communication

Symbols: White Flowers (especially Lotus); Marigolds; Swans

About Sarasvati: A Hindu goddess of eloquence and intelligence, Sarasvati extends a refreshing drink from her well of knowledge to complete the month with aptitude. In Hindu tradition, Sarasvati invented all sciences, arts, and writing. In works of art she is depicted as white-skinned and graceful, riding on a swan or sitting on an open lotus blossom.

To Do Today: Today is an excellent time to embark on any course of study or to reinforce your learning in a specific area. In Hindu tradition, Sarasvati's festival is held on or around this date. During the celebration, students gather in the Katmandu Valley (Nepal) bearing gifts for the goddess, who visits here today. Traditional offerings at the temples include lotus and marigold blossoms and incense, while students often bring pens or books to invoke Sarasvati's aid with their studies. Adapting this a bit, try dabbing your personal tools or educational books with a little lotus oil, and burn any sweet-scented incense to improve your awareness (rosemary is one good choice).

To generate Sarasvati's assistance in matters of communication, find a white flower and remove its petals. Place these in any moving water source, saying,

> Sarasvati, let my words bear gentle beauty and truth,
> falling lightly on others' ears, even as these petals to the water.

Let the water (which also represents this goddess) carry your wish.

February

February gets its name from the word *februare*, meaning "to purify." This is likely due to the fact that February was the traditional month of cleansing in Rome, when people repented of holiday excesses. The official day for focusing on purification is February 15 (I suspect the ancient cure for hangovers, onion juice, saw a lot of use this day). This cleansing theme also explains the prevalence of water-themed celebrations during this month, along with festivals for the dead.

By now the hectic pace of the holidays has begun to settle down, and life returns to some semblance of normalcy. Nonetheless, the need for the Goddess does not go away during day-to-day activities. If anything, making life an act of worship means including her in even the simplest of things. In terms of energy, any magic focused on growth, well-being, purification, cleansing, or initiation is suited to this month's aspects.

February 1

✳

Imbolc (Ireland)

BRIGIT

Themes: Health and Inspiration

Symbol: A Cauldron

About Brigit: Brigit is an Irish goddess known throughout Europe as "the bright one" because of her inspiring beauty and fiery qualities. Today is Brigit's festival in Ireland because it's the traditional first day of spring here, when lingering winter shadows are banished by the sun's radiance. Anyone desiring fertility, health, or creativity should invoke Brigit's blessings today, as the ancients did.

To Do Today: During the winter months it's easy to get a case of the blahs or sniffles. Brigit comes to our aid by offering us the spiritual elixir in her cauldron. Make yourself a nourishing broth today (like chicken bouillon) and serve it in a cauldron (a three-legged bowl). If you don't have one, any cup or mug would do. Bless the broth by holding your hand over the top, visualizing golden light filling the liquid, and saying,

> Brigit, hear my prayer and bless the cauldron [or cup] of inventiveness.
> Renew my body, inspire my heart.
> Throughout my life, your wholeness impart. So be it.

Drink the broth to internalize inspiration.

For health, take any candle (a green one is ideal for healing) and carve nineteen crosses into it. The number nineteen and the symbol of a cross are both sacred to Brigit. Light this candle for a few minutes every day for the next nineteen days. Or, you can let the candle burn for nineteen minutes instead.

February 2

Candlemas (*Europe*)

PROSERPINA

Themes: Divination; Protection; Purification

Symbols: Candles; Corn; Pomegranate

About Proserpina: In ancient Roman mythology, Ceres (an earth and vegetation goddess) sought out her daughter, Proserpina, in the underworld where Hades held her captive. During this time nothing grew on the earth. As she searched, Ceres illuminated the darkness of Hades' realm with candles (see also January 6 and January 27). Symbolically, this indicates a time of soul-searching, of finding any dark corners in our spiritual lives and filling them with purity and light. In works of art, Proserpina is depicted as a young, lovely corn goddess. In Greek stories she's known as Persephone.

To Do Today: In magical traditions, people light candles in the Yule log today, giving strength to the sun and chasing away some of the figurative dark clouds that winter left behind. If candles aren't prudent, turn on every light in the house for a few minutes for a similar effect. Do not burn the Yule log, however; keeping it intact protects your home from mischief.

Another traditional activity for Candlemas is weather divination, which we commonly recognize on this day as Groundhog Day. So, get up and look out the window! Poor weather portends a beautiful spring and a mild, enjoyable summer. Snow today foretells twelve more snowfalls before April 22 (Saint George's Eve).

February 3

❄

Homstrom (Switzerland)

ARTIO

Themes: Spring; Abundance; Providence

Symbols: Bear; Fruit

About Artio: Artio is a Swiss bear goddess who awakens in the spring to announce the season and share fruit from her storehouse. This is the fruit of daily providence and abundance, even as the earth itself will soon show signs of abundant life and fruitfulness. In Celtic tradition, she is also the goddess of wildlife, and she was likely called on during hunting rituals.

To Do Today: As Artio emerges from her sleep, the Swiss burn an effigy of winter to literally destroy the cold with fire and light. An easy way to do this yourself is to burn a fruity cookie (carefully) in the oven, then disperse the ashes to the earth.

If you've spent a lot of time at home lately, definitely emerge from that "cave," experience life fully, and begin preparing the soil of your spirit for spring's growth-oriented energy.

Put together a fresh fruit salad today and invoke Artio's providence, saying,

Artio, see my needs and bless, bring to me fruitfulness!

Share the fruit with family and friends to permeate their life with Artio's abundance. If you want to preserve your resources as well as inspire abundance, use canned fruit instead (which equates with Artio's stores during hibernation).

February 4

Bean-Throwing Day (Japan)

SHIRATA

Themes: Luck; Protection; Cycles; Happiness

Symbols: A Snowflake; Beans; White

About Shirata: This Japanese goddess embodies the first snow, where she glistens and shines with incomparable beauty until she freely and joyfully gives herself to spring's warmth and melts away. By so doing, Shirata reminds us that while the year has only just begun, the wheel of time is ever-moving, and that we should make the most of every moment.

To Do Today: For happiness, cut a snowflake pattern out of a quartered piece of white paper and carry it with you in your wallet as a charm. Make sure to visualize the snowflake being filled with brilliant white light, like that which is seen when the sun shines off new-fallen snow.

In Japan, this day is a time to chase away any malevolent influences that might hinder Shirata's joyful nature within us. People scatter beans and make loud noises to banish evil and carve lanterns with wishes to light the way for a better tomorrow. For our purposes, scatter seeds on the ground or plant beans instead so something as beautiful as Shirata can replace any negativity in your life with abundant growth.

To internalize Shirata's happiness, prepare any white beans and eat them as part of a meal today. If you hold any rituals, use beans to mark the magic circle, scattering them counterclockwise to banish any unwanted influences.

February 5

✳

Saint Agatha's Day (Italy)

AGATHA

Themes: Health; Well-Being; Protection

Symbols: Any Health-related Items

About Agatha: Saint Agatha was a third-century Italian martyr who now presides over matters of health and protects homes from fire damage. Many nurses and healers turn to her for assistance in their work. While this saint was a historical persona (not simply a rewritten goddess figure), she certainly embodies the healthy guardian energies of the goddess.

To Do Today: Traditionally, candles are taken from a central location to people's homes to bring Agatha's blessings. So, get yourself a special Agatha candle, of any color, and light it in a safe place whenever you feel under the weather.

Take out your first-aid kit or bandages and bless it today, saying,

> Restore vitality, well-being impart,
> Saint Agatha, hear the cry of my heart.
> On these tools of healing your blessing give,
> That I may stay healthy as long as I live.

When you use any item in the first-aid kit, you can activate the restorative magic by repeating the incantation.

To protect your home from fire, take a sprig of mistletoe left over from the holiday season and put it near your hearth. Invoke Saint Agatha's protection by saying,

> Saint Agatha, let my home be protected,
> Let these fires ne'er be neglected.

If you don't have mistletoe, substitute any red-colored stone.

February 6

✼

Mardi Gras (New Orleans)

AYIZAN

Themes: Pleasure; Playfulness; Divination

Symbol: Palm Leaf

About Ayizan: Ayizan is the first priestess of voodoo tradition, governing the public places where people gather to celebrate the goddess. As such, she oversees the Mardi Gras exuberant revelry, offering psychic insight and protective energy to keep us out of trouble.

According to tradition, Ayizan is the moral governess of humankind, helping us to balance our desire for pleasure with culpability.

To Do Today: Combine Ayizan's psychic side with a traditional Mardi Gras activity: fortune-telling! And, since it's unlikely that you have a palm leaf handy, use your own palm for divination instead. Get a palmistry guidebook (these are often handy at the supermarket checkout) and see what future your hand predicts.

Mardi Gras is traditionally a time of unbridled fun before the serious lenten season begins—so much so that the festivities are overseen by a lady and lord of misrule, who make sure folks really let loose. One activity in particular inspires Ayizan's energies—that of dancing and tossing grain so that pleasure rains down on all participants. This also banishes evil. Try this yourself, tossing rice or any grain-based cereal around the outside of your home. Then the birds can carry your wishes directly to Ayizan in their beaks!

February 7

Li Ch'un (*China*)

HSI HO

Themes: Spring; Harvest; Luck; Divination; Hope; Weather

Symbols: Water Buffalo; Bear

About Hsi Ho: Hsi Ho is the Chinese mother of the sun, who stretches out her son's golden arms to warm and revitalize both the earth and its people. In Chinese mythology, Hsi Ho bathes her child each morning in the eastern-shore lake so he can shine brightly through the day, strengthening hope and discernment. Her sacred animals are the water buffalo and the bear, both of which represent spring.

To Do Today: Li Ch'un literally means "spring is here." What better time to remember Hsi Ho and her gift of sunlight? Take out a yellow candle, bathe it with a fragrant oil, then light it for a day filled with Hsi Ho's clarity. Or carry a yellow-colored stone (zircon is ideal) for astuteness.

In China, people light a candle today and thank the star under which they were born. This candle can represent Hsi Ho, mother to the morning star. According to tradition, if you try this and the flame burns brightly, it indicates good luck in the coming months. Should the flame spark, it portends important news or a visitor. A flame that smolders or dies out is a negative omen.

Also make note of what the first person you meet today wears. A hat indicates rain, shoes reveal downpours throughout the spring and summer, warm clothing portends a cold year ahead, and light clothing foretells warm weather.

Mass for the Broken Needles (Japan)

WAKAHIRU

Themes: Needlecraft; Arts; Creativity

Symbols: Needles; Thread; Yarn; Embroidered or Woven Items

About Wakahiru: Wakahiru, the Japanese goddess of weaving, takes a much-deserved break from her toils today to enjoy the beauty of handcrafted items, and she suggests you do likewise. Legend has it that she is also the dawn goddess—a suitable job for the younger sister of Amaterasu (the sun goddess), who favored Wakahiru because of her excellent weaving skills. When Wakahiru died, Amaterasu refused to shine until lured out of her hiding place by the invention of mirrors.

To Do Today: Find a pocket sewing kit and use it as a Wakahiru charm for creativity. Energize the charm by leaving it in the light of dawn, saying,

With inventiveness fill, by your power and my will.

Carry the token often, touching it when you need extra ingenuity to handle a situation effectively.

The Japanese hold the art of needlecraft in such high regard that all the needles broken in the previous year receive honor at Buddhist temples today, along with an array of sewing gear. To venerate the needles' sacrifice in the name of beauty, no needlework is done on this day. In keeping with this spirit, take out any artistic tools you have, clean them up, and bless them in any way suited to your path. By so doing, you encourage Wakarhiru's genius to shine through them each time you work.

February 9

Iemanja Festival (Brazil)

IEMANJA

Themes: Foresight; Divination; Psychic Abilities

Symbol: Water

About Iemanja: In Brazil, Iemanja is considered the ocean's spirit. Every drop of saltwater bears her imprint and calls us back to Iemanja, our ancient mother and home. As a water elemental, Iemanja gives her followers vision, inspiration, and the ability to flow smoothly through life's torrential times.

To Do Today: At daybreak on this day, mediums in Brazil begin singing and dancing to summon the spirit of Iemanja, who provides glimpses of the year ahead. Worshipers take offerings carved with wishes to rivers or to the ocean. Here, Iemanja's spirit accepts the gifts, and the magic of the wish begins. To follow this custom, take any small natural token and toss it in moving water with your wish; the water should be flowing toward you if you wish to bring energy and flowing away from you if you want it to carry away problems.

In keeping with today's theme, soak in a mild saltwater bath to cleanse away any unwanted energy and heighten your senses. Then try your favorite divination tool. Pray to Iemanja beforehand to bless your efforts. See what messages she has for you, especially on emotionally charged matters (water equates with emotions in metaphysical traditions).

Finally, to honor Iemanja, wear ocean-blue clothing today, carry a blue-toned stone (like lace agate or lapis), put a seashell or coral in your pocket, dance in the rain (if the weather cooperates), or play in your sprinkler. Rediscover the element of water.

February 10

Argungu (Nigeria)

YEMAJA

Themes: Providence; Blessing; Luck; Fertility

Symbols: Fish; the Color Blue; the Crescent Moon

About Yemaja: Yemaja, the Nigerian goddess of flowing water, bears a name that literally means "fish mother"! As such, Yemaja generates providence and fertility, especially on the physical plane. In legends she gave birth to eleven deities, the sun, the moon, and two streams of water that formed a lake. In art she's often shown as a mermaid or a crescent moon, and her favorite color is blue.

To Do Today: The theme for the day is definitely fishy. Not surprisingly, new year festivities in Nigeria mark the beginning of the fishing season. Having a teeming net today portends prosperity for the rest of the season. So, what is it that you hope to catch today? Cast out your spiritual line to Yemaja for help in meeting or exceeding any goal.

To bite into a little luck, follow the example of Nigerian children. They make candies in fish shapes before this event, then dunk for them. The one to retrieve the most gets the most good fortune. Check out your local supermarket's bulk candy section. Ours carries gummy fish that work very well for this activity.

Consider including some type of fish in your menu today (even canned tuna will do the trick). Eat it to internalize good luck and a little of Yemaja's blessings.

February 11

Miracle at Lourdes (France)

NANTOSUELTA

Themes: Health; Miracles; Providence; Abundance

Symbols: Spring Water; Cornucopia

About Nantosuelta: This Gaulish goddess's name literally translates as "of the winding stream." We can go to Nantosuelta's cool, clean waters when our body, mind, or soul requires refreshment and healing. Additionally, artists often depict Nantosuelta carrying a cornucopia, giving her the symbolism of providence and abundance.

To Do Today: What do you need in your life right now? If it's love, drink a warm glass of spring water to draw Nantosuelta's energy and emotional warmth to you. If you need a cooler head, on the other hand, drink the water cold.

On this day in 1858, a young girl had a vision of Mary (a goddess type) near a grotto in Lourdes, France. According to magical tradition, this is an area where the Goddess was worshiped in ancient times. After the vision, the water became renowned for its miraculous healing qualities, reinforcing the fact that the Goddess is alive and well.

While most of us can't travel to Lourdes, we can enjoy a healing bath at home. Fill the tub with warm water (Nantosuelta exists in the streaming water), a few bay leaves, a handful of mint, and a pinch of thyme (three healthful herbs). Soak in the water, and visualize any sickness or dis-ease leaving your body. When you let out the water, the negative energy neatly goes down the drain!

February 12

❄

Powamu Festival (Arizona)

IYATIKU

Themes: Earth; Harvest; Providence; Health; Weather

Symbols: Corn; Beans; Seeds; Soil

About Iyatiku: Iyatiku is the Pueblo corn and underworld goddess who protects not only future crops but the future in general by safeguarding children. During the early months of the year, Iyatiku extends arms of compassion to embrace us with nurturing support, just as the earth nurtures seeds.

To Do Today: If you have a garden, today is an excellent time to dance on the land and invoke Iyatiku's blessings on your crops or flowers. The Pueblo and Hopi Indians have spirit dancers waltz around the land to instill the crops with energy through sacred movements.

The Hopi also plant beans on top of underground ritual rooms called kivas, which house Iyatiku's nurturing energy. When children go into kivas for rites of passage, they emerge as adults thanks to the goddess's care and guidance within. Using this symbolism to foster maturity or any other of Iyatiku's attributes, go today to some place close to the earth, taking a bean with you. Plant the bean, then sit on top of the ground covered with a blanket (a mock cave/womb/kiva). Meditate here, focusing on the bean, the rich earth below you, and the earth's generative energy. Allow Iyatiku to meet you in this sacred space and begin manifesting what you most need.

February 13

❇

Birthday of Humankind (China)

NU KWA

Themes: Luck; Opportunity; Abundance; Order; Divination

Symbols: Clay; Serpent

About Nu Kwa: Nu Kwa is an ancient Chinese creatrix who formed people out of yellow clay and invented the flute. Today she plays her music bearing good fortune, opportunity, and the organizational skills with which to make both useful. She also serenades the earth back to fullness after winter.

In legends, this serpent-bodied goddess reestablished order on the earth after a terrible rebellion. Nu Kwa used melted stones to refashion the sky, tortoise toes to mark the four winds, and reeds to hold back overflowing rivers. Once this was done, the earth returned to its former beauty.

To Do Today: The eighth day of the Chinese new year celebrates the birthday of humanity, fashioned by Nu Kwa, and is filled with omens about human fate. For example, any person or animal born on this day is considered doubly blessed and destined for prosperity. So, consider taking out a divination tool today and seeing what fate holds for you.

To generate Nu Kwa's luck or organizational skills in your life, make and carry a clay Nu Kwa charm. Get some modeling clay from a toy store (if possible, choose a color that suits your goal, like green for money). Shape this into a symbol of your goal, saying,

> From Nu Kwa blessings poured,
> Luck and order be restored.

If you can't get clay, bubblegum will work, too.

February 14

✻

Lupercalia (*Rome*)

VENUS

Themes: Love; Passion; Romance; Sexuality

Symbols: Doves; Flowers; Berries; Trees; Pine Cones

About Venus: Venus was originally an Italic goddess of blossoms; hearts and flowers have slowly become attributed to her loving, passionate energies. In fact, her name became the root for the word *venerate*—to lift up, worship, or esteem. So it is that Venus greets prespring efforts for uplifting our hearts with positive relationships.

To Do Today: During Lupercalia, an ancient predecessor of Valentine's Day, single girls put their names in a box, and unmarried men drew lots to see with whom they would be paired off for the coming year. To be more modern-minded, try pinning five bay leaves to your pillow instead to dream of future loves. If you're married or otherwise involved, steep the bay leaves in water and drink the resulting tea to strengthen the love in your relationship.

To encourage balance in a relationship, bind together Venus's symbols, a pine cone and a flower, and put them somewhere in your home. Or, to spice up a passionate moment, feed fresh berries to each other and drink a berry beverage from one cup (symbolizing united goals and destinies).

In Roman tradition, anywhere there's a large stone adjacent to a tall tree, Venus is also there. Should you know of such a place, go there today and commune with her warm, lusty energy.

February 15
❄
Losar (Tibet)

SHAKTI

Themes: Protection; Banishing; Communication

Symbols: The Number Six; Magic Charms; Lotus

About Shakti: The Tibetan supreme feminine power, Shakti does not stand by idly when we are in distress. She is an active, loving force for change. When called upon, Shakti manifests within us as intelligence, instinct, willpower, energy, action, and ultimately, magic. Shakti especially energizes communication skills, so that our words will be heard clearly and understood.

To Do Today: Losar is the Tibetan new year celebration, highlighted by monks casting out negative influences using brilliant-colored costumes, masks, and joyful dancing. Burn lotus incense (or any sweet, floral scent) to remember Shakti today, and fill your living space with her abundant power for positive transformation. Alternatively, boil some pleasant-smelling cooking spices in water to release their aroma and energy throughout the sacred space of your home.

If possible, make a mask or a token that represents what you want Shakti to banish. Put it on (or carry it) early in the day, and remove it vigorously sometime during your festivities. Bury this with six stones (to represent Shakti's control) to symbolically bury the bad habit or situation, giving it into Shakti's care.

In keeping with today's celebrations, wear bright-colored clothing to chase away evil influences, which cannot bear the sight of radiant beauty.

February 16

Victoria's Day (Rome)

VICTORIA

Themes: Victory; Success; Excellence

Symbols: Wings (or Feathers); Laurel

About Victoria: Victoria, as her name implies, is the Roman goddess of attainment. Early in the year she inspires resolve within us to do everything we undertake, with excellence as a goal. In works of art, Victoria is often depicted with wings that allow her to surmount any obstacle or problem.

To Do Today: Drink a tea made from lemon balm, ginger, and a pinch of cinnamon to generate a successful attitude. Remember: if you think you can, *you can!*

Put a bay leaf (a form of laurel) in your shoe so that Victoria's triumphant energy can walk with you all day long. Later in the day, burn a few bay leaves on a fire source to fill your home with success. Alternative aromas that invoke Victoria's favor are rose and red sandalwood.

To make a victory charm, find a feather (or cut paper in the shape of a feather) and empower it with this incantation:

> With the wings of Victoria, I will rise
> above all areas where trouble lies.
> Through diligence and mastery I will see
> today begins my victory!

Carry this token anytime you feel your confidence waning, or when you need a boost to get over any seemingly insurmountable obstacle.

February 17

Fornacalia (Rome)

FORNAX

Themes: Home; Love

Symbols: Stove; Fire; Wheat

About Fornax: In Rome, Fornax guided the baking of bread, which, being the proverbial staff of life, was no small matter. Today Fornax still stands ready to watch over our hearths, as the goddess of the oven, which is the true heart of any home. If her fires go out, folklore says, warmth among the home's occupants dwindles soon thereafter.

To Do Today: Fornacalia was the Roman festival of ovens, in which Fornax was invoked by baking wheat breads and other grain-related foods. So think about dusting off your cookbooks, especially any recipes from your family, and start baking! Even people pressed for time can usually make a batch of bread from frozen dough. If you only own a microwave, have no fear—microwaveable soft-dough pretzels are readily available in the freezer section of your supermarket. Or, simpler still, have toast for breakfast this morning to internalize Fornax's warm emotions. On the other hand, if you'd like to give Fornax a much-needed break from her toils at your place, go out and eat! Just make sure to have some bread as part of the meal to welcome Fornax to your feast. Finally, take any dried bread you have and crumble it up for the birds. Focus on your desire for love and closeness in your life. The birds will convey your wishes to Fornax, the heavens, and the four corners of creation.

February 18

✻

Parentalia (Rome)

LARA

Themes: Peace; Death; Protection

Symbols: Rose; Violet; Wine; Crossroads

About Lara: Lara, whose name means "mother of the dead," was the guardian of ancestral spirits in whose care is the home, the family, and by extension, the community. According to tradition, crossroads are sacred spots for Lara, being the meeting of two roads, symbolic of an area where the temporal world and spirit world "cross" over one another.

To Do Today: In Rome, Parentalia was part of a weeklong observance dedicated to one's ancestors. So, pull out the scrapbooks, discuss your family tree, and fondly remember those who have been a part of your family history. If possible, light a white candle in one of your windows to greet the ancestors and Lara. Or, leave an empty chair at your dinner table tonight with some of the deceased's favorite foods in the empty place at the table to welcome them and Lara into your home.

This is also a time to visit grave sites, leaving roses, violets, wine, and other gifts for the deceased. These actions propitiate the spirits and ensure the family of ongoing harmony through the year.

Finally, Romans settled any arguments with family members or friends today, so follow their example. If you can, arrange to meet the person with whom you've argued at a crossroads, so that your two minds can "meet in the middle." Scatter rose or violet petals where you meet to inspire Fornax's warmth.

February 19

✳

Pisces Begins (*Various Locations*)

SAGA

Themes: Foresight; Divination; Inspiration; Femininity; Psychic Abilities; Kindness; Tradition

Symbols: A Cup; Fishes; Water

About Saga: Saga, an attendant of Frigg, is a Scandinavian goddess whose name means "seeress." Saga is a student of the Universe, ever watchful and ever instructing us about the value of keen observation. She is directly connected with the sign of Pisces, which governs artistic expression, psychic abilities, and sensitivity toward others' needs.

In artistic representations, Saga bears a long Viking braid, an emblem of womanhood and honor. According to the Eddas, Saga lives at Sinking Beach, a waterfall, where she offers her guests a refreshing drink of inspiration from a golden cup. Later, her name got applied to the sacred heroic texts of the Scandinavian people.

To Do Today: Tend your sacred journals today. Write about your path, your feelings, where you see yourself going, and where you've been. Saga lives in those words—in your musings, memories, and thoughts—guiding them to the paper to inspire you now and in the future.

Invoke any of Saga's attributes in your life today simply by practicing the art of observation. Really look at the world, your home, and the people around you. As you do, remember that little things count. Saga's insight lies in the grain of sand and the wildflower as well as the stars.

February 20

✤

Winterlude (Ottawa, Canada)

ONIATA

Themes: Recreation; Good Sportsmanship

Symbols: Early-blooming Flowers; Snow

About Oniata: Oniata, an Iroquois goddess, embodies what it means to be a good sport. According to legend she came to live with the Iroquois, who found her beauty distracting, so much so that men left their families just to catch a glimpse of her radiance. When Oniata found out about this, rather than getting angry with the men, she left the earth. The only trace of her beauty she left behind was the sprouting of spring flowers peeking out from melting snow.

To Do Today: Plant some early blooming seeds today so that when they blossom, Oniata's good humor and temperament can also bloom in your life.

In Canada, people take this opportunity to enjoy the last remnants of winter by participating in various sporting activities (especially skating) and by making snow sculptures. Try the latter activity yourself; perhaps create a flower out of packed snow to honor and welcome Oniata. If you live in a warm climate, you can blend up some ice cubes to a snowy consistency for sculpting, and make it into a snowcone afterward to internalize the energy! Or, consider going to an ice rink for a little rest and relaxation. Return outside and appreciate any flowers nearby. Oniata lives in their fragrance and loveliness.

February 21

Feralia (Rome)

LIBITINA

Themes: Death; Freedom

Symbol: Fire

About Libitina: Libitina is the kindly natured Roman goddess of funerals and pyres. In poetic writings, her name metaphorically equates with figurative or literal demise. Turn to her this month to "die" to outmoded ideas or be freed from bad habits. Or call on her to invoke peace for the spirits in Summerland.

To Do Today: In Rome, Feralia was part of a weeklong festival honoring, appeasing, and communicating with the spirits of dead ancestors. If there's something you want to say to a departed loved one or a token you want to give them, today is an excellent time to try this Libitina mini-ritual. Following Roman custom, toss a message or gift into a fire source, focusing on the individual for whom it's intended. Libitina bears the energy of the gift or note safely to the desired spirit. Emotionally, this type of ritual liberates you from lingering guilt and generates a sense of closure.

Use the same ritual to rid yourself of old ideas or characteristics that fetter spiritual growth. Take any flammable object that represents this characteristic. Hold it in your hands and channel that obsolete energy into it. Toss it into a fire, saying,

Libitina, liberate me; as this burns, my spirit is freed.

Turn your back to the fire and don't look back until the symbol is completely destroyed.

✳

Brotherhood Day (United States)

BINAH

Themes: Peace; Cooperation; Communication; Unity; Spirituality

Symbols: Bees; Lilies; Lead

About Binah: In Cabalistic tradition, Binah embodies spiritual discernment, love, stability, and awareness. As the third *sephirah* of the Tree of Life, Binah becomes a divine mother, guiding her children toward attainment and comprehension. Her name literally translates as "the understanding," which gives form and function to all other aspects of life. Bees are sacred to her (as divine messengers), as are lilies (white in purity), and lead (which gives us a foothold in reality).

To Do Today: Binah's energy was present in 1934 when Brotherhood Day began to bring people of diverse faiths together in an atmosphere of tolerance and respect. The thrust of the day is universal brotherhood, accenting our likenesses instead of our differences. So, take time today to learn more about other faiths and foster an open exchange of ideas. Perhaps visit a church or temple and observe quietly, seeing that the Goddess is there, too.

To promote strong spiritual roots in your own life, as well as the understanding to nurture those roots, try this spell: Take a piece of lead (maybe from a pencil) and hold it in your dominant hand, saying,

> *Binah, walk with me; understanding impart.*
> *Every day be part of my heart.*

Write this down and put the incantation in your shoe so that Binah will walk with you wherever you may be.

February 23

Terminalia (Rome)

MINERVA

Themes: Earth; Home

Symbols: Owl; Geranium

About Minerva: This Etruscan/Italic goddess blended the odd attributes of being a patroness of household tasks, including arts and crafts, and also being the patroness of protection and of war. Today she joins in prespring festivities by helping people prepare their lands for sowing and embracing the figurative lands of our hearts, homes, and spirits with her positive energy.

To Do Today: In ancient times, this was a day to bless one's lands and borders. Gifts of corn, honey, and wine were given to the earth and its spirits to keep the property safe and fertile throughout the year. In modern times, this equates to a Minerva-centered house blessing.

Begin by putting on some spiritually uplifting music. Burn geranium-scented incense if possible; otherwise, any pantry spice will do. Take this into every room of your home, always moving clockwise to promote positive growing energy. As you get to each room, repeat this incantation:

> *Minerva, protect this sacred space*
> *and all who live within.*
> *By your power and my will,*
> *the magic now begins!*

Wear a geranium today to commemorate Minerva and welcome her energy into your life.

✳

Festival of Shiva (India)

KALI

Themes: Rebirth; Cycles; Joy; Courage; Hope; Cleansing; Change

Symbols: Flowers; Dance; Iron; Sword; Peacock Feathers; Honey

About Kali: Kali, a Hindu goddess whose name means "time," is the genetrix of natural forces that either build or destroy. Even in destruction, however, she reminds us that good really can come of bad situations. If you find your hopes and dreams have been crushed, Kali can change the cycle and produce life out of nothingness. Where there is sorrow, she dances to bring joy. Where there is fear, she dances in courage.

To Do Today: Hindus gather today at Shiva's temples to honor his celestial dance of creation, and Kali dances with them in spirit. Beforehand, they fast and bathe in holy waters for purification. Doing similarly (in your tub or shower) will purge your body and soul of negative influences. Add some flower petals or sweet perfume to the bath to invoke Kali's cleansing power.

To invoke Kali's assistance in bringing new life to stagnant projects or ruined goals, leave her an offering of honey or flowers, and make this Kali amulet: Take any black cloth and wrap it around a flower dabbed with a drop of honey, saying,

> *Kali, turn, dance, and change.*
> *Fate rearrange.*
> *End the devastation and strife;*
> *what was dead return to life.*

Carry this with you until the situation changes, then bury it with thankfulness.

February 25

Ta'Anith Esther (Israel)

ASHERAH

Themes: Kindness; Love; Divination; Foresight

Symbols: Lion; Lilies; a Tree or Pole

About Asherah: Asherah, a Canaanite goddess of moral strength, offers to lend support and insight when we are faced with inequality or overwhelming odds. In art, she is often depicted simply as an upright post supporting the temple. This is a fitting representation, since her name means "straight." Traditionally, Asherah is a mother figure often invoked at planting time, embodying a kind of benevolent, fertile energy that can reinforce just efforts and good intentions. Beyond this she is also an oracular goddess, specifically for predicting the future.

To Do Today: In Israel, this festival commemorates Esther's strength and compassion in pleading with King Ahasuerus to save her people held captive in Persia. It is a time of prayer when one looks to the divine to instill similar positive attributes within us. For help in this quest, we turn to Asherah with this simple prayer:

> *Lady, make me an instrument of kindness and*
> *mercy; let my words be gentle and true, my actions*
> *motivated by insight and fairness. Where there is*
> *prejudice, let me be the bearer of tolerance. Where*
> *there is uncertainty, let me share your vision.*
> *Where there is disharmony, let me sow love. Amen.*

Plant a tree today to remember Asherah, and tend it often. As you do, you tend her attributes in your heart.

February 26

✳

Ku-omboko (Zambia)

OBA

Themes: Protection; Manifestation; Movement; Energy; Restoration; Flexibility

Symbol: Water

About Oba: Oba is the Nigerian and Santarian goddess of rivers, which figuratively represent the flow of time and life. Turn to her for assistance in learning how to "go with the flow," or when you need to inspire some movement in sluggish projects or goals.

To Do Today: This holiday's name literally translates as "getting out of the water." Due to the annual flood cycle, people must make their way to higher ground around this date. So consider what type of figurative hot water you've gotten into lately. Oba stands ready to get you onto safer footing. To encourage her aid, take a glass half filled with hot water, then slowly pour in cold water up to the rim, saying,

> By Oba's coursing water, let _____ improve,
> to higher and safer ground, my spirit move.

Drink the water to internalize the energy.

Oba can abide in any body of flowing water, including your tap or shower. When you get washed up or do the dishes today, invoke her energy by uttering this chant (mentally or verbally):

> Oba, flow—blessings bestow.
> Pour, pour, pour . . . restore, restore, restore

Let Oba's spiritual waters refresh your energy and your magic.

Cherry Blossom Festival (*Hawaii*)

LAKA

Themes: Tradition; Heritage; Weather; Arts

Symbols: Lei Flowers; Dance; Yellow

About Laka: Laka is the Hawaiian goddess of Hula, through which the myths, legends, and histories of the Hawaiian people are kept intact. Today she charges us with the sacred duty of collecting the treasures of our personal legacies and recording them for sharing with future generations.

In stories, Laka is the sister of Pele (the volcano goddess) and a nature goddess who can be invoked for rain. Artistic renditions show her wearing yellow garments, bedecked with flowers, and always dancing.

To Do Today: The cherry blossoms of this festival in Hawaii are spiritual, not real, symbolizing the power of tradition among the predominantly Japanese community. On this day people gather together and honor their heritage by participating in martial arts, Japanese dances, weaving, and arts competitions. So, if there's any art or craft you learned from an elder in your family, take the time to display that craft or work on it today to commemorate Laka's attributes.

If possible, get together with members of your family and begin creating a family journal that will record all the important events in your lives. Cover the journal with yellow paper dabbed with fragrant oil to invoke Laka's tending care on the sacred documents.

February 28
✻
Kalevala Day (Finland)

LUONNOTAR

Themes: Creativity; Tradition; Fertility; Beginnings

Symbols: Egg; East Wind; Poetry

About Luonnotar: A Finno-Ugric creatrix, Luonnotar closes the month of February with an abundance of creative, fertile energy. Her name means "daughter of earth," and according to legend she nurtured the cosmic eggs from which the sun, moon, and stars developed. In the Kalevala, Luonnotar is metaphorically represented as the refreshing east wind— the wind of beginnings. She also created the first bard, Vainamolen.

To Do Today: The Kalevala is the epic poem of more than twenty thousand verses that recounts the history and lore of the Finnish people. Luonnotar appears in the creation stanzas, empowering the entire ballad with her energy. If there's anything in your life that needs an inventive approach or ingenious nudge, stand in an easterly wind today and let Luonnotar's power restore your personal muse. If the wind doesn't cooperate, stand instead in the breeze created by a fan facing west!

To generate fertility or internalize a little extra resourcefulness as a coping mechanism in any area of your life, make eggs part of a meal today. Cook them sunny-side-up for a "sunny" disposition, over easy to motivate easy transitions, or hard boiled to strengthen your backbone!

February 29

Leap Year (*Various Locations*)

LILITH

Themes: Freedom; Courage; Playfulness; Passion; Pleasure; Sexuality

Symbol: Apple

About Lilith: In Hebrew legends, Lilith is a dangerously beautiful goddess who refused to subordinate herself to Adam, feeling she was created as an equal. This makes Lilith perhaps the first true liberationist, and she resolves to make modern life similarly equal for all people. She also boldly instructs us to stand up for what we believe in, unbridled and courageous, no matter the cost. According to legend, Lilith was turned away from paradise for her "crime," and she has been depicted in art as a demon.

To Do Today: Leap Year day occurs every four years to keep our calendar in sync with the solar year. Customarily, women break loose today, asking men out or proposing marriage. In today's liberal society, actions like this aren't overly surprising. Nonetheless, Lilith charges us with the duty of ever seeking after equality, not just for women but for all of earth's people. If there's someone you've wronged with presupposition or prejudice, make amends today.

To internalize Lilith's fairness, bravery, or exuberant lustiness, eat an apple today. Quite literally take a bite out of life, and enjoy some daring activity to its fullest without fear or guilt. Like Lilith, you are the master of your destiny.

March

Britons call March a "loud and strong" month because of its blustery nature. Before the calendar changed to the present system, the new year took place during March, likely due to the official beginning of spring, which is ushered in by March's winds.

In terms of magical energy, think growth and prosperity! Everything that dwells on the planet is showing signs of life and fruitfulness. Let the Goddess inspire your spirit similarly. Other characteristics for March include cultivating the spirit of adventure and fertility, and focusing on personal maturity in any area of your life.

March 1

Matronella (Rome)

BONA DEA

Themes: Femininity; Blessing; Fertility; Divination; Abundance

Symbols: Vines; Wine

About Bona Dea: Bona Dea's name literally means "good goddess." Her energies come into our lives at the outset of this month, offering all good things, especially fertility and a greater appreciation of the goddess within each of us.

Traditionally, Bona Dea is a women's goddess who received offerings of wine in exchange for prophetic insights during her observances.

To Do Today: On March 1, February was escorted out of Rome with a flourish of adaptable activities. Exchange sweet gifts as the Romans did to ensure yourself of a sweeter future. Greet a friend with Bona Dea's name to invoke her blessings on them. Put up a grapevine wreath fashioned like a heart (or other symbol of something you need), and leave a glass of wine on your altar to honor Bona Dea's presence in your home and your life.

In Rome, female slaves would get this day off, and the head of the house would wait on them. In modern times this equates to switching roles for a day at home. Whoever normally gets up and fixes breakfast gets to sleep in, whoever normally does chores gets to go out and socialize, and so forth. Bona Dea appreciates the considerate gesture as much as you do and will rain her goodness upon your home.

March 2

🌺

Anthesaria (*Greece*)

SEMELE

Themes: Fertility; Grounding; Joy; Playfulness; Pleasure; Youthfulness

Symbols: Wine or Grape Juice; Soil

About Semele: In Greek mythology, Semele is a young earth goddess who, in mortal form, gave birth to the ever-exuberant party animal Dionysus (the god of wine). Today Semele flows into our lives bringing spring's zeal, joy, and playfulness carefully balanced with the exhortation to keep one foot firmly on terra firma. Semele's name translates as "land," giving her additional associations with fertility and grounding.

Semele became a goddess after insisting on seeing Zeus (Dionysus' father) in his full glory. This killed Semele, but Zeus rescued her from Hades and made her a goddess.

To Do Today: A three-day celebration began in Athens around this time to celebrate spring. The first day of the observance was called the "opening of the casks"! So, if you have a favorite wine, today is definitely the time to take it out and enjoy it with some friends. Toast to Semele for giving the world a wine god who lives in every drop poured!

To "grow" any of Semele's virtues within yourself, find a small planter, some rich soil, and a flowering seed. Name the seed after that characteristic, and water it with a bit of wine or grape juice. If you use diligent care and maintain a strong focus on your goal, when the seed blossoms that energy should show signs of manifesting in your life.

March 3

Anniversary of
Pioneer 10 Launching (United States)

TARA

Themes: Universal Unity; Peace; Cooperation; Destiny; Energy; Spirituality

Symbol: Star

About Tara: In Hindu mythology, Tara is a star goddess who encompasses all time and the spark of life. She extends this energy to us, fulfilling our spiritual hunger. In so doing, Tara strengthens our understanding of the Universe and its mysteries and gives us a glimpse of our destiny.

Tara's name literally means "star." In works of art she is depicted as beautiful as the silver turret points of the night sky, young and playful. From her celestial home Tara challenges us to live life fully no matter the day or season, looking to the stars and our hearts to guide us.

To Do Today: I cannot help but believe that Tara was standing by whispering in scientists' ears as they launched *Pioneer 10* into space on this date in 1972, bearing a message of peace to anyone who might find it. In this spirit of exploration and hope, today is definitely a time to reach for the stars! Try something new or set some bold goals for yourself.

If you live in an area where you can observe the night sky, go out tonight and absorb Tara's beauty firsthand. As you watch, let the starlight and Tara's energy trickle into your soul. Make a wish on the first star that appears, and then find concrete ways to help that wish come true. If you see a falling star, it is Tara coming to join you!

March 4

※

Omizuturi (Japan)

KISHI-MUJIN

Themes: Protection from Evil; Meditation; Balance; Banishing

Symbols: Water; Pine

About Kishi-mujin: Kishi-mujin is a mother goddess figure in Japan who wraps us in arms of warmth and safety, as welcoming as the spring sun. She is a compassionate lady whose goal is to bring life into balance by replacing sadness with joy, fear with comfort, and darkness with light.

To Do Today: Follow the Japanese custom, observe this day as a time of reflection: a time to meditate, recite sacred verses, and present offerings of water for blessing. Additionally, on this day, Buddhist monks shake sparks off a pine branch for people to catch. Each ash acts as a ward against evil influences. A safer alternative for banishing negativity or malintended energies is simply burning pine incense or washing your living space with a pine-scented cleaner.

To invoke Kishi-mujin's presence in your life, find a small-needled pine twig and dip it in water. Sprinkle this water into your aura, saying,

> *Away all negativity, darkness flee!*
> *Kishi-mujin's light shines within me!*

Dry the twig and use it as incense for protection anytime you need it.

Finally, before going to bed tonight, honor Kishi-mujin by stopping to meditate about your life for a few minutes. Are you keeping your spirituality and everyday duties in balance? Are your priorities in order? If not, think of creative, uplifting ways to restore the symmetry.

March 5

🎕

World Day of Prayer

TASHMIT

Themes: Prayer; Blessing; Unity; Hope

Symbol: Folded Hands

About Tashmit: The Goddess is timeless and eternal, and she has many faces with which she conveys the concepts of truth and beauty to the world's people. Tashmit, the Chaldean goddess of wisdom and teaching, in particular, stands ready today. Her name means "hearing"; it is she who listens intently to our prayers.

To Do Today: On the first Friday in March, people in over 170 countries join in prayer, and the goddess asks that we do similarly. Prayer is something that seems to have gone by the wayside in our "instant" world. Yet it takes only a moment to honor the sacred. This prayer is but one example; change or adapt it liberally to suit your needs and vision:

> Lady of Wisdom, Tashmit, I come to you for guidance. Shine on my path today that I might see others in an equal light, that I might speak with truth and kindness, that I might walk the Path of Beauty with a loving heart and peaceful spirit.
>
> Hear the voices of your people raised together today in oneness; hear our prayers. Let us find unity in diversity; heal the world; let us know peace and guard it as sacred. With a thankful heart, so be it.

March 6

🐋

Whale Festival (*California*)

WHALE GODDESS

Themes: Nature; Meditation; Rebirth; Movement

Symbols: Water; Whale

About the Whale Goddess: In Arabic tradition, the Whale Goddess swallowed Jonah, neatly giving him time to consider his life and actions seriously before his figurative rebirth. Let's hope she doesn't have to go that far to get our attention this month (or anytime, for that matter).

In some stories, the earth rests on this goddess's back, and earthquakes result when she gets upset and shakes her tail. Symbolically, when your life seems on shaky ground, consider what this goddess is trying to tell you!

To Do Today: Around this time of year in Northern California, people examine the coastline with renewed interest and anticipation. They're watching the annual whale migration—a breathtaking sight. Since many of us cannot experience this firsthand, consider the whale as a magical symbol instead. The gods ride whales to carry messages to the mortal world. Witches ride them to bear their magic on the water. In both instances the whale carries something—either to your heart or toward a goal. Use this image in meditations for movement, and consider the symbolism if whales show up in your dreams tonight.

If possible, visit an aquarium and watch whales there. Or send a donation to an accredited facility to give something back to the Whale Goddess and her children.

※

Phra Buddha Bat Fair (Thailand)

CHIHNU

Themes: Arts; Creativity; Tradition; Excellence

Symbols: Woven Items; Thread or Yarn; Home Crafts; Lyres

About Chihnu: In China and surrounding regions, Chihnu's name means "weaving woman." According to myths, Chihnu's talents in this art are so great that she can weave seamless garments for the gods. From her heavenly domain in the constellation Lyre, she acts like a refreshing spring wind to inspire excellence in our inherited arts and crafts.

To Do Today: This annual Thai festival features folk dancing and traditional handicrafts in honor of Buddha's footprint, which is enshrined nearby. Generally, it is a time to rejoice in Thai tradition, so if you have a Thai restaurant in the neighborhood, by all means indulge yourself, saying a brief prayer of thanks to the provider of your feast—Chihnu.

To make a Chihnu-inspired creativity charm, take three strands of yellow thread or yarn (yellow is the color of inventiveness). Braid these together so that the strands cross four times, saying,

> *One, Chihnu's power absorbs;*
> *two, inside the magic's stored;*
> *three, the magic's alive in me;*
> *four, bear Chihnu's creativity!*

Carry this when you need more ingenious energy, or leave it near your artistic endeavors so they can absorb Chihnu's compelling excellence.

Finally, wear woven or handmade items to honor Chihnu's talents today.

March 8

Mother Earth Day (China)

H U T U

Themes: Earth; Nature; Ecology; Fertility

Symbols: Globe; Soil; All Natural Items; Marble

About Hu Tu: Literally "Empress Earth" in Chinese mythology, this goddess embodies and personifies the earth in spring
and its fertility. Through her we can learn how to live abun-
dantly, while maintaining a reciprocity with nature. Hu Tu
also teaches us how to see and integrate nature's lessons.

To Do Today: According to tradition, this is the birthday of Hu Tu,
in the form of Mother Earth. Celebrate it as you might any birthday,
with a little twist. Make a fertilizer cake for the earth and light a
candle on it. Blow out the candle, making a wish to Hu Tu for earth's
revitalization. Then, give the fertilizer to the soil to start the process!

This celebration bears many similarities to Earth Day in the
West, so organize litter patrols, educate yourself on recycling techniques, take a long walk to truly enjoy Hu Tu's beauty. As you walk,
feel the sacredness of the ground beneath your feet and say a silent
prayer of thankfulness to Hu Tu for her care and providence.

Finally, make yourself a Hu Tu charm that stimulates grounding
and draws figurative or literal fertility to you. Find any marble (blue
is best) to represent Hu Tu. Cleanse and energize this today by
putting it in rich soil to connect it to Hu Tu's foundational energy.
Carry the charm whenever you feel flighty or need to be more productive.

March 9

🦋

Butter Festival (Tibet)

ADITI

Themes: Luck; Change; Perspective; Time; Protection; Prosperity; Overcoming Obstacles; Divination.

Symbols: Butter; the Number Twelve; Anything that Changes Shape

About Aditi: Aditi means "unfettered." In India she represents the infinite sky and the boundlessness of time and space. She offers us this expansive perspective—one in which we are citizens of eternity. Additionally, Aditi is a protector who aids in averting or surmounting difficulties. In regional prayers, people refer to her as the ever-young protectress who guides life's boat safely through the roughest waters.

To Do Today: Buddhists believe that the world is transient—that only spirit is eternal. The Butter Festival illustrates this concept with huge butter statues of heroes that are torn, distributed to participants for luck, or tossed in a river to melt away into time. Following this custom, take out an ice cube. Relax and watch the ice as it melts. Consider: Is the ice still there, even though it's gone? Similarly, does the spirit exist outside its "shape"—the body?

For a less ponderous way of honoring Aditi, light twelve candles (yellow is ideal) and watch the flame. Hindus use butter lamps instead, but this is far easier! If the flames appear dark red, your spirit is filled with strife. Mottled flames indicate weakness, tall flames symbolize mental clarity, crescent-shaped ones reveal a peaceful soul, and round ones proclaim magical power.

March 10

Daedala (Greece)

HERA

Themes: Love; Romance; Forgiveness; Humor

Symbols: Oak; Myrrh; Poppy

About Hera: Hera rules the earth, its people, and the hearts of those people. Using passion and creativity, Hera nudges star-crossed lovers together, chaperones trysts, and helps struggling marriages with a case of spring twitterpation!

Legend tells us that Hera refused to return to Zeus's bed because of a quarrel. Zeus, however, had a plan. He humorously dressed up a wooden figure to look like a bride and declared he was going to marry. When Hera tore off the dummy's clothes and discovered the ruse, she was so amused and impressed by Zeus's ingenuity that she forgave him.

To Do Today: Ancient Greeks honored Hera and Zeus's reconciliation today, often in the company of old oak trees. Small pieces of fallen wood are collected to symbolize the divinities, then burned on the ritual fire to keep love warm. To mirror this custom, find a fallen branch and burn a small part of it as an offering to Hera. Keep the rest to use as a goddess image year-round, burning a few slivers whenever love needs encouragement.

Present someone you love or admire with a poppy today to symbolically bestow Hera's blessings on your relationship. If you have a loved one away from home, burn some myrrh incense in front of their picture so Hera can watch over them and keep that connection strong.

March 11

Nyambinyambi (West Africa)

HARA KE

Themes: Spring; Weather; Providence; Harvest; Growth

Symbols: Seeds; Soil; Rain Water; Dragon Images

About Hara Ke: An African goddess of sweet water (which also equates with the gentle spring rains) Hara Ke comes into our lives and spring with gentle, growth-inspiring refreshment. According to legend she lives under the river Niger with two dragons in attendance, caring for the souls who await rebirth, just as earth awaits its reawakening with spring.

To Do Today: People in Namibia pull out all their garden tools and seeds and bless them today before the sowing season starts. This ensures a good harvest and plentiful rains, the water of Hara Ke's spirit. If you garden or tinker with window pots, this tradition holds merit. Just sprinkle your tools and seeds with a little spring water or rainwater, then visualize the seeds being filled with pale green light (like new sprouts).

Alternatively, sprinkle your own aura, first going counterclockwise to wash away residual sickness or tension, then going clockwise to invoke Hara Ke. As you sprinkle the water, say,

> Hara Ke, renew in me a sense of refreshed ability.
> To my spirit, growth impart; make your home in my heart.

If you're pressed for time, you can recite this in your morning shower or while doing the laundry (during the rinse cycle). The latter allows you to figuratively don Hara Ke's attributes with your clothing whenever you need them.

March 12

Eagle Dance (New Mexico)

WHITE SHELL WOMAN

Themes: Magic; Overcoming; Spirituality; Freedom; Hope; Success; Protection; Joy; Dreams

Symbols: Eagle; Rattle; White

About White Shell Woman: In Native American tradition, White Shell Woman came to earth bearing elemental blankets and the sunshine of protection, dreams, and renewed hope. When she arrived a rainbow appeared, banishing sadness with the promise of eventually reuniting humankind with the gods. Today she renews this promise to us, whispering her message on March's winds and bearing it on the wings of an eagle.

To Do Today: Sometime in spring, the Pueblos of New Mexico hold an Eagle Dance to bring rain and ensure the tribe's success in difficult situations. The mimelike movements of the dance unite the dancers with the Eagle spirit, connecting them with the sacred powers. To adapt this in your own life, grab a feather duster and dance a little of White Shell Woman's hope into your heart while you clean up the house!

If you have young children in your life, work with them on a Shell Woman anti-nightmare blanket or happiness charm. Take four strips of cloth in elemental colors, or seven in the colors of the rainbow. Sew them together to form a blanket or portable swatch. Bless the charm, saying,

> Love and joy within each seam brings me only happy dreams;
> Shell Woman, shine through the night; keep me safe till dawn's
> first light.

Buergsonndeg (*Luxembourg*)

N E R T H U S

Themes: Spring; Cycles; Health; Energy; Peace; Prosperity

Symbols: Fire; Chariot; Soil

About Nerthus: This Germanic earth goddess welcomes the season with her presence. She was so important in Danish regions that no weapons or iron tools could be left out during her festivals, because that was thought to invoke her displeasure. During spring rites, her statue was covered on a chariot until the priest determined she had arrived to oversee the festivities.

To Do Today: Traditionally, today is spent before a bonfire that greets the sun and banishes the last vestiges of winter. So, take down your heavy winter curtains, and let some light into the house! This restores Nerthus's positive energy and expels any lingering sicknesses. If it's cloudy out, turn on some lights, don dazzling-colored clothing, and find ways to brighten up your living space with flowers and decorations that speak of earth (Nerthus) and spring's beauty.

Another customary activity is turning the soil, mixing it with an offering of milk, flour, and water. Even if you don't have a garden, turn a little dirt near your apartment or home and leave a similar gift. This action rejoices in Nerthus's awakening and draws the goddess's peace and prosperity to your residence. To take a little of that same blessing with you, just collect a bit of the soil-milk mixture in a container and put it wherever you need peace or prosperity the most.

🌿

Ghanaian New Year

ALA

Themes: Luck; Harvest; Joy; Cleansing; Death; Cycles

Symbols: Yams; Crescent Moon

About Ala: This West African earth-goddess represents the full cycle of earth's seasons from birth to death, gently reminding us that spring is transitory—so enjoy it now! Serious crimes are an abhorrence to Ala, and the spirits of the dead go to her womb to find rest. Votive candles are a suitable offering for this goddess figure.

To Do Today: When you get up this morning, light any candle to welcome both Ala and spring. If possible, include yams in your dinner meal to internalize the joy and good fortune Ala brings with the warmer weather. Bless your yams by putting your hands (palms down) over them, focusing on your goals, and saying,

> Ala, be welcome. In this your sacred food, place
> the energy of happiness, luck, and protection for
> the months ahead. So be it.

The people of Ghana believe in celebrating the new year over thirteen days instead of one. During this time they dance to banish evil, honor their dead ancestors, encourage serendipity, and petition Ala for a good harvest season. Ala's shrines and other sacred places are bathed on the last day of festivities to wash away the old, along with bad memories. For us this equates to dusting off our altars, bathing any god or goddess images we have, and generally cleansing away old energies so Ala can refresh us.

March 15

Anna Parenna Festival (Rome)

ANNA PARENNA

Themes: Cycles: Peace; Kindness; Grounding; Longevity

Symbols: Circular Items (Rings, Wheels, Wreaths); Wine

About Anna Parenna: Ana Parenna, like Ala, symbolizes the entire year's cycle. Even her name translates as "enduring year." Legend tells us that Anna was once a real woman who showed benevolence to refugees from the Roman aristocracy by giving them food until peace was reestablished. It is this gentle spirit with which Anna comes into our lives, offering the spiritual harmony engendered by random acts of kindness.

To Do Today: Romans honored Anna Parenna around this date because March was the first month of the Roman calendar. In true Roman fashion—that looks for any excuse for a party—they spent the day praying that Anna would let them live one more year for each cup of wine drunk this day. Wine (or grape juice) remains a suitable libation to Anna Parenna when asking for longevity. As you pour the liquid, say,

> A long life of health, blessed from winter to spring,
> Anna Parenna, longevity bring!

To encourage inner peace and security in your life, keep a pinch of the soil-wine mixture in any round container as a charm. Open the container and put the blend under your feet when you feel your foundations shaking, or when stress wreaks havoc in your heart.

Wearing any ring, belt, or other circular item today stimulates a greater understanding of Anna's cycles in nature and your life.

March 16

🌸

Holi (India)

GAURI

Themes: Spring; Protection; Fertility; Harvest; Beauty; Humor; Youthfulness; Wishes; Equality

Symbols: Balsam; Golden-colored Items; Milk; Mirrors; Lions

About Gauri: This fertile Hindu goddess extends springlike youth, beauty, fairness, and tenderness into our lives. Gauri has a sympathetic ear for all human needs and wishes. In works of art she is depicted as a fair maiden, attended by lions and bearing wild balsam and a mirror. She was born of a milky sea, and her name translates as "golden one," indicating a connection with the sun. She is offered rice to ensure a good rice crop.

To Do Today: Holi is India's most colorful festival, filled with Gauri's equitable spirit. It celebrates an epic tale in which the sun (Gauri) is freed from a god's mouth by getting him to laugh! Customarily, caste restrictions are shed today in order for people to simply have fun. Everyone squirts colored water at one another, and by the end of the day, no one can tell who is a servant and who is a king! This translates into a good-humored water-balloon toss. Focus on a goal while you play. When a balloon breaks, it releases Gauri's youthful joy and productivity into your life.

Hindu custom suggests eating sweets to generate Gauri's beauty and pleasantness in your spirit today. Or, pour her a libation of milk while making a wish for something you'd like to "harvest" in your life. Hang balsam in your home to foster Gauri's fairness in your family's interactions.

March 17

❧

Easter (Date and Location Vary)

OSTARA

Themes: Fertility; Rebirth

Symbol: Egg

About Ostara: The Teutonic goddess Ostara presides over personal renewal, fertility, and fruitfulness. Now that spring is here, it's a good time to think about renewal in your own life. Ostara represents spring's life force and earth's renewal. Depicted as lovely as the season itself, in earlier writings she was also the goddess of dawn, a time of new beginnings (spring being the figurative dawn of the year). One of Ostara's name variations, Esotara, slowly evolved into the modern name for this holiday, Easter.

To Do Today: All spells and foods that include eggs are appropriate today. If you've been ill, try an old folk spell that recommends carrying an egg for twenty-four hours, then burying it to bury the sickness.

To improve fertility of all kinds, make eggs for breakfast at dawn's first light, the best time to invoke Ostara. As you eat, add an incantation like this one:

> *Ostara, bring to me fertility;*
> *with this egg now bless my fruitfulness!*

Or, if you're feeling down and need a little extra hope, get up before the sun rises and release a symbol of your burden to the earth by dropping or burying it. Don't look at it. Turn your back and leave it there. Turn toward the horizon as the sun rises, and harvest the first flower you see. Dry it, then carry it with you often as a charm to preserve hope in your heart.

Sheelah's Day (Ireland)

SHEELAH-NA-GIG

Themes: Fertility; Sexuality; Protection; Passion; Femininity

Symbols: Nakedness; Lust-inspiring Scents; Whiskey

About Sheelah-Na-Gig: The image of this Irish goddess of fertility tells us much about the unbridled nature of feminine passion that Sheelah inspires with springlike whimsy. She is shown smiling broadly, holding her legs wide open, completely naked. Nonetheless, this is not irresponsible lust; it is the gate of life through which we all pass. Interestingly enough, Sheelah's image, in an amulet, offers protection, too—perhaps she was the first goddess of safe sex?!

To Do Today: Sheelah's Day is celebrated in true Irish fashion by drinking abundant whiskey and drowning a shamrock in the last glass consumed, to end the festivities. This particular custom denotes the idea of consuming one's luck, increasing fecundity, and internalizing the goddess's protective energies before the day is over. So if you can tolerate whiskey, toast Sheelah, take a sip, and warm up your passion! Otherwise, offer her a libation of whiskey, asking for her energy to be likewise liberated in your body.

If you have a significant other, one of the best ways to honor Sheelah is through passionate encounters that are balanced with wisdom and foresight. Take a condom and bless it, saying,

> *Sheelah, my hunger see, let my body love freely.*
> *But keep us safe, fertility bind,*
> *no matter our haste, keep protection in mind.*

Carry this condom with you to your tryst.

❦

Sacaea (Babylon)

ANAITIS

Themes: Spring; Relationships; Equality; Fertility; Sexuality

Symbols: Green Branches; Water

About Anaitis: This Babylonian goddess of fertility embraces the attributes of fruitful, warm waters that flow from the celestial realms into our lives, especially as the earth is renewed. Her name translates as "humid immaculate one," and art shows her as a strong maiden who creates life and pours out blessings. During the height of Babylonian civilization, she was also the patroness of civic prostitutes.

To Do Today: This day marked the Babylonian new year, during which time heaven and earth were considered married. Therefore, this is an excellent date to plan a wedding, handfasting, or engagement, or just to spend time with someone you hold dear. Bring them a small green branch from a tree to extend Anaitis's love and equality into your relationship.

Traditional roles are often reversed today to emphasize fairness between people. So, if you're normally passive in your interactions, become a little more aggressive. As you do, feel how Anaitis's passion and energy flow through you.

To increase passion or sexual confidence, take a warm bath before meeting your partner. Perhaps add some lusty aromatics to the water (cinnamon, vanilla, mint, or violet) to put you in the right frame of mind. Let Anaitis's waters stimulate your skin and your interest, then enjoy!

Festival of Isis (Egypt)

ISIS

Themes: Magic; Harvest; Dreams; Divination: Perspective; Faithfulness; Love; Spirituality; Destiny

Symbols: Bloodstone; Amethyst; Silver; Myrrh; Cedar; Hawk; Moon

About Isis: One of the most complete goddess figures in history, Isis breathes on us with spring winds to revitalize and fulfill our spirits in every way. Egyptians venerated Isis as the Queen of Sorcery, Life of the Nile, Mother Moon, and Protectress. Isis taught humankind the basic skills necessary to build civilizations, and she came to represent the powerful attributes of faithfulness, love, inner beauty, oracular insight, and spiritual awareness (to name just a few). She could also change her followers' destinies.

To Do Today: Today was the spring harvest festival in Egypt, honoring the giver of all life, Isis. Put a bloodstone or amethyst in your pocket today to inspire any or all of Isis's characteristics in your soul and life. If you have any silver or white clothing, wearing them will also foster Isis-centered energy, because these colors are associated with the moon.

One traditional activity today is fortune-telling, an art under Isis's dominion. To encourage visionary dreams from her, put some rose petals under your pillow before going to bed, and burn some myrrh or jasmine incense. Keep a dream diary handy, and write your impressions immediately upon waking so you won't lose the insight.

March 21

Sun Enters Aries (*Various Locations*)

ISHIKORE-DOME

Themes: Arts; Excellence

Symbols: Stone; Mirror

About Ishikore-Dome: This Shinto goddess is the protectress of all stonecutters and smiths, having fashioned the mold from which an eight-petaled mirror was made for Amaterasu (the sun goddess). The beauty of Ishikore-Dome's creation was such that Amaterasu came out of hiding, bringing spring's wonderful sunshine with her! Similarly, Ishikore-Dome tempts us to come out of our home-cave today, explore and express our talents, and enjoy the warmer weather.

To Do Today: The sign of Aries is said to produce a feisty, courageous spirit, which is exactly what it takes sometimes to stop being the proverbial wallflower and try new things. If there's an art form you've always wanted to try, or one that you love but hesitate to try because of perceived shortcomings, let Ishikore-Dome's encouraging energy nudge you into action today. Remember, Buddhists believe that developing artistic proficiency comes down to three things: practice, practice, practice!

To conduct yourself with greater courage and a unique artistic flair, make a simple Ishikore-Dome charm from a small mirror. Face-down on the mirror, glue a symbol of the area in your life in which you need more creativity, mastery, or mettle and carry it with you. This symbolically reflects your desire to the goddess.

March 22

✥

Vernal Equinox (*Various Locations*)

BUTTERFLY MAIDEN

Themes: Rebirth; Beauty; Fertility; Balance; Freedom; Nature

Symbols: Butterflies; Seedlings; Rainwater; Spring Flowers

About Butterfly Maiden: In Hopi tradition, the Butterfly Maiden is a *kachina* (spirit) who rules the springtime and the earth's fertility. Butterfly Maiden flutters into our life today to reconnect us with nature and to help us rediscover that graceful butterfly within each of us—the one that effortlessly rises above problems, making the world its flower.

To Do Today: In magical traditions, the equinox celebrates the sun's journey back to predominance in the sky and the return of fertility to the earth. It is a joyous fire festival when the elements are in balance, giving us the opportunity to likewise balance our lives. If anything has held you back from real spiritual growth, now is the time to banish it and move on. Visualize yourself as the caterpillar who becomes a butterfly, then let the Butterfly Maiden give you wings with which to overcome anything!

To inspire Butterfly Maiden's beauty within and without, wash your face and chakras (near pulse points as well as at the top of the head, in the middle of the forehead, over the heart, near the groin, behind the knees, and at the bottom of the feet) with rainwater first thing in the morning (dawn is best). Go outside afterward and toss some flower petals into a spring breeze, saying,

> *Butterfly Maiden, liberate me;*
> *let my mind and spirit ever be free!*

The winds will carry your wish to heaven.

March 23

⚜

Marzenna (Poland)

MARZENNA

Themes: Spring; Weather; Protection; Winter; Death; Rebirth; Cycles; Change; Growth

Symbols: Doll (poppet); Water (including ice and snow)

About Marzenna: The Polish goddess for whom this holiday is named represents an odd combination of winter, death, and the fruit field's growth and fertility. As such, she oversees the earth's transition from death to rebirth and likewise oversees the transitions we wish to make in our lives.

To Do Today: Marzenna is a Polish spring festival during which an effigy of Marzenna is tossed into a river to overcome her wintery nature and ensure that there will be no floods that year. This tradition is likely an antecedent of ancient river sacrifices made to appease the water spirits. Following suit, resolutely throw a biodegradable image of something you wish to overcome this season into any moving water source (even your toilet!). Let Marzenna carry it away, slowly breaking down that negative energy and replacing it with personal growth. Burying an image has the same effect.

To invoke Marzenna's protection until next winter, write your name and birthdate on a piece of paper and freeze it in an ice cube. Keep the cube in a safe place in the back of your freezer to keep yourself surrounded by Marzenna's safe barrier. Melt the ice cube later in the year if you need a boost of spring's revitalizing energy.

❧

Crane Watch (Nebraska)

TAMRA

Themes: Air; Earth; Nature; Health; Longevity; Devotion; Wishes; Relationships

Symbols: Feathers; Birdseed

About Tamra: In Hindu tradition, this goddess was the ancestor of all birds. As such, she can teach us their special language, which often bears communications from the divine. As the consort of the turtle god, Kashyapa, she also represents a potent union between earth and air elements.

To Do Today: People in Nebraska spend six weeks watching the cranes who rest and feed here during the migratory season. This region of the United States boasts the largest group of sandhill cranes, about fifty thousand birds. Magically speaking, these creatures represent health, longevity, and devotion. Visualize a crane residing in your heart chakra anytime you feel your eyes straying from the one you love, or whenever you need improved well-being.

Birds offer numerous magical applications. For warmth in a relationship, scatter feathers to the winds with your wish. The birds will use the feathers in their nests, symbolically keeping your nest intact and affectionate. Or, disperse birdseed while thinking of a question. As the birds fly away, watch their movement. Flight to the right indicates a positive response; to the left is negative. If the birds scatter, things are iffy. If they fly straight up overhead, a heartfelt wish is being taken to Tamra.

※

Hilaria (Rome)

CYBELLE

Themes: Love; Health; Humor; Victory; Strength; Relationships

Symbols: Pine; Meteorite Stone; Key

About Cybelle: A black stone that personified this Roman earth goddess is credited with a successful battle against Hannibal. It is this strength, especially in difficult relationships, that Cybelle augments in us as this month draws to a close.

Legend tells us that Cybelle loved a shepherd named Attis who went mad and killed himself. Cybelle, in distress, asked Jupiter to restore him. Jupiter responded by making Attis into a pine tree. Symbolically, this allowed him to eternally embrace Cybelle, with his roots in the earth.

To Do Today: Following the story of Cybelle and Attis, this festival begins in sorrow over Attis's death and ends in joy. Today, laughter and fun activities are considered healthy. So, rent a good comedy flick, go out to a comedy club, or do something that really uplifts your spirit. Your laughter invokes Cybelle's attention and blessings.

To create stability in a relationship, make this Cybelle charm: Take an iron key (or a piece of iron and any old key bound together). Hold them in your strong hand, visualizing the key being filled with radiant red light (love's color). Say,

> *Cybelle, let this key to our hearts be filled,*
> *love and devotion here instilled.*

Wear the key on a long chain so it rests over your heart chakra.

❦

Slavic Plowing Season

LESHACHIKHA

Themes: Earth; Nature; Harvest; Birth; Protection

Symbols: Soil; a Leaf; Seeds

About Leshachikha: A goddess who sometimes appears as a Slavic forest, a wild animal, or a leaf, Leshachikha is said to have died in October and revived around this time in spring. She fiercely protects her lands, not taking kindly to any who abuse them. In this manner she teaches us about reciprocity and nature's fury. Additionally, Leshachikha's watchful aspect can be applied to our figurative lands—for example, safeguarding our homes.

To Do Today: Whenever you need a little extra protective energy, pick up a fallen leaf and put it in your pocket. This will keep Leshachikha's guardian powers with you all day. To bring that protection into your home, wax the leaf to preserve it, symbolically sustaining the magical energy forever. Put the waxed leaf near your entryway or in the room where you spend the most time.

Go to a nearby field or park today and scatter some seed to Leshachikha to greet her as she awakens. Today marks the beginning of the plowing season in Slavic regions. Before this date the earth is regarded as pregnant. It is a crime against nature and Leshachikha to plow the soil with iron tools when it still bears a magical child (spring). Once earth has given birth, the fields can then accept new seed, which the birds will also appreciate!

March 27

Smell the Breeze Day (Egypt)

NUT

Themes: Air; Health

Symbols: A Pot; Turquoise; Musk; a Star; Wind; Cow Images

About Nut: This great Egyptian sky goddess bears a star-spangled belly that stretches over the earth like a protective atmosphere. Today she breaths on us with a late-March zephyr bearing health and well-being.

Legend tells us that when Ra went to escape the earth, Nut offered her aid by becoming a huge cow who lifted him into heaven. When Nut found herself dizzy from the effort, four gods rushed to her aid. They later became the four pillars of creation—the four winds.

To Do Today: If the weather permits, I highly recommend a brisk, refreshing walk. Breathe deeply of the air, which has rejuvenating, healthy energies today. As you exhale, repeat the goddess's name, Nut, and listen as she responds in the breeze.

Any type of wind magic honors Nut, and it is certainly fitting today. If the wind blows from the west, sprinkle water into it for emotional healing. If it blows from the east, toss a feather out so it can return to you with healthy outlooks. If it blows from the north, sift a little soil into the wind to give fruitful foundations to a generating idea, and if it blows from the south, burn musk incense to manifest vital energy and a little passion.

❦

Bali Temple Offering

VAC

Themes: Purification; Protection; Offerings; Communication

Symbols: The Spoken Word; Fresh Flowers

About Vac: The Balinese/Hindu goddess of charms and incantations, Vac joins in today's celebrations using her powers to banish any lingering shadows or negativity from our lives. Traditionally, Vac is present in any sacred words that convey occult power or knowledge. This is especially true of mantras that reaffirm, sustain, and shelter one's soul.

Artistic renderings reveal Vac as a mature, graceful woman bedecked in gold (an allusion to solar energy). She sometimes also appears as a cow, which is her mother-goddess aspect.

To Do Today: Bali legends say that hellish beings roam freely during this time of year, so everyone cleanses themselves and the land through magic and supplications. In this spirit, periodic spiritual "house cleaning" is a good habit to get into, especially if you live in the city. Leave an offering of flowers on your altar, saying Vac's name as you put them out. This begins the process of purging any clinging bad vibes and restoring your home's sanctity.

Use noise makers to chase out any malintended magic or spirits. Burn sweet-smelling incense to welcome Vac to your home, saying,

> *Vac, charge my speech with security so no darkness can dwell in my home or me.*
>
> *Vac, be welcome in and through my words. Let the magic e'er be heard!*

❦

Masquerade (*Africa*)

MUJAJI

Themes: Balance; Restoration; Weather; Cleansing; Fertility

Symbol: Rainwater

About Mujaji: Mujaji is an African rain goddess who exudes gently with fertility, or fiercely with cleansing, depending on the need. Her power and presence is so impressive that it led H. Rider Haggard to write the novel *She*, based on her cult.

To Do Today: To purify any area and ready it for ritual, sprinkle rainwater as you move clockwise, saying,

> *Mujaji, flow through me;*
> *Mujaji, cleanse me;*
> *Mujaji, rain lightly here on all I love and hold dear.*

To expel unproductive emotions (represented by the sky's tears), do the same thing, but move counterclockwise—this is the traditional direction of banishing.

If it does rain gently today, it is a sign of blessing. Go out and skip, dance, or sing in the rain (think Gene Kelly with a magical twist). This will renew your spirit and lift any dark clouds overshadowing your heart.

Africans observe this holiday as a time to reinstate symmetry in the world and in themselves. They wear elaborate costumes to appease the divine, praying for the necessary rainfall to ensure rich soil, and consequently an abundant harvest. To adapt this, pray to Mujaji to enrich the soil of your soul so that come the fall, you can harvest her productive nature.

March 30

Iranian New Year

AHURANI

Themes: Luck; Health; Longevity; Harvest; Fertility

Symbol: Water

About Ahurani: Persians invoked Ahurani for prosperity, growth, fertility, and insight through water libations, and we can do likewise. Her companion, Ahura Mazda, is the Lord of Wisdom and helps us distinguish good from evil.

To Do Today: People in Iran welcome the new year over thirteen days around the spring equinox with festivities similar to those of many other cultures, including rituals for portents, luck, health, and long life. Rain today indicates Ahurani's pleasure and thus a good harvest. Eating sweet wheat breads or a nut compote today brings Ahurani's fortune and fertility. It is also very important to go outside today; otherwise, all bad luck stays within the house!

Quaff a full glass of fresh, clean water today to internalize any of Ahurani's attributes you need. Keep your mind strongly focused on your goal as you drink. To improve this little spell, dye the water with food coloring to match the magic. Use green for growth, abundance, and fertility, or blue for wisdom. In keeping with Iranian custom, give a little of this water to the earth as you invoke Ahurani's blessings.

Wear water-toned clothing today (blues and purples) to help you flow easily through the day and to accent Ahurani's energy.

March 31

🌺

Feast of the Moon (Rome)

LUNA

Themes: All Lunar Attributes—Instinct; Creativity; Luck; Femininity; Water Element; Miracles (on a Blue Moon)— also Safety in Travel

Symbols: Silver or White Items; Water; Moon Images; the Number Thirteen

About Luna: The Roman goddess personifying the moon, Luna had the additional unique quality of being a protectress of charioteers, which in modern times could make her a patroness of automobiles!

While March came in like a lion, Luna escorts it out lamb-ishly, with her soft, shimmering light. She is the full moon, which symbolizes the growing awareness developed this month, the fullness of loving emotions, and charms and enchantments empowered by the silvery light of the moon.

To Do Today: Go moon gazing (okay, if it's a dark moon, meaning the moon can't be seen, you'll have to wait for another day). To encourage any of Luna's attributes, recite this invocation to the moon:

> *Moon, moon, Lady moon, shine your light on me.*
> *Moon, moon, Lady moon, bring _____ to me.*

Fill in the blank with your heart's desire. If possible, gear your request to match the energy in today's moon phase. A waxing moon augments spells for any type of growth or development. A full moon emphasizes maturity, fertility, abundance, and "ful"-fillment. Waning moons help banish unwanted characteristics or shrink problems, and dark moons emphasize rest and introspection.

April

April gets its name from the goddess Aprilis, who is the Romans' version of Aphrodite. Her name means "to open," which is exactly what Aprilis does . . . she opens the path to playfulness and the way to personal enrichment.

We all know the rhyme "April showers bring May flowers." So consider what energies you want Aprilis to sprinkle on you this month for personal flowering. Overall, any magical efforts aimed toward growth, love, pleasure, improvements, and developing one's inner child will benefit from working during this month.

April 1

April Fool's Day (*Various Locations*)

LAUFEY

Themes: Humor; Playfulness; Youthfulness

Symbols: A Piece of Wood; any Humorous Items

About Laufey: On this day of pranks and foolery, look to Laufey to show you how to hone your funny bone. As the mother of the great trickster Loki, if anyone understands and can teach the value of raillery and good-intended tricks, it is she!

To Do Today: Spring's upbeat theme continues into April, offsetting the rains with laughter. If it's been a while since you really chuckled, consider renting a good comedy movie. As you watch it, light a candle and ask Laufey to join you!

Or, improve your sense of humor and draw a little luck your way by making a Laufey charm. In Teutonic tradition, Laufey's name means "wooded isle," because she furnished her son with firewood. So, to represent her, begin with a stick no larger than the palm of your hand and a small feather (any kind). Draw an ascending spiral on the stick with a green magic marker (green is spring's color and encourages growth). Attach the feather to the end of the stick to "tickle your fancy." Energize the token, saying,

> *Laufey, in this stick of green, place a sense of humor ever keen.*
> *And when upon the stick I knock, bring to me a bit of luck.*

Hold the token whenever you find your humor failing; knock on the wood when you need better fortune to bring a smile back to your face.

April 2

✳

Rejoicing Day (Germany)

RINDA

Themes: Spring; Overcoming; Protection; Fire; Spirituality; Change

Symbols: Fire; Solar Images; Gold and Yellow

About Rinda: In Scandinavia, Rinda represents winter struggling to retain control, even as people sometimes fight positive change because they find the process uncomfortable. Eventually, Rinda succumbs to Odin's advances, which warm and fertilize her, bringing spring. Rinda teaches us to likewise accept personal transformations gracefully.

To Do Today: Sometime around the fourth Sunday after lent, many German villages stage a battle between the forces of winter and spring (of course, spring always wins). This might equate to a ritual tug-of-war game in which the winter puts up a good battle, but loses. Have people focus on something they similarly want to lose in their lives (like a negative characteristic).

To clear away the cold and old ways, follow the German custom of creating an effigy of winter out of straw and burning it in the fire of spring. Just gather a few strands of straw from the kitchen broom. Tie them together with a white string (for protection), visualizing whatever situation you want "warmed up" or the habits/ideas you want "burned away." Ignite this in a fire-safe container, saying,

> As Rinda accepts Odin, I now accept change.

Let the straw burn to ash, then scatter it to disperse the energy.

April 3

✳

Sizdar Bedah (Iran)

AHERAH

Themes: Luck; Health; Blessings; Wisdom; Divination

Symbols: A Wooden Pole; Brick

About Aherah: Aherah is the Phoenician/Mesopotamian Mother of all Wisdom and Proprietress of Universal Law. On this day she offers her perspective on the present and future to begin settling the first quarter of the year sagaciously.

In Iranian stories, Aherah could walk on water, gave birth to over seventy deities, and taught people the arts of carpentry and brick building.

To Do Today: This festival is part of the new year festivities in Iran. Follow Iranian tradition and generate Aherah's fortuitous, healthy energy in your life by going on a picnic (or have one in the living room if the weather doesn't cooperate, but leave the windows open). It is bad luck to stay inside today! Or, to make a spring wish, toss any type of springwater sprouts in water while focusing on your goal. If it is meant to be, the wish will manifest before the next Sizdar Bedah. The alternative to sprouts is any newly sprouting seed, which should be planted afterward to encourage the magic to grow.

For wisdom, find a small piece of wood or brick to represent Aherah. Lie down and meditate with the token over your third eye (located in the middle of the forehead and reputed to be a psychic center), visualizing purple light pouring through it. Chant

> *Aherah abide in me;*
> *with your wisdom let me see!*

Carry the token when you need to act judiciously.

April 4

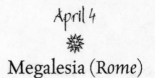

Megalesia (Rome)

THE CARMENAE

Themes: Divination; Protection; Victory; Children; Birth; Communication

Symbols: The Written Word; Divination Tools (any); Fertility Symbols

About the Carmenae: This group of goddesses correspond to the Muses of Greek tradition: they know our past, see what's in store in the future, foretell children's fates, and teach us the effective use of "letters" (the alphabet), the arts, and how to tell fortunes. They also oversee midwives.

To Do Today: Megalesia celebrates the accuracy of the Sibylline oracles, who predicted the way for the Roman victory in the Punic war. Romans traditionally honored the goddess today with music and song, so put on some magical tunes! The Carmenae will saturate the music and uplift your spirit.

Ask the Carmenae to help you write personalized invocations or spells today. Put pen to pad and let these goddesses inspire sacred words suited to your path and needs. Keep these in a magic journal for future use.

The Roman oracles often drew lots to determine a querent's answer. If you have a question weighing heavily on your heart today, follow this custom and take out some variegated beans. Hold them. Concentrate on the question, then pick out one bean. A black one means "no"; white means "yes." Red means that anger is driving action, brown means things are muddled, and green indicates growth potential. If you don't have beans, colored buttons are a suitable alternative.

April 5

✳

Festival of the Goddess of Mercy
(China/Japan)

KWAN YIN

Themes: Children; Kindness; Magic; Health; Fertility

Symbols: Lotus; Black Tea; Rice; Rainbow

About Kwan Yin: Kwan Yin is the most beloved of all Eastern goddess figures, giving freely of her unending sympathy, fertility, health, and magical insight to all who ask. It is her sacred duty to relieve suffering and encourage enlightenment among humans. In Eastern mythology, a rainbow bore Kwan Yin to heaven in human form. Her name means "regarder of sounds," meaning she hears the cries and prayers of the world.

To Do Today: If you hope to have children or wish to invoke Kwan Yin's blessing and protection on the young ones in your life, you can follow Eastern custom and leave an offering for Kwan Yin of sweet cakes, lotus incense, fresh fruit, and/or flowers. If you can't find lotus incense, look for lotus-shaped soaps at novelty or import shops.

For literal or figurative fertility, try making this Kwan Yin talisman: During a waxing-to-full moon, take a pinch of black tea and a pinch of rice and put them in a yellow cloth, saying,

> As a little tea makes a full cup, so may my life be full.
> As the rice expands in warm water, so may my heart
>   expand with love and warmth.
> The fertility of Kwan Yin, wrapped neatly within.

Tie this up and keep it in a spot that corresponds to the type of fertility you want (such as the bedroom for physical fertility).

April 6

※

Boat Festival (France)

SEQUANA

Themes: Wishes; Youthfulness; Luck; Health; Movement

Symbols: Ducks; Boats

About Sequana: A Celtic river goddess, Sequana flows in with April showers, raining good health and improved fortunes upon us. Statuary of her shows Sequana standing in a duck-shaped boat (the duck is her sacred animal) with open arms ready to receive our prayers.

To Do Today: Children in France run merrily to the Rhine river around this date to launch miniature boats with candles inside. Each boat represents life's voyage being filled with joy. Anyone finding a boat later may make a wish as they bring it to shore. This is a charming custom that you can re-create if you have a stream, river, pond, or lake nearby. Or, fill a children's pool with water. Make a wish to Sequana as you launch your boat. Putting the boat on the water invokes Sequana's happiness and motivational energy for achieving a personal goal. Coax the boat toward a friend or partner on the other side so they can make a wish!

If neither of these options works out, float a rubber duckie in your bathtub and soak in Sequana's revitalizing waters. Add to the bath pantry herbs that match your goals. For wishes add sage, for youthful energy add rosemary, for luck, allspice, for health, fennel, and for movement, ginger. No time for a bath? Make these five herbs into a tea and quaff them to internalize Sequana's powers for the day.

✳

Romanian Water Offering

COVENTINA

Themes: Wishes; Water; Purity; Innocence

Symbol: Water

About Coventina: This British/Celtic goddess of sacred water sources flows with the Blajini (water spirits) to enrich our life with clarity and virtue and to answer our heart's desires. In works of art she is depicted as a water nymph floating on a leaf while holding vessels teaming with water. Customary offerings to encourage Coventina's favor include pins, votives, coins, and semiprecious stones.

To Do Today: In this region of the world, water spirits are called Blajini, or "gentle ones," because they kindly reward people who give them an offering (much like wishing wells in Europe). These are citizens of the Coventina's fairy realm, whose motivations are pure and guileless. To keep the Blajini happy and encourage Coventina's sanction, present a special offering to them while whispering your hopes and dreams. Go to any fountain (perhaps one at the mall) and toss in a coin. The Blajini will bear the coin and the wish to Coventina for manifestation.

For personal clarity or to inspire principled actions in a situation in which you might be tempted to be a proverbial "bad witch," start the day off with a glass of water. Recite this incantation over it before drinking:

> *Coventina, keep my magic pure;*
> *within my spirit let goodness endure.*

Repeat this phrase throughout the day anytime you have water.

April 8

❋

Geranium Day (England)

BLODEUWEDD

Themes: Beauty; Relationships; Charity; Hope

Symbols: Flowers (any); Owl

About Blodeuwedd: This intensely beautiful Welsh goddess's name means "flower face," because magicians fashioned her visage from oak, primrose, meadowsweet, and broom flowers. Folktales say that Blodeuwedd was unfaithful to her husband. As punishment for her crime, the same magicians who gave her a flower face chose to be merciful and transformed Blodeuwedd into an owl rather than inflicting some other punishment. She has forever remained in this form, mourning the loss of love and reminding people of two important lessons: relationships are fragile, and beauty is indeed only skin deep.

To Do Today: The English sell geraniums today to collect funds for charities, specifically those that support services for the blind, who cannot see Blodeuwedd's radiance as we do. In the language of flowers, geraniums represent solace—which is what any act of charity stimulates today. It provides hope to those in need and inspires Blodeuwedd's beauty within your soul. Even if your pocket is empty, extend assistance to someone or something in need. Offer to help an elderly friend with chores, give some returnable bottles to a homeless person, act as a big brother or sister to orphans, give water to a stray cat. Benevolence has many forms, and it makes the world a much nicer place in which to live.

April 9

※

A-ma Festival (Portugal/China)

A-MA

Themes: Water; Providence; Protection; Magic; Weather

Symbols: Fish; Red Cloth

About A-ma: This goddess is the patroness of all fishers and sailors in the region of Macao, where today is her festival day and her birthday. Also sometimes called Matsu, this divine figure offers safety in any of life's literal or figurative storms, often by teaching magical weather charms. Legend says that A-ma achieved enlightenment and a mastery of magic at the young age of twenty-eight, after which she went to nirvana and became a goddess.

To Do Today: In Portugal, the day is spent enjoying parades for the goddess, eating lots of seafood, adorning altars with food and incense, and setting off firecrackers in A-ma's honor. So by all means, have some type of fish today (if you're allergic, eat fish-shaped candy instead). Before eating it, thank the founder of your feast with this prayer:

> A-ma, thank you for your providence and protection.
> Let the seas of my soul find solace in you;
> Let the waters of my spirit be refreshed in you. So be it.

Wear any red-colored clothing today to commemorate A-ma's birthday and inspire her magical assistance. Ties or scarves are especially nice for this, as you can bind one of A-ma's attributes within the knot for the day. Anything bearing a fish motif is also suitable.

April 10

✳

Humane Day (United States)

POLUKNALAI

Themes: Kindness to Animals; Nature

Symbols: All Animals

About Poluknalai: In Afghanistan, Poluknalai is the goddess of all animals, being both their creatrix and their protectress. Now that the warm weather has many people walking their pets or taking them to parks, Poluknalai walks alongside, watching over the animals who give us love and companionship.

To Do Today: People in the United States dedicate the first Sunday in May to commemorating the Humane Society, which was established to prevent cruelty to animals, in the true spirit of Poluknalai. Numerous organizations schedule fund-raising events today and extend compassion to both animals and people, in keeping with the festivities. If you have the means, adopt an animal today or make a small donation to the Humane Society in your area so they can continue their work. Both actions honor Poluknalai.

Back up your actions spiritually with this spell for animal welfare: Gather any pictures of endangered species you can find. Put them inside a Ziploc bag while visualizing the white light of protection surrounding each. As you close the bag, say,

> *Protected by Poluknalai's command, these creatures are safe across the land.*
> *Sealed with love and magic within, by my will this spell begins.*

As long as the bag remains sealed and safe, it will continue generating protective magic for those animals.

April 11

※

Fortuna's Festival (*Rome*)

FORTUNA

Themes: Luck; Wealth; Abundance; Destiny; Success

Symbols: Wheel; Cornucopia

About Fortuna: Fortuna, whose name means "she who brings," is the keeper of our destiny and the guiding power behind all fortunate turns of events. She stands on top of Fortune's wheel, steering us toward success and victory all year long.

To Do Today: Who of us couldn't use a little of Fortuna's assistance with tax day on the horizon? For a little extra cash, dab your automobile's, bike's, or motorcycle's wheels with almond oil or pineapple juice. Symbolically, this invokes Fortuna's help by keeping money "rolling" in! Also dab your steering wheel similarly—this way you can keep a "handle" on personal finances.

Romans traditionally asked Fortuna about their fate and difficult problems today, then received replies on slips of paper, often baked into small bread balls akin to a fortune cookie! This is fun for a gathering of people to try. Each person should write a word or short phrase on a piece of paper (all of which are equal in size). These get dropped in a bowl, and at the end of the day everyone can reach in to see what Fortuna has to say!

Wear colors that indicate to Fortuna what you need most (green for prosperity and luck, blue for victory, red for success, yellow for communication and creativity, and purple for spirituality and leadership qualities). Or, don lucky clothing and carry your lucky charms. Fortuna's energy is already housed within them.

April 12

✳

Chhau Festival (India)

MAHESVARI

Themes: Protection; Overcoming; Prayer

Symbols: Masks; Drum; Prayer Wheel

About Mahesvari: An epic mother-goddess figure in the Hindu pantheon and a protective aspect of Lakshimi, Mahesvari hears our prayers for assistance in risky, threatening, or seemingly impossible situations. When your back's to the wall, Mahesvari opens a doorway for a clever, smooth exit.

To Do Today: Consider following the Indian custom of dancing to drums while masked and enacting a pantomime in which you victoriously overcome some negativity in your life. If you're trying to quit smoking, for example, dance over your cigarettes and destroy them. To overcome a broken heart, jump over a paper heart, then carry it with you to manifest Mahesvari's life-affirming energy in your heart.

A fun version of the Buddhist prayer wheel can be fashioned from a children's pinwheel. Write your prayers to Mahesvari on the blades of the wheel. Then focus on your intent and blow! The movement releases your prayers so Mahesvari can begin answering them.

Finally, find something that can act as a drum in this spell for protection and victory. Sprinkle the head of your makeshift drum lightly with rosemary and powdered cinnamon. Then tap it, saying,

Away, away, Mahesvari, take the problems away.

Continue until the herbs have been cleared off completely, symbolically clearing away that obstacle.

April 13

✸

Songkran (Thailand)

TOU MOU

Themes: Cleansing; Luck; Charity; Karma; History

Symbols: Pen (or Quill); Books; Light

About Tou Mou: The Chinese/Thai goddess of record keeping takes special notice of our actions (or inactions) today, keeping careful notes for the karmic bank account. In works of art, Tou Mou is depicted sitting behind books and glowing with the beautiful light of the aurora. It is this brightness that shines on our lives today, revealing both the good and the bad. Suitable offerings for this goddess include rice, fruit, and all acts of goodness.

To Do Today: In Thailand, this water festival begins with tossing water down the street to chase away evil influences. I suggest using your driveway instead, or a glass of water on the kitchen floor that is judiciously mopped up later.

People in Thailand traditionally wash their parents' hands with scented water today to bring them honor and long life. So, remember your elders today, and do something nice for them—it's good karma, and it definitely catches Tou Mou's attention. Another activity extends good deeds to the natural world—that of freeing songbirds, who then bear their liberator's prayers directly to Tou Mou's ear. You might want to simply scatter some birdseed instead for similar results.

Finally, it might be a good day to balance your checkbook to make sure your financial karma stays in good standing. Burn a green candle nearby for prosperity.

April 14

✳

Nara Varsa (Nepal)

SRI

Themes: Joy; Protection; Fertility; Insight; Wealth

Symbols: Blue; Pink Lotus

About Sri: In this region, Sri, which means "prosperity," is said to protect the Dalai Lama. Invoke her to bring abundance for tax paying! Sri is portrayed as having three eyes, giving her the additional power of perspective when ours is lacking.

To Do Today: Celebration of the Nepalese new year, Nara Varsa, includes heartfelt greetings for luck and ritual bathing for fertility. As you see people today, smile brightly and wish them a good day. This provokes Sri's fortunate energy and a little extra felicity wherever you go.

Wearing something blue today makes Sri happy, which in turn sharpens Sri's shrewdness in you to promote a safe, frugal day. Or, carry a tumbled soldalite for Sri's focus, a blue topaz for her help in maintaining financial reserves, or a turquoise so that Sri will preserve your well-being.

Try this visualization when you need Sri's attributes to begin blossoming in your spirit: Envision an unopened pink flower in the region of your heart. Above, the sun shines with the pink-blue light of dawn and beats with the rhythm of your blood. You feel your heart's petals open to embrace it, accepting the warmth and energy without reservation. As your soul-flower absorbs the light, you can see it is a lotus, Sri's flower. She is there with you now, in your heart, to call on as needed.

April 15

✳

Awuru Odo (Nigeria)

ASASE YAA

Themes: Death; Truth; Morality; Fertility; Harvest

Symbol: Soil

About Asase Yaa: In West Africa, Asase Yaa means "old woman earth." As such, she governs the soil's fertility, and consequently, the harvest. This goddess represents the earth's womb, who gives us birth and to whom we all return at death. In life she presides over and motivates truth and virtue; upon death, she cares for and judges our spirits. Thursday is the traditional day for honoring her in the sacred space.

To Do Today: Every two years in April, people in Nigeria honor the spirits of the dead in a special festival that resembles a huge, extended family reunion—which is exactly how we can commemorate Asase Yaa in our own lives. If you can't assemble with your family because of distance, pull out photographs of loved ones and wrap them in something protective. Lay these down and sprinkle a little rich soil over them so that Asase Yaa's presence (and, by extension, yours) can be with them this day, no matter where they may be.

To keep Asase Yaa's honesty and scruples as an integral part of your life, take any seed and a little soil and wrap them in cotton, saying,

> Into your womb I place the seed of self,
> to be nurtured in goodness and grown in love.

Carry this token with you to keep Asase Yaa close by.

April 16

✳

Ludi (Rome)

POMONA

Themes: Rest; Pleasure; Nature

Symbols: All Flowers; Gardens

About Pomona: A Roman goddess of orchards and gardens, Pomona is symbolized by all gardening implements. Pomona's consort was Vertumnus, who likewise presided over gardens. Together they embody the fruitful earth, from which we gather physical and spiritual sustenance. First fruits are traditionally offered to them in gratitude.

To Do Today: Public games in ancient Rome were dedicated to taking a much-needed rest from toil and war. This particular segment of the festival celebrated the beauty of flowers before people returned to the fields and their labors. So, wear a floral- or leafy-print outfit today and visit a greenhouse or an arboretum. Take time out to literally smell the flowers and thank Pomona for the simple pleasure this provides.

Make yourself a Pomona oil to dab on anytime you want to better appreciate nature or cultivate some diversion from your normal routine. Prepare this from the petals of as many different flowers as you can find, gathered early in the day. Steep the petals in warm oil until they turn translucent, then strain. Repeat and add essential oils (fruity ones for Pomona are ideal) to accentuate the aroma and energy you've created.

April 17

※

Academy of Arts Day (United States)

THE GRATIAE

Themes: Arts; Creativity; Honor; Love; Excellence; Beauty

Symbols: Sweet Aromas; Arts (all); Wine

About the Gratiae: The Gratiae are akin to the Greek Graces, who inspire all arts, from a dancer's elegance, a model's beauty, and a diplomat's words to a terminal romantic's loving presentation. They arrive as earth is blossoming to encourage a flood of creativity that leads to excellence. It is traditional to offer them the first draught of wine at a gathering to invoke their blessing and aid.

To Do Today: The Gratiae were present in spirit on this day in 1916 when the American Academy of Arts Charter was signed by Woodrow Wilson to honor excellence in the industry. Toast the occasion with wine or grape juice, giving the first glass to these creative ladies to encourage their energy to visit your home.

Wear a sweet-smelling perfume or cologne today as an aromatherapeutic supplication to the Gratiae. Each time you catch that fragrance it will motivate beauty in any of your artistic skills. Better still, through the aroma the Gratiae can attract the attention of potential lovers!

Consider stopping at an art exhibition today or doing something creative yourself (even coloring!). Otherwise, do a little decorating. Hang a new poster, put out some fresh flowers, rearrange your knickknacks in a way that is aesthetically pleasing. These kind of actions appeal to the Gratiae's sense of style and tempt them to join you!

April 18

✵

Burmese New Year

SIPE GIALMO

Themes: Cleansing; Luck; Playfulness; Water

Symbols: Water; Bowl

About Sipe Gialmo: A pre-Lamist mother figure, Sipe Gialmo rules with a gentle, nurturing heart. Art traditionally depicts her as having three eyes to keep track of things (as any good mother does) and bearing a sword to protect her children and a bowl of water for refreshing them.

To Do Today: Around this time, people in Burma hold a three-day festival of water during which all sacred statues are cleansed, as are all participants, often with a playful flair. I see no reason not to follow suit. Gather any god or goddess images (or other symbolic items) you have in your home and polish, clean, scrub, and pamper them. Indirectly, this pampers the divine persona represented and pleases Sipe Gialmo (all good children remember to clean up after themselves!).

The splashing of water chases bad luck away and keeps people blissfully cool during one of the hottest months in Burma. While it's not quite that hot in other areas today, splash a little water (ideally, from a bowl) wherever you go anyway to encourage Sipe Gialmo's presence. Splash it at the work fountain to banish office politics. Splash it on your doorway so only good fortune enters your home. Splash it on your car to keep luck with you when driving, and in your wallet for financial good fortune.

April 19

❋

Bali Temple Offering

RANGDA

Themes: Thankfulness; Magic; Fertility

Symbols: A Pregnant Goddess; Round-shaped Fruit; Hibiscus; Yellow

About Rangda: A witch goddess in Bali, Rangda takes on a function many witches have throughout history, that of a woman's helpmate, especially in conception. To men, Rangda offers physical fertility or improved energy for magical workings.

To Do Today: Now that the earth is fertile, Rangda's power is even more abundant. To commemorate this and generate some literal or figurative fertility in your life, do as the Balinese do. Wear saffron-dyed (yellow) clothes, and leave Rangda an offering of fruit or flowers somewhere special. As you do, pray for an unborn child's well-being, for pregnancy, or for fruitful productivity in whatever area of your life needs it most.

Rangda can fulfill your desire for successful living. To manifest her profuseness, take a round watermelon and cut it in half. Make melon balls, and add any other round-shaped fruit (especially tropical fruit). Before eating, add this incantation:

> Rangda, fulfill me; Rangda, complete me.
> As my hunger is filled, let my spirit find satisfaction.

Eating the fruit salad internalizes her sweet, helpful energy.

Finally, to invoke Rangda's blessing and aid in conception, decorate your bedroom with yellow highlights before making love. Find a yellow light bulb, put yellow-toned sheets on your bed, and place yellow flowers (or hibiscus) by the bed.

April 20

✹

Furukawa Matsuri (Japan)

THE TENNIN

Themes: Protection; Anti-theft

Symbols: Drum; Feathers

About the Tennin: These semidivine beings are a kind of angel in Buddhist tradition. They like to make music, and their singing voices are as lovely as their stunning visages. Art renderings show them wearing feathered robes and sprouting wings a bit like oversized sylphs. On this day they join their voices to our celebration and wrap us in wings of safety.

To Do Today: Follow Japanese conventions and go through your home or entire town making as much noise as possible by banging pots, blowing horns, ringing bells. This protects you from the threat of thievery and unwanted ghostly visitations, as will singing sacred songs that draw the Tennin's attention and aid. A flurry of lantern lighting (or in our case, lamp lighting) often accompanies this activity, to shine a light on the darkness and reclaim the night with divine power.

To remember the Tennin specifically and invite their protective energy, put a lightweight item (like a silk scarf, a sheer curtain, or something else with diaphanous qualities) in the region that needs guarding. Put on a tape, record, or CD of vocal music (or sing yourself), and they will come. To protect yourself, carry a feather in your purse or wallet.

April 21

✳

Taurus Begins (*Various Locations*)

TAUROPOLOS

Themes: Work; Patience; Strength; Courage

Symbol: Bull

About Tauropolos: No goddess could better represent this date other than Taruropolos, the Cretan bull goddess whose name literally means "Bull Lady" (and that's no bull!). Teaching us the virtues of diligence and the rewards of hard work, Tauropolos also has a strong connection to the fields (the plow) and the hearth, where food from the fields gets prepared.

To Do Today: The Cretans were well known for having bull-leaping festivals that honored this goddess, probably as a fertility rite and test of one's bravery. Oddly enough, this is how we come by the saying "seize the bull by the horns!" So, if there's an area of your life in which you want to really seize the day, try this simple symbolic spell. Find any image of a bull (in a magazine, carved out of stone, or in some other form). Put it on the floor, and put a symbol of your aspiration on the side of the image across from you. Say,

> Tauropolos, *prepare the fields for success;*
> *help me now to do my best.*

Leap over the image and claim victory!

If you can't find bull images, any harvested item may represent Tauropolos instead. If you choose this option, be sure to consume the food later. This way you can internalize this goddess's tenacity, persistence, and fortitude, then apply them toward successfully achieving your goals.

April 22

❀

Festival of Ishtar (*Babylon*)

ISHTAR

Themes: Love; Fertility; Passion; Sexuality; Moon

Symbols: Star; Moon; Lion; Dove

About Ishtar: In Babylon, Ishtar encompasses the fullness of womanhood, including being a maternal nurturer, an independent companion, an inspired bed partner, and an insightful advisor in matters of the heart. Having descended from Venus (the planet that governs romance), she is the moon, the morning star, and the evening star, which inspire lovers everywhere to stop for a moment, look up, and dare to dream. Saturday is Ishtar's traditional temple day, and her sacred animals include a lion and a dove.

To Do Today: Babylonians gave Ishtar offerings of food and drink on this day. They then joined in ritual acts of lovemaking, which in turn invoked Ishtar's favor on the region and its people to promote continued health and fruitfulness. If you'd like to connect with this fertile energy but have no bed partner, a magical alternative is using symbolism. Place a knife (or athame, a ritual dagger often representing the masculine divine or the two-edged sword of magic) in a cup filled with water. This represents the union of yin and yang. Leave this in a spot where it will remain undisturbed all day to draw Ishtar's loving warmth to your home and heart.

If you have any clothes, jewelry, or towels that have a star or moon on them, take them out and use them today. Ishtar abides in that symbolism. As you don the item, likewise accept Ishtar's mantle of passion for whatever tasks you have to undertake all day.

April 23

First Day of Summer (Iceland)

S I F

Themes: Summer; Kinship; Arts; Passion; Sun

Symbols: Sun; Gold; Hair

About Sif: This Scandinavian earth goddess has long golden hair that shines even more brightly now that the sun is reclaiming its dominance in the sky. On warm nights, especially in summer, she enjoys making love beneath an open sky in the fields, symbolically giving life and adoration to the earth.

To Do Today: People greet the traditional first day of summer exuberantly in Iceland, as winter has been very long and often very difficult. They exchange gifts wrapped in gold to celebrate the sun's return, gather with family and friends, and revel in regional arts, especially dramas. A non-Icelandic version of this might be performing a ritual drama in which you slowly raise a golden sphere with trailing gold ribbons (representing the sun and Sif). Once the sphere is in full view, high in the room, say,

> *Sif, be welcome;*
> *Sif is here.*
> *She shines her golden warmth on us and the earth,*
> *warming both, nurturing all.*

Afterward, try this Sif-centered spell for unity and passion at home: Have a small, enclosed fire source burning (this represents the sun's blessing). Each person in your household then takes one strand of hair and gives it to the flame. As this burns, add dried lemon peel and basil to emphasize harmony (and offset the scent of the hair). Sprinkle the ashes in the soil around the living space.

April 24

Peppercorn Ceremony (*Bermuda*)

ERZULIE

Themes: Prosperity; Abundance; Love

Symbol: Blue

About Erzulie: This Haitian love goddess extends her beneficent springlike energy whenever we need it, especially when our pockets or hearts are empty. When life gets out of kilter, petitioning Erzulie sets everything back on track, slowly but surely. Blue is Erzulie's sacred color, and she is sometimes called "the loving one."

To Do Today: Use peppercorns somehow, of course! This festival began in 1816 when the mayor of Bermuda was given use of the state house for the annual rent of one peppercorn. This rent must be delivered annually, and with all due pageantry, to preserve the island's prosperity beneath Erzulie's watchful gaze. For us this might translate into eating a peppercorn dressing on a green salad (lettuce represents money) to internalize financial abundance, or keeping a peppercorn in your wallet to safeguard your money and its flow.

Definitely wear blue today to catch Erzulie's attention, and add blue foods to your diet—blueberries, blue juice drink, or even blue-colored water. You can also encourage Erzulie's blessing through selfless actions. Give a friend a hug, pamper your pets, take the kids out for some quality time, and remember to kiss your partner goodbye in the morning. You'll feel better and find your heart naturally filling with Erzulie's love.

April 25

✸

Sechselauten (Switzerland)

LADA

Themes: Spring; Protection; Overcoming; Kinship; Energy; Joy

Symbols: Birch; Bells

About Lada: Lada bursts forth from her winter hiding place today in full Slavic costume and dances with joy, grateful for spring's arrival. As Lada moves, her skirts sweep away sickness and usher in the earth's blossoming beauty. She bears a birch tree and flowers to honor the earth's fertility and to begin planting anew.

To Do Today: This spring festival is overflowing with Lada's vibrancy and begins with the demolition of a snowman, symbolic of winter's complete overthrow. If you live in a region where there's no snow, take out an ice cube and put a flowering seed atop it. Let it melt, then plant the seed with "winter's" water to welcome Lada back to the earth.

Bells ring throughout this day in Switzerland to proclaim spring and ring out any remaining winter maladies and shadows. Adapt this by taking a handheld bell (you can get small ones at craft stores) and ringing it in every room of the house, intoning Lada's revitalizing energy. Or, just ring your doorbell, open the door, and bring in some flowers as a way of offering Lada's spirit hospitality.

Finally, wear something with a floral print today or enjoy a glass of birch beer. Better still, make a birch beer float so the ice cream (snow) melts amid Lada's warmth, bringing that transformative power into you as you sip.

April 26
✺
African Fertility Festival

MAWU

Themes: Creativity; Universal Law; Passion; Abundance; Birth; Inspiration

Symbols: Clay; Moon

About Mawu: Mawu arrives on an elephant's back, expectant with spring's creative energy. Hers is a wise passion and a timely birth, being ruled by natural laws and universal order. In Africa, she is a lunar-aligned creatrix who made people from clay. As a mother figure, Mawu inspires the universe's abundance and every dreamer's imagination.

To Do Today: Rituals for Mawu rejoice in her life-giving energy, often through lovemaking. In Africa, people take this seed generation literally and sow the fields, knowing that Mawu will make the land fertile. So get yourself a seedling today and bring it into the house to welcome Mawu and her creative powers. Name the sprout after one of Mawu's attributes that you want to cultivate. Each time you water or tend the plant, repeat its name and accept Mawu's germinating energy into your spirit.

Alternatively, get some nonhardening clay and begin fashioning a symbol of what you need. Devote yourself to spending time on this over twenty-eight days (a lunar cycle), until it's complete. Each time you work, say,

> Mother Mawu, make me whole,
> help me obtain my sacred goal.

By the time this is finished, you should see the first signs of manifestation.

April 27

✿

Landsgemeinden (Switzerland)

MATI-SYRA-ZEMLYA

Themes: Community; Divination; Promises; Justice; Morality

Symbols: Oil; Soil

About Mati-Syra-Zemlya: This goddess's name means "moist mother," alluding to her fertile aspects. She attends today's festivities to hear oaths and witness legal decisions that may affect the rest of the year. Any promise or sentence made with one hand on the earth, or in her name, is completely binding. In some areas her motherly nature is expressed through healing qualities, while in others she has prophetic ability. An appropriate gift for her is hemp oil.

To Do Today: This is a civic-oriented holiday during which people gather to conduct regional business, including voting, budgets, and tax proposals. It's a very old custom adorned with lavish clothing, ceremonial swords, and, I suspect, an eavesdropping goddess (just to keep everyone honest). If you need to tie up some pending business, work on your personal budget, or balance the checkbook, honor Mati-Syra-Zemlya and draw her ethical energies to you by getting busy!

Alternatively, if you've been thinking about getting more involved with your local or magical community, make a commitment to Mati-Syra-Zemlya to start making efforts in that direction. Simply place a hand on the ground and speak your pledge to her ears. The goddess will respond by giving you the time and energy needed to fulfill that commitment.

April 28

✸

Floralia (Rome)

FLORA

Themes: Beauty; Sexuality; Love; Spring; Fertility

Symbols: All Flowers

About Flora: Roman prostitutes considered Flora their own goddess, protecting all acts of beauty, especially heartfelt lovemaking. She is also a spring goddess from whom we get the word *flora*, meaning blossom or plants. Symbolically, this flowering pertains to the human spirit too, one that can appreciate beauty in the body without necessarily making it into a sex object.

To Do Today: Wearing bright colors on this day is customary, as is decorating everything with a plethora of flowers, each of which has Flora's presence within. If flowers prove difficult to obtain or too costly, think floral aromas instead. Pull out a blossoming air freshener, light floral incense, or wear a floral perfume. Flora is as much a part of the scent as she is the petals, conveying love and passion on each breeze!

Another traditional activity for this day is erotic dancing. If you have someone special in your life, tantalize them a bit with slow, sexy movements. Let Flora's passion fill both of you to overflowing, then let nature take her course.

Finally, make yourself a Flora charm that incites the interest of those from whom you seek it. Take three flower petals and tuck them in your clothing, keeping an image of your partner in mind, and say,

> One for interest,
> two for Flora's desire,
> three to light passion's fire.

April 29

✳

Tako-Age (Japan)

SHINA TSU HIME

Themes: Wishes; Freedom; Playfulness; Air Element; Movement

Symbols: Wind; Sailing Ships

About Shina Tsu Hime: This Japanese wind goddess disperses the morning fog. She also keeps away evil, distracting winds, winds that threaten to uproot or blur our spiritual focus. Because of this, Shina Tsu Hime has become the patroness of sailors and farmers, the latter of whom pray to her for fertile winds bearing seed and rain.

To Do Today: Join our Eastern cousins in kite-flying festivities. Shina Tsu Hime will be glad to meet with you in a nearby park and give life to your kite. As it flies, release a wish on the winds. Or cut the kite free and liberate a weight from your shoulders.

While you're out, gather up nine leaves that Shina Tsu Hime banters about (one for each remaining month). Turn clockwise in a circle, releasing all but one leaf back into Shina Tsu Hime's care while saying,

> Come May, bring movement in my goals,
> come June—playful love makes me whole.
> Come July, my wishes I will see,
> come August—hope grows in me.
> Come September, all distractions you abate;
> come October, my spirit, you liberate.
> Come November, my health is assured;
> come December—in my heart you endure.

Keep the last leaf with you, releasing it only when you need one of this goddess's attributes to manifest quickly.

April 30

Walpurgisnacht (*Germany*)

GEFN

Themes: Sun; Winter; Spring; Protection; Health; Love; Divination; Magic; Fertility; Foresight; Growth

Symbols: All Green or Growing Things

About Gefn: A goddess whose name means simply "giver," Gefn was regarded by the Norse-Germanic people as a frolicsome, fertile figure and seeress who embodied the earth's greenery. Gefn brings this abundance to us today: abundant well-being, abundant companionship, and abundant goddess-centered magic!

To Do Today: This holiday originated with a German saint (Saint Walburga), who had curative powers and taught people how to banish curses. For our purposes, Gefn stands in, offering to heal the curse of a broken heart by filling our lives with love and hope-filled foresight. If someone has completely overlooked or trashed your feelings recently, ask Gefn for help in words that you find comfortable. She's waiting and willing to apply a spiritual salve to that wound.

Also try the German custom of ringing bells and banging pots to frighten away any malicious or prankish magic (or the people who make it) before your spring activities really start to rock 'n' roll. Make this as playful as possible to encourage Gefn's participation. Burning rosemary and juniper likewise cleanses the area, and if you can get either of these fresh, Gefn's presence lies within. The burning releases her energy.

May

May gets its name from the Roman goddess Maia (see May 1), who embodies the earth's renewal during spring. Next to New Year's Eve, May Day was among the most popular holidays in the old world, marking the time when the sun's warmth and nature's fertility began appearing in the land. Later, well over one hundred nations chose to celebrate Labor Day on May 1, giving everyone a much-needed rest from winter's tasks.

For the purpose of your magical escapades, the theme is definitely blossoming and liveliness. Use as many flower parts as possible in spells and rituals, and go outside frequently to get closer to nature. Energies emphasized by this month include creativity, inventiveness, fertility, health, and metaphysically "spring cleaning" any area of your life or sacred space.

May 1

May Day (Beltane)

MAIA

Themes: Sexual Prowess; Playfulness; Wishes

Symbols: Braided or Knotted Items

About Maia: This Roman goddess, whose name means "mother," offers all who seek it fulfillment and renewed zest. Maia gave her name to the month of May. She is the queen of the flowers, and today was one of her festival days, celebrated suitably with an abundance of blossoms. In later times, Maia became strongly associated with Bona Dea, whose name literally translates as "good goddess" (see March 1).

To Do Today: As a child, on this day I left bundles of wildflowers anonymously at neighbors' homes. As a random act of beauty and kindness, this still holds merit today and certainly honors Maia.

In magical circles people customarily braid wishes into the ribbons of the Maypole and leave them there to germinate and grow until fall. To do this yourself, find three strands of blue ribbon and braid them together so they meet five times, saying,

> 'Tis the month of May, for____ [health, love, money, or whatever] I wish today.
> Ribbons of blue, help my wish come true.
> Braided within, the spell begins.
> Bound to and fro, the magic grows.
> When in Fall untied, this wish is mine!

Wear a flowery shirt, skirt, or tie today to welcome Maia and brighten your day.

May 2

Apple Blossom Festival (*Washington State*)

ESTSANATLEHI

Themes: Fertility; Beauty; Blessing; Summer; Weather; Time; Cycles

Symbols: Apples; Apple Seeds; Apple Blossoms; Rainwater

About Estsanatlehi: This Native American goddess inspires the earth's blossoming, and that of our spirits, with her productive energies. Having the power of self-rejuvenation, she warms the earth with wind in the spring, then brings soft summer rains to keep the fields growing. As the seasons change, so does her appearance, reminding us of time's movement and the earth's cycles.

To Do Today: The Apple Blossom Festival is the oldest flower fair in the United States and actually takes its conceptualization from a New Zealand custom of celebrating the apple orchards in bloom—a place filled with Estsanatlehi's glory. When you get up today, check outside. If it's sprinkling lightly, it is a very good omen, meaning Estsanatlehi is fertilizing the earth. Gather a little of this rainwater and use it in a ritual for cleansing and blessing the sacred space, or as a libation.

If you can get outside to appreciate the spring flowers, it pleases Estsanatlehi and initiates her renewal in your spirit. At some point in the day, have a tall glass of apple juice (apples plus water) to quaff a bit of Estsanatlehi's resourcefulness. Or, enjoy a fruit salad that includes apples and a garnish of fresh flowers (many of which are edible) so her beauty will grow within you.

Hakata Dontaku (Japan)

AMATERASU

Themes: Sun; Tradition; Unity; Blessings; Community; Kinship

Symbols: Mirror; Gold or Yellow Items

About Amaterasu: Amaterasu is unique among goddesses, being one of the few women to personify the sun. In Japan she rules over cultural unity, kinship, and the blessings that someone with the name "Illuminating Heaven" might be expected to bestow. It is Amaterasu's sun that nudges the greenery to reach toward her light, just as her gentle energy prods us toward reestablishing harmony in all our relationships.

To Do Today: The first week of May in Japan is called Golden Week, and it's a time when Amaterasu's solar beauty really shines. The Hakata festival is a national holiday that includes celebrations for children and a special parade depicting Japan's legendary deities. Take a moment to join the festivities long-distance. Remember Amaterasu by wearing gold-colored items today and opening as many curtains as possible to let in her glorious light.

Once the curtains are opened, take a hand mirror and reflect the light into every corner of your home. This draws Amaterasu's unifying energy into your living space and guards against discord among all who dwell therein. Also, to ensure that no malevolence enters from outside the home, put a mirror facing outward in an eastern window (where Amaterasu rises). This is a Buddhist custom for turning away negativity and evil influences.

Fairy Gatherings (Ireland)

MAEVE

Themes: Fairies; Magic; Protection; Leadership; Justice (Law)

Symbols: Birds; Gold

About Maeve: As the Fairy Queen, Maeve oversees today's merrymaking among the citizens of fey. She also attends to human affairs by providing protection, wise leadership, and prudent conventions. Works of art depict Maeve with golden birds on her shoulders, whispering magical knowledge into her ear.

To Do Today: Near the beginning of May, the wee folk of Ireland come out of hiding for a grand celebration of spring. If you don't want the Maeve and the citizens of fey to pull pranks on you today, take precautions, as the Europeans do: avoid traveling, put a piece of clothing on inside-out, wear something red, and leave the fairy folk an offering of sweet bread, honey, or ale. In some cases, this will please the fairies so much that they will offer to perform a service or leave you a gift in return!

When you need to improve your command of a situation or inspire more equity, call on Maeve through this spell: Take a piece of white bread and toast it until it's golden brown. Scratch into the bread a word or phrase representing your goal (for example, if raises at work haven't been given out fairly, write the words *work* and *raises*). Distribute the crumbs from this to the birds so they can convey your need directly to Maeve's ears.

May 5

Rain Festivals (Mexico/Central America)

XTAH

Themes: Weather; Harvest; Fertility; Prayer

Symbols: Rainwater

About Xtah: The Guatemalan goddess of rain and water sprinkles herself into today's celebration in answer to her people's fervent prayers. As she does, her rain also bears constructive, fulfilling energy to maintain the gardens of our spirit with spring's growth-centered magic.

To Do Today: This is the time of the year when peoples in this region begin praying to the sacred powers for rain. In Guatemala, specifically, they pray and make offerings to the goddess so the crops will not fail from draught.

If your spiritual life has seemed a bit "dry" lately or lacking in real substance, pray to Xtah with words like these:

> Xtah, as you pour forth from the heavens, see my need. [*Pour out a glass of water here—this is a type of sympathetic magic that encourages Xtah to follow your example*].
> Rain upon my life and heart with your fruitful waters so I may grow with clarity of spirit.
> Thank you for your bounty, for refilling my inner well with your richness. So be it.

If it's raining outside, dance in the rain as you pray so you can literally touch Xtah's presence. Alternatively, pray in the shower or in the rains created by a lawn sprinkler.

Wear water-colored clothing today (blue, purple, dark green) to accent whichever of Xtah's attributes you want to develop.

Family Week (United States)

CHANTICO

Themes: Kinship; Unity; Cooperation; Communication; Divination; Protection; Home

Symbols: Fire; Metals; Minerals

About Chantico: A classical Mesoamerican goddess, Chantico personifies and safeguards the hearth fires and the home, the place where families gather. The name Chantico means "in the house." Men going to battle pray to her that they will return and still find those home fires burning! Children petition her to know the future. She also became the guardian of lapidaries and some metalsmiths.

To Do Today: Around the first Sunday in May, Catholic and Jewish congregations celebrate family week, a time to focus our attention on family solidarity and how to improve the quality of family life. With our society having become so mobile, Chantico is a very timely goddess to entreat for assistance in this endeavor. Gather with your family or friends today, light a candle (symbolizing Chantico's presence), and rededicate yourselves to oneness.

Carrying or wearing silver, copper, red-toned agate, amethyst, or jade today draws Chantico's presence and encourages the warmth of kinship no matter where you may be. To extend this idea, take a piece of paper with the word *earth* written on it and wrap it around one of these metals or stones. That way you share Chantico's unifying energy with all the earth's inhabitants.

Sealing the Frost (*Guatemala*)

IX CHEL

Themes: Weather; Children; Fertility; Health

Symbols: Water; Turquoise; Jade; Silver, Blue or White Items

About Ix Chel: The aqueous Mayan goddess of water, the moon, medicine, and childbirth, Ix Chel lives in the land of mists and rainbows. Art shows her wearing a skirt that flows with fertile waters, dotted with water lilies, and adorned with tiny bits of turquoise and jade. This skirt reaches all the way to earth, filling our lives with Ix Chel's well-being and enrichment.

To Do Today: Believing that the Frost Spirit lives in the cliffs of Santa Eulalia, people brave the sheer stones once a year and make prayers to the weather deities to keep away further intrusion by the frost, which would ruin crops. Ix Chel is present to witness, being part of the frost and part of the nurturing rains, for which the priests also pray. For our purposes this equates to calling on Ix Chel's energy to "defrost" a frozen or emotionally chilly situation, or to rain on us with her healing power.

To protect your health specifically, carry a turquoise, which also safeguards you during travel today. To inspire productivity or fertility, wear blue and white items, repeating this incantation as you put them on:

> Ix Chel, be in this _____ of blue, so my thoughts stay fixed on you.
> Ix Chel, be in this _____ of white, bring abundance both day and
>   night.

Furry Dance (England)

TANAT

Themes: Unity; Joy; Luck

Symbols: Flowers; Triangle

About Tanat: In Cornwall, Tanat is the mother goddess of fertility who has given all her attention to nursing spring into its fullness. She also staunchly protects her children (nature and people) so that our spirits can come to know similar fulfillment.

To Do Today: The Furry Dance is an ancient festival that rejoices in Tanat's fine work manifested in spring's warmth and beauty. To bring this goddess's lucky energy into your life, it's customary to dance with a partner. In fact, the more people you can get dancing, the more fortunate the energy! Usually this is done on the streets throughout a town as a show of regional unity, but when propriety won't allow such a display, just dance around a room together instead. Don't worry about the steps—just do what feels right.

Wearing something with floral or triangular motifs (guys, wear a necktie, and gals, pull out a square scarf and fold it in half crosswise) activates Tanat's happiness in your life and in any region where you have the token on today. As you don the item, say,

> *Liberate happiness in and around,*
> *by Tanat's blossoming power, joy will be found!*

Or, if you want to use the same thing to generate unity and harmony, use this incantation:

> *Harmony and unity,*
> *Tanat's blessings come to me!*

Lemuria (Rome)

SECURITA

Themes: Protection; Ghosts; Grounding

Symbols: Amulets and Protective Sigils

About Securita: As the name implies, Securita is a protective goddess who watches over not only individuals in need but also entire empires. In the true spirit of security, she also actively promotes stability and firm foundations in our lives.

To Do Today: In ancient Rome, lemures were considered to be the ghosts of family members who like to pester the living, if given the chance. So, in all due prudence, the Romans took time once a year to put ghosts back where they belong and invoke Securita's protection by tossing beans behind them nine times. We can use this symbolism today in banishing any ghosts that linger in our figurative closets. Just name a handful of beans after your "ghost," toss them behind you in an open area, and walk away. This appeases the spirits and leaves the troubles behind you in the past, where they belong.

Today is an excellent day to make Securita amulets for protection against mischievous spirits. Take any one or all of the following and bind them in a white cloth with red wool: sandalwood, sage, violet, or peach pit. As you tie the wool, say,

> Securita's power lies inside.
> Where this amulet sits, no ghosts may abide.

Put the token wherever you need it. Eating leek soup keeps away spirits, too.

Bun Bang Fai (Laos)

SAOQUING NIANG

Themes: Weather; Harvest; Hope

Symbols: Rain; Clouds; Stars (or Light); Brooms

About Saoquing Niang: Known as the Broom Lady in the Far East, Saoquing Niang lives among the stars, sweeping away or bringing rain clouds, depending on the land's needs. From a spiritual perspective, Saoquing Niang's moisture fills us with refreshing hope when our soul is thirsty.

To Do Today: A traditional rain ceremony in Laos, this festival is very ancient and ensures a good harvest. It includes all manner of festivities, such as fireworks that carry people's prayers into the sky. In keeping with this, if sparklers are legal in your area, light one or two and scribe your wishes with light for Saoquing Niang to see.

For weather magic, tradition says that if you need Saoquing Niang's literal or figurative rains, simply hang a piece of paper near your home with her name written on it (ideally in blue pen, crayon, or marker). Take this paper down to banish a tempest or an emotional storm.

To draw Saoquing Niang's hope into your life, take a broom and sweep your living space from the outside in toward the center. You don't actually have to gather up dirt (although symbolically getting rid of "dirt" can improve your outlook). If you like, sing "Rain, rain, go away" as you go. Keep the broom in a special place afterward to represent the goddess.

May 11

Kattestoet (*Belgium*)

BAST

Themes: Animals; Magic; Overcoming; Playfulness; Joy; Humor

Symbol: Cat

About Bast: Bast is the Egyptian cat-faced goddess of sorcery, beneficence, joy, dance, and fertility. Being a cat in nature, Bast teaches us to land on our feet in any situation, using a positive, playful attitude as our best ally. Bast and her minions were so revered in Egypt that to kill cats was a crime punishable by death. Archaeologists uncovered mummified cats there, whose owners wanted the companionship of cats even in the afterlife. May is one of Bast's traditional festival months.

To Do Today: In this region of the world, people dress as cats today and hold a parade in which Bast is featured as the Queen of Cats. So think cat magic! If there's a cat in your life, pamper the creature today and include it in spellcraft as a magical partner (a traditional "catty" role in history). For example, if you find any of your cat's whiskers, keep them. These may be burned for Bast in return for a wish. Or, carry a pinch of cat hair to tickle your funny bone.

Painting the image of a cat on a paper lantern and lighting it (with either a bulb or a flame) draws Bast's attention and energies to you. Or, carry a cat's eye in your pocket today to begin developing catlike instincts and playfulness.

May 12

Garland Day (England)

DAMARA

Themes: Fertility; Health; Luck; Kindness; Abundance

Symbols: Flowers; Green Items

About Damara: Throughout England, Damara is celebrated as being intimately connected with May and its abundant fertility for the fields, herds, and home. Through this productive energy, Damara brings well-being and improved fortune throughout the month.

To Do Today: Children in England believe that Bringing in the May also conveys Damara's blessings. To try this, make small floral garlands or bouquets with ribbons and leave them anonymously on doorsteps, especially at the homes of people who have given much to the community or to you. By doing so, you return some of that person's positive energy and lay Damara's health and luck at their feet.

This activity also opens the fishing season in England, where the garlands get cast into boats to bring a good harvest there, too! So, leave a flower anywhere you need improved abundance—in your wallet, in the pantry, at the office for abundant energy, or close to your heart for abundant love.

Finally, bring a bundle of fresh flowers into your living space today to attract Damara's healthy energy. Gardenias, roses, violets, geraniums, or tansies are all excellent choices, being metaphysically associated with vitality.

Pilgrimage to Fatima (*Portugal*)

MARY

Themes: Miracles; Sun

Symbols: Sun (or Yellow/Gold Items); Rosary

About Mary: It is no coincidence that many of the world's goddesses have "ma" as part of their name, being mothers of humankind. The Virgin Mary became the maiden, virginal goddess archetype in Christianity, faithfully interceding for people with the gods and attending to our needs.

To Do Today: If you feel like you need a miracle, be sure to wear yellow- or gold-colored items today. As you don each one, say,

> Mary hear me,
> Mary see me,
> Mary free me.

This date commemorates the appearance of Mary in Fatima, where children praying for peace began a cycle of visitors all looking for this goddess to appear again. According to the story, when seventy thousand people were gathered there on this day, the rain stopped and the sun began to dance for joy as if guided by Mary's hand. Whenever the sun shines again today, it is a sign of her blessing.

To make your own prayer beads (to beseech Mary or any goddess), cook rose petals in a little water in an iron pot until nearly black and pasty. Add a little orris powder and rose-scented oil, and shape the beads to two times the size you want them to be when dry. Pierce them with a needle and string them, turning them regularly until they're dry. Bless them in a manner suited to your path, then use the beads to energize your prayers by holding them as you entreat the goddess.

Midnight Sun (Norway)

DAG

Themes: Sun; Blessings; Cycles; Movement; Travel

Symbols: Gold or Yellow Items; Horse

About Dag: Northern Scandinavian legends describe Dag, whose name means "day," as shining so brightly that she lights both the heavens and the earth, which is certainly what occurs around this time of year. As the northern hemisphere approaches late spring, Dag's inspiring light and warmth are welcome and notable. Dag navigates the sky with the help of a horse, her sacred animal, giving her additional connections with movement and safe travel.

To Do Today: This date begins a "day" for Norwegians that will actually last for ten weeks, emphasizing Dag's power. Correspondingly, people's activity level increases around the clock, as they sleep less to adjust to the change in earth's cycle. So, when your inner resources lag or you're out of kilter with natural or biological clocks, turn to Dag for assistance. Wear gold or yellow items to tune into her vibrations, and get out in Dag's sunlight today (if the weather cooperates). It's very healthy and naturally generates more of Dag's positive energy for anything you undertake.

It's an excellent day to take a short trip anywhere. If you enjoy horseback riding and have a stable nearby, take a jaunt and ride with Dag and the wind at your back. Alternatively, use "horse power" and take a short drive in your car!

May 15

Barbecue Festival (Kentucky)

FIRE WOMAN

Themes: Sun; Fire; Family; Love

Symbols: Fire; Hearth (Stove/Grill)

About Fire Woman: Since the United States is a melting pot of culture, we turn to the Fire Woman of Borneo to instruct us in making fires by rubbing wood together, followed by subsequent lessons in cookery! Today she continues her warming ways by teaching us how to keep lovin' in the oven!

To Do Today: Cook outdoors! Fire Woman, by her very nature, is part of that grill or hibachi. I must confess this festival is included for my sake, since weekend barbecues are my summer fire rituals. Kentucky is considered the barbecue capital of the world (they've never been to Buffalo), and over the course of this festival in a town by the name of Owensboro, over ten tons of meat will be cooked and consumed, as the day takes on the ambiance of a huge "family" picnic.

In choosing your menu, think either hot, spicy foods to emphasize Fire Woman's fiery aspect or foods that metaphysically engender love. One combination that stresses both is strawberry-garlic grilled chicken (add crushed berries to honey, ginger, and garlic for a sauce). Vegetarians can use this sauce on potatoes or shitake mushrooms instead.

If you don't have time for a barbecue, light any candle briefly sometime today to honor Fire Woman and draw her loving energy into your home.

May 16

Thargalia (*Greece*)

HOSIA

Themes: Cleansing; Offering; Forgiveness; Magic

Symbols: Ritual Tools

About Hosia: As the Greek goddess who created all sacred rituals and ceremonies, Hosia oversees today's rite and directs our magical energy toward successful manifestation.

To Do Today: Follow Greek tradition and leave Hosia an offering of fruit, bread, or wheat to encourage her assistance. Next, consider creating a personal ritual for cleansing or forgiveness. Hosia will guide your hand in choosing words and actions suited to the working. Alternatively, take out your ritual tools and ask for Hosia's blessing on them, saying,

> *Hosia, these are the tools of my hand, heart, and spirit.*
> *They symbolize the elements and the corners of creation.*
> *Today I ask that you empower them for working magic, and regulate their use for the greatest good.*
> *May they always direct my energy in perfect love and trust. So be it.*

In Greece, a scapegoat (often a criminal) was often identified to bear the sins for an entire community, then banished into the wilderness. A way to adapt this is by designing an image of something you need to banish, then "driving it away" by putting it in the car and leaving it in a remote spot. As you turn away, ask Hosia to witness the rite and to empower your efforts for positive change.

May 17

Mut I-art (Morocco)

NEJMA

Themes: Protection; Health; Courage; Organization

Symbols: Caverns; Water

About Nejma: In Morocco, Nejma oversees all other health and healing spirits, organizing their efforts to ward off spring colds and other maladies. Local legends claim that she lives in the grotto of d'El Maqta, which is likely representative of a motherly womb in which our spirits are made whole.

To Do Today: On the first day of summer in this region, locals use the solar symbolism to avert evil and danger. We can adapt their customs by taking baths, which invoke Nejma to strengthen the body, and by staying awake longer than usual, which purportedly raises courage. Additionally, eating carrots, turnips, beets, or other vegetables internalizes Nejma's protective qualities for year-round well-being.

You can honor Nejma, inspire her energy, and help yourself by seeing to matters of personal health today. Get a checkup, eat well-rounded meals instead of junk food, review your diet, take a healthy walk, start an exercise program, let some fresh air into the house or smudge it with sage for purification, visualize yourself being washed clean by white light. And don't forget to think positively! An upbeat mental outlook puts you much closer to the goal of being whole in body, mind, and spirit.

May 18

Gawai Dayak (*Malaysia*)

BORU DEAK PARUDJAR

Themes: Harvest; Blessing; Longevity; Courage; Opportunity

Symbols: Soil; Rice

About Boru Deak Parudjar: The Malaysian creatrix and guardian of life, Boru Deak Parudjar grew bored of the upper realms and jumped away from them as soon as an opportunity opened up. It is this type of adventurous spirit and leap of faith that she inspires today.

In local legend, Boru Deak Parudjar's father sent a bit of soil to the water to await his daughter in the lower worlds. The earth grew to sustain the goddess. This change in the waters made the Naga (a primordial sea serpent) very angry—he wiggled until Boru Deak Parudjar's earth began to cleave, creating mountains and valleys. Which just goes to show that stirring things up sometimes has a good outcome!

To Do Today: Following ancient custom, the elder of a house makes sacrifices and prays poetically for direction, the goddess's blessings, health, and a good harvest. Foods include rice dishes and rice wine. So, add any rice dish to your diet today: rice cereal for Boru Deak Parudjar's growth-oriented energy, rice pudding for her sweet blessings, herbed rice to spice up your life with a little adventure.

When you need a bit of this goddess's courage, place a piece of rice in your footprint (someplace where it won't be disturbed). As you put the rice in the imprint, say,

Let courage guide my feet all this day.

May 19

Hay on Wye (Wales)

FUWCH GYFEILIORU

Themes: Creativity; Communication; Arts; Learning; Knowledge

Symbols: Cow; Milk

About Fuwch Gyfeilioru: Fuwch Gyfeilioru is the Welsh goddess of knowledge, inspiration, wisdom, and happiness. Appearing sometimes as an elfin cow, she has an endless supply of magical milk that refreshes ailing dispositions with joy and creativity.

To Do Today: The Hay on Wye is a Welsh festival of words and language, specifically in the form of plays, music, debate, poetry, and other creative written and verbal forms that certainly honor Fuwch Gyfeilioru in spirit. In keeping with the theme, take out your magic diary today. Place one hand on the cover, asking for this goddess's insight, then read it over. You'll be pleasantly surprised by your awareness of metaphysical matters and your growth in the last few months. Drink a glass of milk, consume milk by-products, or include beef as part of a meal to physically accept Fuwch Gyfeilioru's powers into yourself. Focus intently on your goal as you eat or drink, and don't forget to thank the goddess for her gift by way of a mealtime prayer.

To motivate a little extra creativity, make a milk shake (any flavor, but add a pinch of cinnamon for energy or nutmeg for luck). The blender "whips up" Fuwch Gyfeilioru's energy in the shake as you incant,

> *Creativity I claim, by my will and in the goddess's name!*

Drink expectantly.

Ch'un Hyang (Korea)

BAI MUNDAN

Themes: Love; Devotion; Romance; Femininity; Promises

Symbols: Any Items Associated with Love and Romance; Peony

About Bai Mundan: This goddess is beautiful and sensual but also filled with only the most honorable intentions. It is her sacred task to tempt the ascetics in the keeping of their vows (turning the tables somewhat on the theme of this holiday). Her name means "white peony," a flower that in Chinese tradition affords this goddess's protection.

To Do Today: This holiday celebrates the heroine in an ancient story, Ch'un Hyang, who secretly married a nobleman's son. Even when beaten by a lusty governor, however, she remained devoted and refused all advances, as if guided by Bai Mundan's fidelity and esteem. For modern-minded people, this basically means "loving the one you're with" and really appreciating their companionship today. If it's been a while since you've given your partner a gift for no reason, or spent quality time alone with them, by all means, do so! Bai Mundan's energy is wherever two hearts emit true, faithful emotions.

If you don't have a partner, try this Bai Mundan love spell. You'll need a white peony (or any other white-petaled flower, like a daisy). Slowly tear off all the petals, saying,

> Bai Mundan, for love I ask;
> help me in this sacred task.

Let the earth and air accept all the petals but one, which you should carry with you as a love charm. Release it in thankfulness when your wish is answered.

May 21

Gemini (*Various Locations*)

IAMBE

Themes: Communication; Creativity; Art; Humor; Playfulness

Symbols: Paired Items

About Iambe: Iambe means "speech," indicating this goddess's intimate connection with the art of communication. In Greek stories, Iambe always had a witty (and sometimes satirical) comeback. This may be why she was credited with creating the writer's bane of iambic pentameter verse (a metered verse with two distinct accents). In mythology, Iambe used this form of poetry to cheer up Demeter, with tremendous success.

To Do Today: Astrologically, the twins personify individuals who have dual natures: they are filled with charm and creativity but also seem elusive, like Iambe and her poetic method. You can remember Iambe and learn more about her style today by reading Shakespeare, one of the few humans to master it (or perhaps rent one of the recent Shakespearean movies)!

If that's not your proverbial cup of tea, use this invocation to Iambe as a prayer, part of a ritual, or whatever is appropriate for you:

> Iambe, I sing your mystic poems.
> From dots and tittles, the magic's sown.
> With celestial pens, you scribe each spell,
> and lessons in joy, may I learn them well.
> Iambe, your metered muse confounds,
> yet where'er it's spoken, magic abounds,
> full and fierce, potent and free,
> and when I hear it I know, that the magic is me!

Bonfire Night (*Scotland*)

MACHA

Themes: Victory; Success; Protection; Fertility; Fire

Symbols: Red Items; Acorn; Crow

About Macha: Macha means "mighty one." Macha used her potency to clear the land for wheat, giving her associations with fertility. She also used her might to protect the Celts' lands against invaders, thereby becoming a war goddess and guardian. Art shows her dressed in red (a color abhorrent to evil) and with blazing red hair, forever chasing off any malevolence that threatens her children's success.

To Do Today: Taking place around this date, this festival originally had strong pagan overtones, the fires being lit specifically for ritual offerings that pleased the gods and goddesses and invoked their blessing. Additionally, the bright, red fire looked much like Macha's streaming hair, and thus it banished any evil spirits from the earth. So don any red-colored clothing today, or maybe temporarily dye your hair red to commemorate this goddess and draw her protective energies to your side. Eating red foods (like red peppers) is another alternative for internalizing Macha's victorious power and overcoming any obstacle standing in your way.

Or, find some acorns and keep them in a Macha fetish bag (any natural-fiber drawstring bag). Anytime you want her power to manifest, simply plant the acorn and express your wish to it. Macha's potential is in that acorn, ready to sprout!

May 23

Tubilustrium (Rome)

BELLONA

Themes: Protection; Victory; Communication; Strength

Symbols: Swords (or Athame); Spear

About Bellona: She who kindles the fire of the sun and the fire in the bellies of warriors, Bellona is both a mother and a battle goddess, being the female equivalent of Mars with a distinct diplomatic twist. Those who call upon Bellona receive strategy, tactfulness, and a keen sense of how to handle explosive situations effectively.

To Do Today: Romans spent today ritually cleansing their trumpets for battle and honoring the people who make the trumpets. In this part of the world, a horn not only signaled a charge but invoked the goddess's attention. So, for what personal battle(s) do you need to sound Bellona's horn today? Find a horn with which to do just that (perhaps a kazoo or a piece of construction paper rolled to look like a megaphone). Shout your battle plans to Bellona so she can respond with all her resources to help you.

If you use a sword, athame (sacred knife), or wand in magic, today is an excellent time to take out that tool and invoke Bellona's blessing upon it. Oil and sharpen the blade, polish the wand, then hold it in your hand as if it were a weapon, saying,

> *Bellona, see this implement of magic, which, as any,*
> *has two edges—for boon and bane. May only good-*
> *ness flow through this tool, and may I ever remain*
> *aware of the responsibility for its use. So be it.*

May 24

Furrow Day (*Cambodia*)

PO INO NOGAR

Themes: Growth; Harvest; Fertility; Community

Symbols: Clouds; Saltwater; Rain; Soil

About Po Ino Nogar: This agricultural goddess's name means simply "great one" in Cambodia, likely due to the fact that she brings fertility to the earth and its people. It is her duty to protect the fields and harvests. Epics sometimes symbolize Po Ino Nogar as a gentle rain, because local myths claim that she was born in the clouds and still controls the water's generative gift to the land and to our souls.

To Do Today: Members of the royal family in Cambodia used to plow the fields today to appease Po Ino Nogar and ensure fertility to the crops. For modern purposes, think about tasks that need to be "plowed" through—paperwork that's been neglected, communicating to someone with a difficult demeanor, a project put on terminal hold. As you till the metaphoric soils of that situation, you also encourage Po Ino Nogar's growth-oriented energy in them.

If your spirit or humor has seemed a bit "dry" lately, try this Po Ino Nogar visualization: Close your eyes and imagine a blue-white cloud overhead with the face of a smiling woman formed by its creases. As you look, the cloud releases small light-drops that pour softly over you. As they do, your skin absorbs the light, as well as this goddess's energy. Continue the visualization until you feel filled to overflowing.

May 25

Shavouth (Israel)

HOLY SPIRIT

Themes: Communication; Mediation; Universal Law; Blessings; Change; Health; Purity; Truth

Symbol: Light

About the Holy Spirit: In both Gnostic and Hebrew writings, the Holy Spirit is a female force. In New Age vernacular, she is seen as white light energy. The Holy Spirit pours upon people to communicate divine missives, including messages of well-being and blessing. She also mediates on our behalf with other facets of the divine, using order, universal law, and wisdom as a force for positive change.

To Do Today: The Feast of Weeks in Jewish tradition centers around the return of Moses from Mount Sinai bearing the Ten Commandments, and the promises made by God for a home "flowing with milk and honey." Consequently, suitable edibles today include dairy products and anything sweetened with honey to internalize divine promises for your life. To know what those promises might be, ask the Holy Spirit to show you: pray and meditate. Visualize a sparkling white light pouring over you. Write down any insights, images, or phrases that come during this time. Don't be surprised if you get words in a different language. This is glossalia (tongues) and may reveal secrets about past lives through the languages represented. If you don't have time for meditation, at least burn a white candle today to honor the Holy Spirit and her spiritual gifts.

Well Dressings (*Europe*)

CORDELIA

Themes: Blessings; Prayer; Beauty; Fairy; Wishes

Symbols: Flowers; Water

About Cordelia: A British nature goddess, Cordelia is part of every spring and summer flower that blossoms. This is the beauty she brings into our lives today, along with all the positive energies of spring. Traditionally, Cordelia does not appear until May, when the earth is fertile enough to sustain her glory. Art sometimes depicts her as being a citizen of fairy realms, and perhaps a flower princess.

To Do Today: Well-dressing festivals go back to animistic times, when people believed sacred wells held beneficent indwelling spirits. To appease these powers, people decked the well with Cordelia's symbols: garlands of spring flowers. They then asked for the gods', goddesses', or spirits' favor. So, if you have any type of fountain or well nearby, today is a day for wishing! Take a small offering (coins if a fountain; a flower if a natural water source) and toss it in while whispering your desire to Cordelia.

To draw the attention of Cordelia and her companions, the fey, into your life, take a dollhouse chair and glue any or all of the following items to it: thyme, straw, primrose, oak leaves, ash leaves, and hawthorn berries or leaves. Leave this on a sunny windowsill (preferably one with a plant on it) to encourage fairy guests, who will bring all manner of spring frolic into your home.

May 27

Festival at Bath (England)

SULIS

Themes: Water; Healing; Sun; Blessings; Wishes; Community; Offerings

Symbols: Water; Wheat Cakes; Fire

About Sulis: The Celtic goddess Sulis oversees all sacred wells and springs, which give healing and other blessings to those who pray at them. She also has associations with the sun, which explains the ever-burning fires in her temples.

To Do Today: One hundred miles outside London, Sulis's ancient natural springs lie as they did for over seven thousand years until they were discovered by the Romans, who used them for ritual, wish magic, socialization, and healing. The Festival at Bath revels in this region's history, especially Sulis's hot springs, which continue to bring thousands of visitors here annually, few of whom know that the springs are ten thousand years old and part of Sulis's spirit. To my mind this equates with enjoying time in a hot tub or sauna (perhaps you can take part of the day at a local spa).

If a spa isn't possible, let your bathroom get really steamy from a hot-water shower, then sit inside for a while absorbing Sulis's cleansing power into your pores. Release your tensions and dis-ease to her. Maybe light a candle to represent Sulis's presence with you, and meditate as you relax. Remember, the bathroom is one of the few places you can be assured of a private moment with the goddess, so take advantage of it!

May 28

Ute Bear Dance (Colorado)

BEAR WOMAN

Themes: Health; Psychic Abilities; Fertility; Unity; Love; Kinship; Instinct; Nature; Rebirth; Energy

Symbol: Bear

About Bear Woman: Among Native Americans, Bear Woman's power is intimately intertwined with the earth, protecting its creatures and helping humans in hunting. Because of the way bears interact with cubs, Bear Woman refocuses our attention on the importance of family unity, warmth, and love (especially in extended families like that of the tribe).

To Do Today: The Bear Dance was once held in February as bears emerged from their caves to commemorate the Utes's common ancestry with bears. Continuing the tradition ensures the tribe's health as well as ensuring ongoing communication with Spirit on important matters through Bear Woman. To adapt this custom, dress up in a furry coat or fuzzy clothing and imitate a bear. This acts as a form of sympathetic magic that draws Bear Woman's energy to you and helps you commune with it for positive personal transformation.

Also stop at a nature or science shop that carries stone carvings and get one today. Carry it to connect with Bear Woman's strength, endurance, and other positive attributes that you need in your life.

Dreaming of bears today reveals a bear totem or spirit guide in your life offering guidance, or a special message of help from Bear Woman.

May 29

Byblos Day (*Lebanon*)

ASHTART

Themes: Love; Prophecy (especially by stars); Hope; Protection; Victory; Romance

Symbols: Star; Fire; Red and White Items; Lion

About Ashtart: A Lebanese goddess for the lovelorn, Ashtart fell from the heavens as a star and landed in Byblos. She became the city's patroness, renowned for her prophetic insight, assistance in relationships, and protectiveness, especially when one faces a difficult battle. This tremendous power explains the artistic depictions of Ashtart riding a lion (a solar/fire symbol) or having the head of a lion.

To Do Today: International music festivals have been held in Byblos since the late 1960s to celebrate it as one of the oldest towns in the world with ongoing inhabitants (and an ever-present goddess!). It was here that a forerunner of the alphabet developed, inspired by the papyrus export trade. With this in mind, take a piece of onionskin paper and describe your emotional needs on it with red ink or crayon. Burning this releases the wish to Ashtart and begins manifesting the magic.

Honor Ashtart and gain her insight by star-gazing tonight. If you see a falling star and can repeat your wish for love three times before it disappears, folklore says it will be granted. If you see a meteor shower, count the sparks you see while thinking of a suitable binary question for this goddess. An even-numbered answer means "yes"; an odd-numbered answer means "no."

May 30

Memorial Day (United States)

SESHAT

Themes: Honor; Learning; History; Time; Karma

Symbols: Books; Writing Implements

About Seshat: Seshat is the Egyptian record keeper of the gods and a goddess to whom history, writing, and books are all sacred. Seshat reminds us that to change both our collective and our individual futures, we must first learn from the past. Measuring time and helping people plan out sacred buildings, Seshat often appears in art with a seven-pointed rosette and a wand (likely to inscribe her notes).

To Do Today: A time to remember people who have died in battle, Memorial Day also affords us a moment to remember those who have fought for freedom in alternative faiths. For the phrase "never again the burning" to mean something, we have to open our "broom closets" and begin educating the public about the beauty of magical traditions instead of using the usual hype. If you know someone who's been curious about magic, sharing your knowledge today honors Seshat and all the people who have kept records of our metaphysical legacy even when risking their lives.

Attend to your magic books today: read, write, make notes of your experiences with all due diligence, and ask Seshat to help you see the bigger picture. Don't dawdle today! Commit yourself to eliminating the phrase "pagan standard time" from your vocabulary. Being timely is something this goddess appreciates.

May 31

Flores de Mayo (Philippines)

SISINA

Themes: Offering; Prayer; Love; Devotion; Home; Relationships

Symbols: Spring/May-Blossoming Flowers

About Sisina: This Filipino goddess oversees the realms of orderliness, beauty, and love. Traditionally, she protects marriages against discord, but she may also be called upon to settle inner turmoil within your soul and restore self-love.

To Do Today: People in the Philippines say good-bye to May with bouquets, flower offerings, and an array of sweet foods to honor the month's sweetness and beauty. Sometimes they ask Sisina to join the festivities by setting a place for her at the table.

This particular custom appears in several other cultures and it is a simple, lovely way of honoring the goddess. Just leave a plate with a fresh flower on your dinner table. This draws Sisina's presence, love, and peaceful nature to your home and family relationships. If you wish, also leave an offering of sweet bread or fruity wine in a special spot to thank her.

As you go about your normal routine today, take time to enjoy any flowers you see, and be very considerate of the special people in your life. Sisina will see the effort and continue blessing those relationships with harmony.

June

J une takes its name from Juno, the Roman goddess of love and marriage (see June 2). Not surprisingly, June became the traditional month for marriage in Rome, and it continues to enjoy tremendous popularity for weddings today. Besides this, June is the favored month for flower festivals, likely due to the abundance of earth's blossoms around this time of year.

June's energies are focused on socialization and activity. It is a capricious month, filled with young love, romance, and the companionship of good friends. Any magic aimed at enhancing one's relationships, communication skills, and the personal energy level necessary for maintaining both will be augmented by working during this month.

June 1

Carna's Festival (Rome)

CARNA

Themes: Health; Kinship; Change; Opportunity

Symbols: Beans; Pork

About Carna: Carna presides over all matters of physical and spiritual health, well-being, and wholeness. Carna is also the patroness of the hinge, meaning she can help us open or close any doors in our life.

To Do Today: Romans traditionally gathered with their family on this day, offering Carna beans and pork to thank her for continued good health. This translates into a meal of pork, beans, and bacon to internalize her well-being! If you're a vegetarian, just stick with the beans.

To get Carna's assistance in getting an opportunity to open up, try this bit of sympathetic magic: Take any bean and go to your door. Stand before the door and say,

> Carna, help this magic begin; my future turns on your hinge.
> Open the way, starting today!

Open the door as you say "open the way," and put the bean outside in a safe place to draw Carna's opportunities to you.

To permanently close a chapter in your life, just alter the spell a bit. This time begin with the door open, saying,

> Carna, help me leave the past behind;
> by this spell this situation bind.
> Away it goes, the door is closed!

Put the bean outside the door and close it as you say "the door is closed," leaving the problem outside your life.

June 2

☯

Festival of Juno (*Rome*)

JUNO

Themes: Femininity; Love; Relationships; Romance; Kinship; Time; Protection (Women and Children); Leadership

Symbols: Cypress; Peacocks; Cuckoo; Luxurious Clothing; Figs; Moon (or Silver Items)

About Juno: The supreme goddess of the Roman pantheon, Juno offers a helping hand in every aspect of our relationships, especially the safety and happiness of women and children in those settings. Juno is also a very modern minded goddess, taking an active role in public life and finances. Beyond this, she rules women's cycles, giving her connections with the moon. Art depicts Juno always wearing majestic clothing befitting the "Queen of Heaven."

To Do Today: According to Roman folklore, marrying today ensures a long, happy relationship. So if you're planning a wedding or an engagement, or even moving in together, Juno can bless that commitment if you time the big step for today! As part of your devotion ritual, don't forget to wear special clothing (perhaps something your partner especially likes) to invoke Juno's attention and loving energy.

If you'd like to connect with Juno's feminine force, her leadership skills, or her sense of timing within yourself, eat some fig-filled cookies today (or just some figs), saying,

> Juno, bring _____ to my spirit, my wish fulfill.
> By your power, through my will.

Fill in the blank with whatever aspect of Juno you most need to develop.

June 3

☯

Pharmakos (Greece)

CHARILA

Themes: Cleansing; Fertility; Luck; Protection; Providence; Kindness

Symbols: Leeks; Onions; Grain; Honey Cake

About Charila: Charila comes to our aid when there is a famine, a drought, or some kind of abuse, be it in the earth or in our spirits. Greek mythology tells us that Charila was a young girl who approached a king seeking food. The king was angered and slapped her. Charila hung herself in disgrace, but not without some notice by the Delphic oracle. The prophetess told the king to change his unsympathetic ways and make offerings to Charila to appease her spirit. Some traditional offerings for her include honey cakes and grains.

To Do Today: During this observance in Greece, a criminal representing the community was ritually driven out of the city with leeks and onions rather than being executed. This act of mercy propitiated Charila, cleansed the city of its "sins," and ensured continuing good fortune for the region. This also brought fertility, onions being an aphrodisiac. So, whether you need Charila's luck, productivity, forgiveness, or protection, definitely add onions and leeks to the menu (followed by a hefty dose of breath mints)!

To draw Charila's kindness or good fortune to your home, take a handful of any type of grain and sprinkle it on the walkway near your living space, saying,

> *Follow me, wherever I roam,*
> *and let tenderness and luck fill my home!*

June 4

☯

Rosalia (Greece)

APHRODITE

Themes: Love; Romance; Passion; Sexuality; Luck; Fertility; Beauty; Pleasure

Symbols: Roses; Copper; Turquoise; Sandalwood

About Aphrodite: Since 1300 B.C.E., Aphrodite has been worshiped as the ultimate goddess to inspire passion, spark romance, increase physical pleasure, augment inner beauty, and improve sexual self-assurance. Consequently, many artistic depictions show her naked, with erotic overtones. Aphrodite's name means "water born" or "foam born," intimating a connection with the ocean's fertility.

To Do Today: Follow Greek custom and shower whatever goddess image you have at home with rose petals, or dab it with rose-scented oil. If you don't have a statue, poster, or painting, any visually beautiful object can serve as a proxy. This gesture honors and entreats Aphrodite, who responds by granting good luck, especially in matters of the heart.

Another tradition is bathing yourself in rose water to emphasize Aphrodite's comeliness (both within and without). Rose water is available at many Asian and international supermarkets. Or you can make it easily by steeping fresh rose petals in warm (*not* hot) water and straining. If you don't have time for a full bath, just dab a little of the rose water over the region of your heart to emphasize this goddess's love and attractiveness where it can do the most good—in your emotional center.

June 5

☯

World Environment Day (*United Nations*)

UTO

Themes: Ecology; Nature; Magic

Symbols: Green Items; Snakes

About Uto: This ancient Egyptian goddess bears a name that means "green one." She embodies the earth's regenerative force, specifically in its vegetation. Art often shows Uto in the form of a snake, ever transforming and renewing herself and the earth. This tremendous magical power comes from being able to draw on the essence of creation and all that dwells therein. As she wields this beneficial energy, she inspires today's activities by assisting our summer efforts to restore the planet.

To Do Today: I suspect this goddess inspired the creation of World Environment Day in 1972, specifically to increase enthusiasm for global environmental causes and natural restoration. The United Nations continues to encourage its members to have special activities today that further earth-first thinking and world healing in all forms. So, put on something green today, get outside, and get busy! Organize a recycling drive, pick up litter in a nearby park, plant some seedlings or trees, begin composting, make a donation to a reputable environmental group. Anything you can do to help restore the earth's greenery honors and welcomes Uto's regenerative spirit to the earth. Let her guide your hands and efforts today, flowing through you with healthy energy, ministering to the earth.

June 6

☯

Ancestor Day (*Yoruba*)

EGUNGUN-OYA

Themes: Destiny; Death; Ghosts; Divination; Foresight; Truth

Symbols: Dance; Fire

About Egungun-Oya: The Yoruban Mother of the Dead and mistress of spiritual destinies, Egungun-Oya helps us peek into our own futures, being a goddess of fate. Traditionally she is venerated through folk dances that show her guiding spirits in the afterlife with the flames of truth in one hand.

To Do Today: As one might expect, the people of Nigeria honor their ancestors on this day, believing that they and Egungun-Oya control the fates of the living. It's a common custom, therefore, to leave food and gifts for both the deceased and the goddess today, hoping both will find pleasure in the offering. In your own home, put out pictures of loved ones who have passed on, and light a candle in front of these today so that Egungun-Oya's truth will fill your home. When you light the candle, observe its flame. If it burns out quickly without your assistance, this indicates that you should take care—you're burning yourself out on too many projects. If it flames up brightly and steadily, anticipate health and longevity. An average-sized flame that burns blue indicates spiritual presences and a normal life span.

To keep any unwanted ghosts out of your house, put a light of any sort in a window, saying,

> *Egungun-Oya is your guide;*
> *return to your sleep and there abide.*

The goddess will safely guide those spirits back to where they belong.

June 7

☯

Sjomannadagur (Iceland)

WAVE MAIDENS

Themes: Providence; Protection (from water); Charity; Fertility; Peace; Cycles; Water

Symbols: Fish; Sea Items

About the Wave Maidens: These northern Teutonic goddesses number nine and rule over the waves, being the joint mothers of Heimdel, the god of the sea. In mythology, the Wave Maidens live at the bottom of the sea, watching over the World Mill that continually turns with the seasons to bring the earth and her people fertility and harmony.

To Do Today: In Iceland, fishermen honor the Wave Maidens today by taking a well-deserved day off and enjoying sports, foods, and dances, the proceeds from which support fishermen's retirement homes. If you're a fish lover, this translates into abstaining from fish today as a way of thanking the Wave Maidens for their ongoing providence.

If you live near a region where you can get to a lake or ocean, consider stopping by for a moment today and greeting the Wave Maidens yourself. Pick up a bit of sand and carry it with you to generate a better understanding of personal cycles and those of the earth. Or, gather a shell, a bit of driftwood, or a tumbled stone to promote the Wave Maidens' flowing harmony in and around your life.

In terms of clothing, think sea-blue or green and something that's loose, to help you physically flow as easily as the Wave Maidens through life's circumstances.

June 8

☯

Dragon Boat Festival (China)

NUGUA

Themes: Balance; Masculinity; Femininity; Cooperation; Equality

Symbols: Yin-Yang Symbol; Opposites

About Nugua: In China, Nugua is known as "she who restores balance." Nugua's energy brings life back into equilibrium when circumstances may have threatened us with chaos. In art she is depicted as being part rainbow-colored dragon and part woman, representing the importance of maintaining balance between the lower and the higher self.

To Do Today: Around this time of year, when the daylight and nighttime hours are growing closer to equal, the Chinese hold a dragon-boat festival that revels in Nugua's balance—the masculine (yin) and feminine (yang), the light and the dark, and the cooperative energies that dance between the two. To commemorate this yourself, be sure to carry a coin with you (the heads/tails represents duality), but keep it where you won't accidentally spend it. Bless it, saying,

> By day and dark,
> Nugua's balance impart.

If negativity threatens your sense of stability, follow Chinese custom and drum out the evil. Use anything that has a drumlike sound, move counterclockwise, the direction of banishing, and visualize Nugua's rainbow filling every inch of your home.

Offerings of beans, peaches, and rice are also customary. So, either leave these in a special spot or eat them to internalize any of Nugua's attributes you need today.

June 9

☯

Rice Ceremony (Japan)

WAKASANAME NO KAMI

Themes: Providence; Harvest; Growth; Patience; Manifestation

Symbols: Rice; Fire

About Wakasaname no Kami: This goddess's name describes her function in Japan—the Young Rice Planting Maiden. It is Wakasaname's duty to oversee the rice transplantings at this time of year, as she was born of a union between the food goddess and the grain god. From a more spiritual perspective, Wakasaname no Kami offers us the providence and fulfillment that come from a job patiently well attended.

To Do Today: Early in June, Japanese farmers transplant their rice seedlings into the paddies, asking for the blessings of the goddess as they go. Prayers are made as ritual fires burn to get Wakasaname's attention, and they probably act as an invocation to the sun. In your home, this might mean going outside (if the weather permits) and starting the grill or hibachi. Burn a little rice in the flame as an offering to the goddess so she can help you fulfill your work-related goals. Make sure you keep your purpose in mind while the rice burns or speak your wishes into the smoke so it carries them before Wakasaname's watchful eyes.

To inspire Wakasaname's patience in your life, make a bowl of rice. Breathe deeply, then try to pick up one grain with chopsticks. This is an old meditative method from the East, and believe me, it teaches much about the benefits of persistence and practice!

June 10

☯

Strawberry Festival (New York)

AWEHAI

Themes: Harvest; Tradition; Growth; Longevity; Community

Symbols: Turtle; Seeds

About Awehai: In Iroquois tradition, this goddess reigns in the sky and the heavens, watching diligently over family life and the community.

Mythology tells us that Awehai grabbed seeds and animals as she fell from heaven, landing on the back of a great turtle. From here, Awehai scattered the seeds and freed the animals, resulting in a growing, fertile earth filled with beauty.

To Do Today: This festival takes place nearly in my backyard, having been instituted by the Iroquois Indians in Tonawanda, New York. Here people come to the longhouse to enjoy ritual dancing, chanting, and the sounding of turtle-shell rattles, a symbol of Awehai. So, if you know any type of traditional ritual dances or chants, consider enacting them outside as you scatter grass seed to the wind. This will manifest Awehai's productivity in your life and in the earth.

Another custom is simpler and a lot of fun: consuming strawberries in as many forms as possible. In Iroquois tradition, these pave the road to heaven, and eating them ensures you a long life and Awehai's fertility. Share strawberries with a loved one to inspire Awehai's community-oriented energy in your home, and consume fresh strawberries to harvest her powers for personal growth.

June 11

☯

Kamehameha Day (Hawaii)

PELE

Themes: Unity; Tradition; Protection; Creativity; Change

Symbols: Fire; Red-colored Items

About Pele: In Hawaii, Pele's fires develop and redevelop the islands through volcanic activity. It is this creative force that comes into our lives today, cleansing, transforming, and rebuilding, augmented by summer's fiery energy.

According to local legend, it is unwise to take any souvenir from Pele's mountain without asking or leaving a gift, lest bad luck follow you everywhere. She is zealously protective of her lands and her children. Traditional offerings include coins, strawberries, hair, sugarcane, flowers, tobacco, brandy, and silk.

To Do Today: King Kamehameha united the Hawaiian people, protecting commoners from the brutality of overlords, much as Pele unites them through her creative, protective power. This festival commemorates him and the traditions of Hawaii through arts and crafts, parades, hula dancing, and luaus. At home, this might translate into having some tropical foods served steaming hot (the heat represents Pele's activating energy). For example, eat pineapple fried in brown sugar for sweet harmony. Or consume fresh strawberries soaked in brandy to ignite your inner fires with Pele's inspiration. Finally, wear something red today to energize Pele's attributes in your efforts all day long.

June 12

☯

Rice Festival (Korea)

KWANSEIEUN

Themes: Luck; Blessings; Harvest; Cleansing; Kindness

Symbols: Fish; Willow; Gold Items

About Kwanseieun: This Korean goddess of goodness, courage, and fortune listens carefully to our needs, intending to meet each with compassion. Art sometimes shows her riding a fish, giving her associations with fertility. In other depictions she bears a willow branch and gold necklaces (lunar and solar symbols, respectively), indicating the diverse powers she can use in answering our prayers.

To Do Today: In a festival similar to that held in Japan this month, Korean farmers go about the task of ensuring an abundant rice crop today. To draw this abundance and Kwanseieun's blessings into your life, follow Korean custom and wash your hair today. This cleans away ill fortune. Change the type of rinse you use to mirror your goals. For example, rinse in Kwanseieun's fertile aspect by using pine-scented water, or increase her fortunate energies for the day by using allspice-nutmeg-scented water. Making these rinses is very easy. Just steep the desired aromatic in warm water, as you would a tea, then refrigerate and use as desired!

Wear gold or eat fish today to commemorate Kwanseieun and activate her positive attributes in your personality. For example, wear a gold necklace to communicate with more kindness, or wear a gold ring to remind you to extend a helping hand to those in need.

June 13

☯

Feast of Epona (Gaul)

EPONA

Themes: Protection of Animals, Especially Those Who Serve Humankind

Symbol: A Horse

About Epona: Epona protects the creatures who faithfully keep humans company. This pre-Roman Gaulish goddess is nearly always shown riding or lovingly feeding a horse and accompanied by a dog—these are her two sacred animals.

Also sometimes depicted with corn in her lap and carrying a goblet, Epona inspires love, fertility, and providence in your life. In some myths, Epona appeared to acknowledge a king's sovereignty, giving her leadership qualities that can help you when you need more authority in a situation.

To Do Today: To generate a little more providence in your life, eat corn today. Say a silent prayer to Epona, asking her to saturate your food with her power, then consume it to internalize the energy.

If you have a pet, consider blessing it today. To do this, find a small silver charm of a horse or a dog (like those from charm bracelets). This image invokes Epona's protection. Alternatively, use a little bell and draw the image of a horse or dog on it.

Hold the token cupped in your hands. Visualize it filled with glittery white light and say,

> Epona, watch over _____ [fill in with the name of the animal].
> Keep them safe and healthy no matter where they may be.

Put the charm on the animal's collar or cage or in its bedding.

June 14

☯

Birthday of the Muse (Greece)

MNEMOSYNE

Themes: Creativity; Knowledge; History; Art

Symbols: Fountains; Springs; the Number Nine

About Mnemosyne: Mnemosyne means "memory." Remembrance is this goddess's gift to us, memories of all the wonderful moments of our lives. In Greek tradition, Mnemosyne also gave birth to the Muses today—the nine creative spirit-children that give our lives so much beauty: song, stories, tradition, humor, dance, and sacred music. Greeks sometimes worshiped Mnemosyne in the form of a spring, alluding to her profuse, flowing energy.

To Do Today: Absolutely anything thoughtful, creative, or inspiring will grab Mnemosyne's attention and encourage her participation in your day. Try donning a unique combination of clothing that really motivates you to do your best, or something that provokes fond memories from the past. Wear an aroma that arouses your inventive nature or cognitive abilities (jasmine and rosemary are two good choices, respectively).

If there are special arts that you've learned from family or friends, celebrate them today. Hum that little ditty from your childhood, dust off that neglected craft item, try those recipes, listen to old songs, and let Mnemosyne fill your hours with the encouragement that comes from fond "musings."

June 15

☯

Hemis Festival (India)

RATNA DAKINIS

Themes: Banishing; Victory; Kindness; Karma

Symbols: The Color Yellow

About Ratna Dakinis: In Tibet, these goddesses rule over all gestures of goodness and compassion, which naturally help improve karma. Collectively, their name means "inestimable," showing us the true power and value in acts of kindness that are driven by a pure heart.

To Do Today: This festival includes a ritual play in which all manner of mythic creatures are poised against the Tibetan lamas, symbolizing the battle between good and evil. Bells, censers, cymbals, and drums draw in positive magic, banish evil, and win the fight for Ratna Dakinis' goodness. In keeping with this idea, string together some yellow-colored brass bells for a Ratna Dakinis house amulet. Hold these in your hand and empower them by saying,

> Let your goodness ring, let purity sing,
> with each wind Ratna Dakinis' blessing bring!

Hang these where they will catch the wind regularly, releasing the magic.

Wear something yellow today to keep Ratna Dakinis in mind so that your actions will be gentle and filled with kindness. Do something nice for someone who's been feeling blue lately, "just because." Give them some yellow flowers, offer a hug, or maybe make an extra bell amulet for them too! This boosts good karma, makes both of you feel good, and invokes Ratna Dakinis' blessings through thoughtfulness.

June 16

❂

Incan Festival of the Sun (Mexico)

CHASCA

Themes: Sun; Fire; Divination: Love

Symbols: Sun; Fire; Flowers

About Chasca: In Incan tradition, this goddess created the dawn and twilight, the gentlest aspects of the sun. Along with her consort, the sun god Inti, she uses light to draw sprouts from the ground and inspire blossoms. Her rapport with Inti and her tender nature give Chasca associations with love. According to lore, she communicates to people through clouds and dew in a type of geomantic omen observation.

To Do Today: In this ancient Peruvian festival, Incans reveled in Chasca's and Inti's power and beauty around the time when the sun reached its zenith. People made offerings to the goddess and god, followed by folk dances around ritual fires. So, if you can hold an outdoor ritual today, build a fire and dance come dusk. Allow Chasca's inspiring, growth-oriented energy to fill you to overflowing.

Incans also burned old clothing in the ritual fire to banish sickness or bad luck. Try this, or burn an emblem of your troubles instead. As the token is consumed, Chasca transforms the negative energy into something positive.

If you're fortunate to have a semicloudy day, go outside and ask a question of Chasca (ideally about relationships). Then watch for a cloud that has a recognizable shape. This shape represents your answer in some form. For example, a heart would indicate that love is on its way!

June 17

The Cleansing Lily (Japan)

DAINICHI-NYORAI

Themes: Beauty; Cleansing; Protection; Spirituality; Weather

Symbols: Lilies; Gold-colored Items; Light

About Dainichi-nyorai: This light-bearing goddess comes in answer to the Japanese people's prayers for sunlight. Having all the sun's power, Dainichi-nyorai embodies pure goodness, her name meaning "great illuminator." With this in mind, call upon this goddess at midyear to assist your quest for enlightenment and keep the road ahead filled with radiance.

To Do Today: In Shinto tradition, today marks a time when people gather lilies as an offering to entreat the goddess to stop flooding rains. This is really a form of weather magic. If you need rain in your area, burn a lily; to banish rain, wave the lily in the air to move the clouds away!

It is customary to anoint one's hearth (the stove) today with lily (or any floral-scented) oil. This welcomes Dainichi-nyorai in all her radiant goodness into the heart of your home and the hearts of all those who live there. Wear something gold while doing this, or decorate your kitchen with a yellow or gold-toned candle. When you light the candle, whisper Dainichi-nyorai's name so she can live through that flame, warming every corner of your life.

By the way, if you feel adventurous, lily buds are edible; they have a nutty taste. Try cooking them in butter and eating them to internalize all the positive energies of this festival and the goddess.

June 18

☯

Father's Day (United States)

HERMAPHRODITOS

Themes: Balance; Masculinity; Femininity; Honor; Reason; Leadership

Symbols: Two-sided Items; Yin/Yang Symbol

About Hermaphroditos: This androgynous deity was once the son of Hermes, but he loved the nymph Salmakis so much that the lovers became of one body and soul, neither the male nor the female being discernible. In this form, Hermaphroditos reminds us that the Goddess is also God, blending the best of both sexes together into powerful, productive energy.

To Do Today: At the midpoint of the year we take a moment's pause from the Goddess to honor her consort and other half, the God, represented by fathers everywhere. Take time to thank the special men in your life and pamper them today. Ask Hermaphroditos to show you the goddess within them, and how god and goddess work together, making each person unique.

In magic traditions, the god aspect is the conscious, logical force of the universe who offers us the attributes of leadership, reason, and focus. This persona and energy is part of the goddess—one cannot be separated from the other. This is a good day to look within yourself, find both aspects of the divine, and concentrate on bringing them into balance. If you're normally headstrong, back off a bit. If you're normally a wallflower, get daring! If you like to plan, become spontaneous—and so forth. Hermaphroditos will show you the way.

June 19

☯

Emancipation Day (*Texas*)

MAAT

Themes: Freedom; New Beginnings; Justice; Morality; Organization; Promises; Universal Law

Symbols: Ostrich Feather (or any feather)

About Maat: In Egypt, Maat is the ultimate representation of fairness, justice, and truth. As the spirit of orderliness and legislation, she assists us by overseeing any legal matters, hearings, promises, and oaths to ensure harmony and honesty. In some Egyptian stories, a person's soul was weighed against Maat's feather to gain entrance to paradise.

To Do Today: On June 19 in 1865, the slaves in Texas were finally told about the Emancipation Proclamation signed three years previously. While freedom was slow in coming, it finally arrived, likely in part thanks to Maat's encouragement.

For all of Maat's spells it's best to have a feather to use as a component and focal point. Change the color of your feather to suit the goal. Pick blue for true seeing (or to encourage honesty with yourself), white for pure promises, black and white for legal equity, and pale yellow to inspire a new beginning filled with Maat's keen insight. Bless the feather, using the following incantation (fill in the blank with your goal), then release it to the wind so the magic begins to move!

> Maat, on this feather light
> bring to me renewed insight.
> To my life _____ impart;
> make a home within my heart.

June 20

☯

Bald Eagle Day (United States)

MOTHER OF ALL EAGLES

Themes: Freedom; Perspective; Overcoming; Health; Power; Destiny; Air Element; Movement

Symbols: Feathers (*not* Eagle—gathering these is illegal)

About Mother of All Eagles: On the warm summer winds, Eagle Mother glides into our reality, carries us above our circumstances, and stretches our vision. Among Native Americans, the Eagle Mother represents healing, her feathers often being used by shamans for this purpose. Beyond this, she symbolizes comprehension, finally coming to a place of joyfully accepting our personal power over destiny.

To Do Today: On this day in 1982, President Reagan declared Bald Eagle Day to honor the American emblem of freedom. In Native American tradition, this emblem and the Eagle Mother reconnect us with sacred powers, teaching us how to balance our temporal and spiritual life on the same platter.

Find a new, large feather for Eagle Mother talismans, one different from those you gathered for Maat, because the two have very different energies (check craft shops). Wrap the pointed end with cloth crisscrossed by leather thonging or a natural-fabric ribbon. Each time you cross the leather strings, say,

> _____ *bound within;*
> *when released by wind, let the magic begin.*

Fill in the blank with the Eagle Mother attributes you desire, then have the feather present or use it in rituals or spells to disperse incense, thereby releasing its magic on the winds.

June 21

☯

Cancer Begins (*Various Locations*)

LADY OF REGLA

Themes: Kinship; Protection; Kindness; Moon; Love; Devotion; Fertility; Relationships

Symbols: Fish; Moon; Silver (lunar) or Blue Items (her favorite color); Crab

About the Lady of Regla: This West Indian fish mother swims in with summer rains as the bearer of fertility, family unity, prospective life mates, and other traditionally lunar energies. Shown in art looking much like a mermaid, the Lady of Regla is also the patroness of this astrological sign.

To Do Today: In astrology, those born under the sign of Cancer have a great deal of compassion, desire family closeness and stability, and are ruled by the moon, all of which characterize this goddess's energies to a tee. How you emphasize those powers depends on what you need. For harmony at home, add blue highlights to your decorating scheme, and wear pale blue clothing when having difficult conversations.

Eat fish or crab today to digest a little extra self-love or empathy, or to encourage fertility in any area of your life. To spice up this magic, serve the fish with a bit of lemon juice—a fruit that emphasizes devotion and kinship.

If you'd like to dream of future loves or get the Lady of Regla's perspective on a difficult family situation, leave her an offering of yams before going to bed. According to local custom, this invokes Regla's favor and you will experience helpful night visions—so take notes!

June 22

☯

Midsummer (*Various Locations*)

SAULES MATE

Themes: Sun; Prayer; Protection

Symbols: Sun; Fire; Yellow/Gold or Red Items; Horses; Birch

About Saules Mate: Saules Mate comes to us from Indo-European tradition, her name meaning "sun." Indeed, with the sun reaching its highest point today, she becomes the center of our festivities. Saules Mate crosses the sky during the day in a carriage drawn by yellow horses, then travels the waters by night in a golden birch boat, hanging a red scarf in the wind to give the sky its lovely color.

To Do Today: In magic traditions, we stop for a moment on this day to mark the sun's halfway point through its annual journey. Traditionally, this is a time to harvest magical herbs, but do so before Saules Mate gets too bright in the sky; her heat diminishes the natural oils in the herbs. Remember to leave an offering for the goddess so she will empower these herbs—perhaps some ground birch wood that acts as plant mulch!

Purify yourself by jumping the ritual fire (or a candle) today, then burn a wish in Saules Mate's fires to release it into her care. And use this invocation to Saules Mate for part of personal magic today (for the southern quarter of the magic circle):

> Powers of the fire, reach ever higher.
> Saules Mate, bring your light; the power ignite.
> Salamanders prance in the magical dance,
> By your power and my will, this sacred space fill!

June 23

☯

Rousalii (Romania)

THE ROUSALII

Themes: Humor; Protection; Weather; Fertility; Fairies; Growth

Symbols: Water; Linen; Green Robes

About the Rousalii: A group of ill-treated women in life, these goddesses often create mischief when they interact with humans, especially those with nasty dispositions. They do, however, have a good side. The Rousalii know the dances that make plants and people grow and thrive, and sometimes they will teach them to humans. In literature, the Rousalii sometimes appear as water fairies, begging linen from passersby, which they use to make green robes for fertility rites.

To Do Today: In Romania, people would tell you that it is best to stay home today and leave the Rousalii offerings of bread and salt to avert their impish ways. If it's windy, definitely stay home; this means the ladies are in a foul mood. To protect yourself, place wormwood under your pillow, pull the covers over your head, and stay put!

On a less drastic level, wear something green to keep them happy and try this spell to encourage the Rousalii's growth or maturity in any area of your life: Take a little piece of linen (or cotton cloth) and dance with it in your hand, moving clockwise and saying,

> *The dance of life, the dance of power, Rousalii, join me this magic hour!*
>
> *To _____ bring growth and maturity; by your power this spell is freed!*

Fill in the blank with your intention. Tuck the swatch of cloth on your person, or close to the area that represents your goal.

June 24

☯

Yam Festival (Nigeria)

INNA

Themes: Harvest; Offering; Protection; Promises; Justice

Symbols: Yams; Harvested Foods

About Inna: In Nigeria, Inna ensures an abundant yam harvest for this festival, as well as good crops for farmers who honor her. During the summer months, she appears as a protectress who oversees our lands, homes, promises, and all matters of justice. Oaths taken in Inna's name are totally binding.

To Do Today: Around the end of June, nearly every group in Nigeria celebrates the Yam Festival with offerings to the goddess and a feast of yams. This is a sacred crop here, and eating yams today will purify your body and spirit. If you can't find yams, try sweet potatoes instead, sprinkling them with a little brown sugar to ensure sweet rewards for your diligent efforts. To get the wheels of justice turning a little faster, forego the sugar and eat the potatoes steaming hot (heat represents motivating energy).

People also traditionally practice yam divination today. You can try this yourself using any potato. Cut it in half the long way, then toss the two sides in the air while praying for Inna's insight. If one lands face up and the other face down, it is a good sign for your family or the entire community in which you live. The coming year will be filled with Inna's abundance and equity. To increase the meaning in this system, draw two personally significant symbols in the potato and see if either comes up!

June 29

☯

White Nights (*Russia*)

HOTOGOV MAILGAN

Themes: Sky; Tradition; Arts

Symbol: Pale Light

About Hotogov Mailgan: In Siberia, Hotogov Mailgan illuminates the night sky with her heavenly sparkle. She is the Queen of the Sky, a creative force for personal empowerment, and the manifester of the life energies in and around us.

To Do Today: Between June 21 and June 29 the skies in Russia always appear light gray at night because of the northern location. The effect throughout St. Petersburg is very magical, casting unique shadows on the lavender, pink, and yellow pastel-colored buildings. To celebrate this beauty, the citizens enjoy traditional Russian ballets, theatrical performances, and music. So, get out the theme music from Dr. *Zhivago*, rent a ballet featuring Barishnikov, or cook yourself up some Russian dumplings (*varnekey*) and invite this goddess to join you.

If you perform any magic today, try putting up some pastel-colored curtains around the space to filter the outside light so it suits Hotogov Mailgan. Or darken the room and use glow-in-the-dark stars to mark the magical circle so you're literally surrounded by her power.

Try taking a bubble bath and dotting the surface of the water with glitter to look like Hotogov Mailgan's night sky. Then sit, relax, and meditate, absorbing the hopeful, dreamy energy that her stars inspire in people everywhere.

June 26

☯

Alaskan Whale Dance

SEDNA

Themes: Thankfulness; Providence; Nature; Abundance

Symbols: Water; an Eye; Fish

About Sedna: The mother of the sea, which is sometimes called the "eating place" in northern climes, Sedna is a very important figure in Alaskan mythology as the provider of nourishment for both body and soul. In narratives, Sedna gave birth to fish, seals, polar bears, and whales, the life-sustaining animals of this region. Artistic renderings show her as having one eye that sees all things in her domain.

To Do Today: At this time of year, fishermen in Alaska dance through town giving out whale meat. According to custom, this dance propitiates the spirits of the food-providing whales who have died in the previous year. It also ensures an abundance of food in the year ahead. Adapting this a bit, abstain from your favorite meat product today and ask for Sedna's blessing on the animals who provide your food year-round. Vegetarians can forego their favorite staple and ask Sedna to bless the earth's greenery instead! Eating fish, however, is perfectly suited to the occasion, as it will fill you with Sedna's nourishment. Remember to eat thankfully!

To keep a small token in your home that will continually draw Sedna's blessing to you, get a goldfish and name it after her! Each time you feed the fish you're symbolically giving an offering to the goddess. When you have a need, whisper it to the fish so Sedna hears you.

June 27

☯

Sun Dance (Northcentral United States)

SHAKURU

Themes: Theft; Divination; Sun; Truth; Magic

Symbols: Sun; Gold/Yellow Items

About Shakuru: Pawnee daughter of the moon and goddess of the sun, Shakuru joins summer celebrations by shining her light on today's ceremony. In Pawnee stories, Shakuru's son became the first man on earth, making her the mother of humankind.

To Do Today: About this time of year the Plains Indians gather to welcome the sun and all its power. All manner of magical practices take place during this rite, including divinations to uncover a thief or murderer using totemic practices. For our purposes this might translate into divining for a totem animal whom we can call on for guidance and energy in times of need. To do this you'll need a lot of animal pictures (cut from magazines or anywhere else you can find them). Make the images the same shape and size to ensure randomness. Sit quietly with these face-down before you and ask Shakuru to guide your hand. Don't move quickly, and wait until the paper below your hand feels warm, a sign of Shakuru's presence. Turn it over and see what animal it is, then read up on that creature in folklore collections to see what message it's bringing you.

As much as possible, try to move clockwise today (imitating the natural movement of the sun through the sky). Walk through your house going to the right, stir your coffee clockwise, clean windows using clockwise strokes, and so forth. This honors Shakuru and draws the sun's blessings into your life.

June 28

☯

Palio Festival (Italy)

RIGANTONA

Themes: Sports; Excellence; Magic; Fertility; Movement; Travel

Symbols: Horse; Moon; White Items; Birds

About Rigantona: A Roman/Italic form of Rhiannon, this goddess travels the earth on a swift white horse, a lunar symbol, sweeping us up to travel along and get everything in our lives moving! Stories portray Rigantona in the company of powerful magical birds, and she also represents fertility.

To Do Today: In Italy, people attend the Palio Festival, a horse race that started in the thirteenth century and has continued ever since as a time to show physical skill and cunning. It's a perfect place for Rigantona to shine. Any type of physical activity that you excel in will please Rigantona today and encourage her motivational energy in your efforts. Get out and take a brisk walk, swim, rollerblade. As you move, visualize yourself atop a white horse, the goddess's symbol, approaching an image of a specific goal. All the energy you expend during this activity generates magic for attainment.

If birds fly into your life today, pay attention to the type of bird and its movements, because birds are Rigantona's messengers. Birds flying to the right are good omens, those moving to the left act as a warning of danger, and those flying overhead indicate productivity in whatever you try today. If any of these birds drops a feather, keep it as a gift from this goddess.

June 29

☯

Mnarja (Malta)

TESANA

Themes: Harvest; Light; Fertility; Abundance; Hope; Beginnings; Growth; Opportunity; Restoration

Symbols: Dawn; Red; Fruit

About Tesana: In Etruscan, Tesana means "dawn." As the first pink rays of light begin to reach through the darkness, Tesana is there, offering the hope of a better tomorrow and the warmth of a new day. Through her steadfast attendance, the earth and its people bear life and become fruitful.

To Do Today: Mnarja is the primary folk festival in Malta and originated as an orange and lemon harvest celebration. The name Mnarja means "illumination," and all the ritual fires ignited today symbolically keep Tesana's fertility burning. So, light a candle this morning at dawn's first light to welcome Tesana and invoke her assistance. Choose the color of the candle to reflect your goal: pink for hope, white for beginnings (a clean slate), and green for growth or restoration. If you like, also carve an emblem of your goal into the wax, leaving the taper to burn until it melts past the symbol (this releases the magic).

In a similar prolific tone, the customary food to encourage Tesana's fertility and continuing good harvests today is rabbit. If this isn't a meat you enjoy, make rarebit instead; this was a substitute for costly rabbits in the Middle Ages.

❽

Arretophoria (*Greece*)

ANTHEIA

Themes: Promises; Friendship; Trust; Honor; Community; Love; Relationships

Symbols: Gold-colored Items; Honey; Myrrh

About Antheia: Since 800 B.C.E. Antheia has been known as the Greek goddess of marriage, companionship, and good council. These attributes manifested themselves in a triple goddess figure who flowered, sought a mate, and reached perfection. Today we ask her to bless our rites by flowering within our souls so we too can obtain spiritual perfection.

To Do Today: In ancient Greece this festival of trust and friendship was held sometime between June and July. Each year, two maidens were given a special honey-laden diet and clothed in golden robes to take on a special trust. They delivered a package untouched to a secret place in a local temple, then spent the year in community service, never peeking inside the box. This sounds like a fun activity for couples or friends. Each person picks out a trust gift for the other and gives it to them to put in a special place, leaving it untouched for a year. The entire time the gift remains there unopened, Antheia will energize it and bless the people in that relationship, so don't get tempted to peek. Believe me when I say it's worth the wait. At the end of the year, don something gold, burn myrrh to create a sacred space in which Antheia dwells, and open the gifts, explaining the significance of the items. I guarantee it's a present you'll never forget.

July

July was named after the great leader Julius Caesar, who was born in this summer month. Because the warm weather continues, activity levels are high, even though the days are beginning to shorten. Consequently, numerous festivals during this month focus on family, friends, and social interaction.

For magical purposes, July directs our attention to personal growth and improvements. This includes increasing your knowledge, continuing efforts for prosperity, creating new ideas and works of art, and also taking time out periodically to really enjoy yourself. Our society sometimes mistakes much-needed leisure time for laziness, but this month's energies know better. Go and have fun, carrying the Goddess with you for a little extra energy.

July 1

Half-Year Day (Hong Kong)

GRISMADEVI

Themes: Cycles; Recreation; Rest; Summer; Time

Symbols: Summer Flowers; Red; Cup

About Grismadevi: The Buddhist goddess whose name means "summer" joins us to welcome the season and energize our efforts for goddess-centered living. In works of art she often appears wearing the color red, the hue of life's energy, and carrying a cup offering refreshment to all in need.

To Do Today: On this day, people in Hong Kong take a much-deserved reprieve from their labors to welcome summer and mark the halfway point in the year; we can do likewise today. This is a moment to pat yourself on the back for the magical goals you've attained thus far and the growing power of the Goddess within you.

Wear something red or flowery today to accent Grismadevi's energies in and around your life. Drink red juices or eat red foods to internalize the vibrancy of summer and this goddess. Suggestions include red grapefruit juice for purification, red peppers for zest, strawberry pie to partake of life's sweet abundance, a tossed tomato salad for love (the dressing brings harmony), raspberries to protect your relationships, and rhubarb for devotion.

Finally, leave a cup filled with reddish-colored liquid or a bouquet of fresh flowers on your altar or family table today to honor Grismadevi and welcome both her and the summer sunshine into your home.

July 2

Seminole Green Corn Dance
(Southeastern United States)

CORN MOTHER

Themes: Abundance; Children; Energy; Fertility; Harvest; Health; Grounding; Providence; Strength

Symbols: Corn; Corn Sheafs

About Corn Mother: Literally the spirit of the corn in Native American traditions, Corn Mother brings with her the bounty of earth, its healing capabilities, it nurturing nature, and its providence. This is the season when Corn Mother really shines, bountiful with the harvest. She is happy to share of this bounty and give all those who seek her an appreciation of self, a healthy dose of practicality, and a measure of good common sense.

To Do Today: Around this time of year the Seminole Indians (in the Florida area) dance the green corn dance to welcome the crop and ensure ongoing fertility in the fields and tribe. This also marks the beginning of the Seminole year. So, if you enjoy dancing, grab a partner and dance! Or, perhaps do some dance aerobics. As you do, breathe deeply and release your stress into Corn Mother's keeping. She will turn it into something positive, just as the land takes waste and makes it into beauty.

Using corn in rituals and spells is perfectly fitting for this occasion. Scatter cornmeal around the sacred space to mark your magic circle, or scatter it to the wind so Corn Mother can bring fertility back to you. Keeping a dried ear of corn in the house invokes Corn Mother's protection and luck, and consuming corn internalizes her blessings.

Festival of Cerridwin (Wales)

CERRIDWIN

Themes: Fertility; Creativity; Harvest; Inspiration; Knowledge; Luck

Symbols: Cauldron; Pig; Grain

About Cerridwin: The Welsh mother goddess, Cerridwin also embodies all lunar attributes and the energy of the harvest, specifically grains. In Celtic mythology, Cerridwin owned a cauldron of inexhaustible elixir that endowed creativity and knowledge. At the halfway point of the year, her inspiration comes along as motivation to "keep on keepin' on." Her symbol is a pig, an animal that often represents good fortune and riches, including spiritual enrichment.

To Do Today: Since most folks don't have a cauldron sitting around, get creative! Use a special cup, bowl, or vase set in a special spot to represent Cerridwin's creativity being welcome in your home. Fill the receptacle with any grain-based product (like breakfast cereal) as an offering. Whisper your desire to the grain each time you see it or walk by. At the end of the day, pour the entire bowl outside for the animals. They will bear your wish back to the goddess.

For meat eaters, today is definitely a time to consider having bacon for breakfast, a ham sandwich for lunch, or pork roast for dinner to internalize Cerridwin's positive aspects. Vegetarians? Fill up your piggy bank with the odd change you find around your house and apply the funds to something productive to inspire Cerridwin's blessing.

July 4

Independence Day (United States)

THMEI

Themes: Freedom; Justice; Honor; Divination; Balance; Equality; Foresight; Morality

Symbols: Scales or Balanced Items; Ostrich Feathers

About Thmei: This Egyptian goddess of law and mother of virtue watches over human conduct, looking for right action, wise decisions, ethical dealings, and just outcomes. On a broader scale, she also tends to matters of universal law, that we might learn its patterns, internalize its ideals, and then use this awareness throughout the year.

In some instances, Thmei is considered a prophetic goddess to call on in determining the outcome of any course of action, especially legal ones. Egyptian art depicts Thmei bearing a single ostrich feather, the symbol of truth with self and others.

To Do Today: Celebrate your personal independence, and break free from any constraints that seem unjust or unethical, asking Thmei for the power and courage to endure.

To make a Thmei charm that draws equity into all your dealings, find a portable token that, to you, represents balance, harmony, and fairness. Put this on your bathroom scale, saying,

> *Balance and harmony within this shine,*
> *Thmei, make impartial dealings mine!*

Carry this token with you, or leave it in the area where you feel inequity or discord exists.

July 5

Tynwald (Isle of Mann)

MALA LAITH

Themes: Justice, Community; Peace; Wisdom; Knowledge; Forgiveness; Maturity; Unity

Symbols: Gray; Pigs; Deer; Horse; Birds

About Mala Laith: Known often simply by the designation "gray one," Mala Laith is the ancient Celtic crone goddess. Mala Laith is said to have made the mountains and formed many stone circles, alluding to her age and power. She travels in the company of birds, pigs, deer, or a gray horse, carrying wisdom, knowledge, understanding, sensibility, and preparation to us as gifts that come with maturity.

To Do Today: On this day, people on Mann honor the old Norse assembly system instituted over one thousand years ago by gathering to discuss legal matters and end internal bickering. As they do, Mala Laith stands by, offering good counsel and sagacity. For us this means taking a moment out to make sure things in our life are in order and being properly attended to. Review your checking account, follow up on legal matters, make peace with someone from whom you've been estranged, and generally spend the day focusing on sound action, wise words, and sensible thinking. This invokes Mala Laith's energy.

Wear something gray today to honor the goddess, and watch to see if any of her sacred animals show up (in logos, on billboards, anywhere) during your day. If they do, pay close attention to their movements and actions. They're bringing a message to you from Mala Laith, and it's well worth heeding!

July 6

Apache Puberty Rites
(Southwestern United States)

WHITE PAINTED WOMAN

Themes: Maturity; Cycles; Femininity; Tradition

Symbols: White-colored Items

About White Painted Woman: White Painted Woman taught her people sacred rituals, and she can change her appearance at will to that of a young girl or an old woman, representing the full cycle of life and all that awaits us in between. When White Painted Woman was a girl, she went away to the mountains, where the sun taught her how to conduct puberty rites, which is her function in today's ceremony.

To Do Today: About this time of year, Apache girls participate in a special coming-of-age ritual that takes place over four nights. Part of the ritual commemorates White Painted Woman's adventure in the mountains, and in another part the young women take on her role so they can prepare for adulthood. In modern times, rites of passage have been somewhat overlooked, but today is definitely a time to consider reinstating them to honor White Painted Woman and draw her blessings into someone's life. If you know a child who has reached an important juncture (going to school, getting their driver's license, graduating) find a way to commemorate that step in their personal growth. For school, bless a special lunch box or book bag with rosemary oil for mental keenness. For a license, make them a protective automobile amulet (perhaps something to hang off the rearview mirror). Whatever you do, fill this person's life with magic!

July 7

Weaving Festival (Japan)

KAMUHATA HIME

Themes: Love; Arts; Relationships; Devotion; Romance

Symbols: Woven Items

About Kamuhata Hime: A Japanese goddess of weaving, Kamuhata Hime braids the strands of fate to help out anyone seeking solid relationships. Through her careful, artistic eye, she binds devotion with love into a beautiful, strong tapestry between two committed people.

To Do Today: The Tanabat weaving festival is a traditional day for marriage in China, commemorating the time when two stellar deities meet and celebrate their love, thanks to the help of celestial magpies who build a winged bridge across the Milky Way, bringing them together this one day out of the year.

Stargazing is a favorite activity that you can participate in, watching as Kamuhata Hime weaves the heavens into a feast for the eyes and soul. As you gaze out into the stars, watch closely the area of the Milky Way. If you see a shooting star, make a wish for love or the improvement of a relationship, and Kamuhata Hime will answer it.

If you're thinking of deepening your commitment to someone, tonight is an excellent time to recite your promises to each other beneath the stars. As you do, braid three strands of cloth or yarn, making a vow at each juncture. Keep this as a Kamuhata Hime amulet to protect the love and devotion in your relationship. Unbind this if the two of you ever part ways.

July 8

Old Dance (Tibet)

BUDDHABODHIPRABHAVASITA

Themes: Wisdom; Mediation; Universal Law; Overcoming; Spirituality; Banishing

Symbols: Yellow; Prayer Wheel

About Buddhabodhiprabhavasita: This Buddhist goddess controls the awareness of Buddha, personifying spiritual regeneration and the power of light to overcome any darkness in our lives. Since Buddhabodhiprabhavasita has the ear of Buddha, she makes an excellent mediator and teacher of universal truths.

To Do Today: In Tibet, this is a time for monks to bring out costumes fashioned after Manchu dynasty tradition and dance in a parade to cymbals, flutes, gongs, and drums. Their dance portrays the demons of hell fighting against the favorite regional deities (who of course win the symbolic battle by the end of the exhibition). To adapt this, go through your living space making lots of noise to banish any negativity that lurks within. Turn on the lights as you go to literally "turn on" Buddhabodhiprabhavasita's power to overcome those problems, tensions, and any residual bad feelings.

Wear something yellow to invoke Buddhabodhiprabhavasita's insight within yourself, and use any wheel as the focus for your prayers. For example, write your needs on your automobile tires, or attach them to bicycle spokes so that each time the wheel goes round, the prayer goes out to the goddess!

Bodmin Riding (*Wales*)

HABONDE

Themes: Abundance; Joy; Health; Fertility; Luck; Magic; Cleansing

Symbols: Ale; Fires

About Habonde: In Celtic tradition, Habonde is a witchy goddess who represents abundance: an abundance of joy, health, fertility, and luck. Customarily, people honored her by dancing around magical ritual fires whose smoke was said to purify both body and soul.

To Do Today: On the first Monday in July, people in Wales prepare for a lunch of ale brewed eight months ago. This is taken joyfully around town and shared to bring joy, prosperity, and longevity to everyone, courtesy of the goddess and the local brewers' guild. If you're a home brewer, this is an excellent day to make ritual beer or wine, both of which have to boil on the hearth, a symbol of Habonde. As you work, stir clockwise to draw positive energy your way. When your schedule's too hectic for this, pour yourself a small glass of beer (you can use the nonalcoholic kind), and lift it to the sky, saying,

Habonde, bring abundance. Habonde, health and luck bring.
When through my lips this liquid passes, let my soul sing!

Drink expectantly.

Lighting any fire source honors Habonde and draws her attention to areas where you feel her energies are needed. Light a candle at home (or light the stove for a moment, or the fireplace). And at the office? Just light a match (make sure it's allowed by company rules, or go to the smoking lounge)!

July 10

Panathenaea (Greece)

ATHENA

Themes: Protection; Victory; Courage; Leadership

Symbols: New Clothing; Olives; Owls; Oak

About Athena: Among the Greeks, especially those dwelling in Athens, Athena was the great protectress, standing for personal discipline and prowess, especially in battles. When you find your self-control lacking, or you need the courage to withstand a storm, Athena stands ready to come to the rescue. Grecian art shows Athena bearing a spear, wearing a breastplate, and accompanied by an owl. She is also the patroness of spinners and many other forms of craftspeople who work with their hands.

To Do Today: The Greeks celebrated this goddess by giving her a new wardrobe today, making offerings, and taking her images out for cleansing. So, if you have any likenesses of the goddess, dust them off and adorn them in some way, perhaps using an oak leaf for a dress to honor Athena.

Wearing a new piece of splendid clothing or adding olives to your diet today draws Athena's attributes into your life. Or, use pitted olives as a spell component. On a small piece of paper, write the word that best describes what you need from Athena. Stuff this into the olive and bury it. By the time the olive decomposes, your desire should be showing signs of manifestation.

Finally, place a small piece of oak leaf in your shoe today so Athena's leadership and bravery will walk with you, helping you to face whatever awaits with a strong heart.

July 11

Bawming the Thorn (England)

NEMETONA

Themes: Wishes; Protection; Joy; Fairies; Magic; Luck; Nature

Symbols: Hawthorn (or trees in general)

About Nemetona: In Romano-Celtic regions, Nemetona guards groves of trees with a special protective presence that marks the area as a sacred site. Within this space, the soul is hushed and calm, becoming one with nature and the goddess. Nemetona's name means "shrine," giving new depth of meaning to William Cullen Bryant's poetic phrase "the groves were God's first temples."

To Do Today: This ritual takes place around this time of year in Appleton, England. It is an occasion for the community to gather together and decorate a hawthorn tree in the center of town. Local people believe this was a spot of ancient pagan worship, which is highly likely since hawthorns are sacred to both witches and fairykind. In magic traditions, carrying hawthorn ensures happiness and promotes good luck (not to mention bearing a bit of Nemetona with you). Wherever the oak, ash, and thorn grow together is a very magical spot filled with Nemetona's power, and one that will be visited regularly by fairies!

To commune with Nemetona, you need go no farther than the nearest tree. Give it a hug! Sit beneath the tree and meditate on its strength, its connection to the earth, and the roots that keep it sure. Accept this security as a gift from Nemetona.

July 12

Good-Luck Day (*Various Locations*)

OSHION

Themes: Luck; Health; Home; Travel; Prosperity; Work; Wealth

Symbols: Your Lucky Number, Clothing, Tokens, etc.

About oShion: Among gypsies, oShion rules over all matters of fortune and fate, including having the good timing it takes to really see a lot of luck! As we go about our summer activities, oShion keeps things interesting by mixing in a little serendipity.

To Do Today: Legend tells us that Gabriel declared this day among the most fortuitous on the calendar, especially for those wanting to travel, find a new home, improve their health, or embark on any prosperous project (like looking for a new job). oShion joins in these efforts by adding even more luck to a day already filled with positive influences. Take out any lucky items and wear or carry them today to augment the energy further.

Add luck-inspiring foods and spices to your diet to help you internalize your good fortune and make it last longer than twenty-four hours. Examples include consuming oranges, pineapples, and strawberries (or juices from these fruits) for breakfast. Or, bake with allspice and nutmeg.

As you dress, add a rose or violet to your outfit; both of these vibrate on lucky levels. Alternatively, carry a piece of turquoise, a piece of jet, or an apache tear in your pocket to transport oShion's good fortune wherever you go today. Leave an extra stone at home to encourage luck there, too!

July 13

Highland Games (*Scotland*)

SCATHACH

Themes: Sports; Strength; Excellence; Kinship; Art; Tradition Magic; Protection; Victory

Symbols: Tartan (plaids); Celtic Music

About Scathach: This Celtic mother figure endows strength, endurance, and the ability to "go the distance" no matter our situation. In Scotland she is also a warrior goddess who protects the land using magic as a weapon, as implied by the translation of her name, "she who strikes fear." Warriors from around Scotland were said to have studied under Scathach to learn battle cries and jumping techniques (possibly a type of martial arts).

To Do Today: In Scotland, the second weekend in July marks the gathering of Scottish clans to revel in their heritage through numerous games of skill, strength, and artistry (including bagpipe competitions). If you have any Scottish or Celtic music, play it while you get ready to energize your whole day with Scathach's perseverance. If you don't have the music, for a similar effect find something to wear with a Scottish motif, like heather perfume, a plaid tie, things bearing the image of a thistle or sheep, or anything woolen.

To make a Scathach amulet to protect your home, car, or any personal possessions, begin with a piece of plaid cloth and put some dried heather in it (alternatively, put in several strands of woolen yarn). Tie this up and keep it where you believe her powers are most needed.

July 14

Linden Festival (*Germany*)

MINNE

Themes: Protection; Love; Luck; Devotion; Unity

Symbols: Linden Tree; Cup; Beer

About Minne: Minne is a German goddess of love and fertility. Her name—meaning "remembrance"—was applied to a special cup for lovers in this part of the world. The cup was filled with specially prepared beer and raised between two people wishing to deepen their love. This gives Minne a strong association with devotion, unity, and fidelity.

To Do Today: During the second weekend in July, people in Geisenheim, Germany, gather around an ancient linden tree (six hundred–plus years old) and celebrate the year's new wine. All aspects of the festival take place beneath the linden's branches, which in magic terms represent safety and good fortune. The linden flowers portray Minne's spirit, having been used in all manner of love magic! To protect a relationship, two lovers should carry dried linden flowers with them always.

When making a promise to each other, a couple may drink a wooden goblet of beer today, linking their destinies. Raise the glass to the sky first, saying,

> *Minne's love upon our lips, devotion in each sip.*

Drink while looking deeply into each other's eyes. Or, exchange pieces of linden wood as a magical bonding that invokes Minne's blessing. If linden isn't native to your area, other trees and bushes that promote Minne's loving qualities include avens, elm, lemon, orange, peach, pear, primrose, rose, and willow.

July 15

Mount Fuji Climbing (Japan)

FUCHI

Themes: Inspiration; Courage; Safety (protection); Fire (ancient); Skill (sports); Relationships

Symbols: Mountains; Fire

About Fuchi: This goddess gave her name to the sacred volcano Fujiyama. As a fire goddess, she rules natural energy (heat) sources, and also those generated in our hearths, homes, and hearts. This energy, along with summer's sun, joins together in our life today, generating strength, endurance, keen vision, and relationships filled with genuine warmth.

To Do Today: July and August mark the climbing season at Mount Fuji. For most people, attempting this is a pilgrimage of sorts dedicated to "climbing the mountain because it's there." On a deeper level, however, the mountain houses the deities of Shinto tradition, challenging all who dare visit to stretch their limits and do their very best. While most of us can't go to Japan to visit the goddess in her abode, we can climb stairs to help us reconnect with Fuchi's uplifting powers. Today, instead of using elevators, climb stairs whenever and wherever possible. As you do, visualize the area(s) in your life that could use a boost from Fuchi's energy, those areas that really challenge you somehow, or those where emotional warmth seems lacking. When you reach the top, claim your reward with some type of affirmation (such as I *am strong*, I *am loving*), and then act on this change with conviction!

July 16

Our Lady of Carmel (Italy)

MEDITRINA

Theme: Health

Symbols: Healing Charms; Herbal Preparations

About Meditrina: This Roman goddess of healing magic specializes in the use of wines, herbs, and empowered charms to restore our health when summer colds or weariness set in.

To Do Today: In Italy, this is a time to go to Madonna del Carmine's church bearing an emblem of one's sickness so the Madonna (a goddess type) can heal the malady. We will be turning to Meditrina instead, invoking her power to make health-provoking amulets for physical protection, and a healthful wine.

To make yourself a Meditrina charm that keeps health with you, place a pinch of caraway, marjoram, nutmeg, and thyme in a green cloth and tie it up. Put this in sunlight (considered healthful) for several hours, then bless it, saying,

Meditrina, see my need. I am open to receive.
Throughout the day good health impart, in my body, mind, and heart.

Carry this often. To change it so it protects you from sickness, use a red-colored cloth filled with apple peel, allspice berries, and a pinch of cinnamon.

To make an aqua vitae (a healthful wine) that will internalize Meditrina's well-being, begin with a base of apple juice or wine. In this base steep a cinnamon stick, cloves, ginger, allspice, nutmeg, and a bit of a honeycomb. Do this during a waxing moon if possible to promote growing health, then drink as desired.

July 17

Tirgul de fete de pe Muntele Gaina (*Romania*)

AMARI DE

Themes: Arts; Humor; Relationships; Love; Fertility; Wealth; Health; Beauty

Symbol: Light

About Amari De: In Romania, Amari De is a Gypsy goddess who is the great mother of all things and the personification of nature. According to lore, she bestows wealth, health, beauty, love, fertility, and insight to those who seek her. Descriptions say that she was so holy that a divine light always shone from her face.

To Do Today: A Transylvanian folk festival, this fete was originally a marriage fair where young people came looking for partners. Over time the custom faded, and now it is simply a crafts, costume, and musical exhibition with lighthearted satire and nightlong bonfires that glow with Amari De's light. In keeping with this tradition, if you're planning a wedding or engagement, today would be a wonderful date to consider for either, as it draws Amari De's positive energy to that relationship.

This is also a good time for single folks to get out and mingle, carrying an Amari De love charm along for a little extra help. Find a little piece of luminescent cloth (like a fine silk that shines) and wrap it around a pack of matches. Bless the token, saying,

Amari de, bring love my way!

Ignite one of the matches before going into a social situation so Amari de can light your way!

July 18

Tabuleiros Festival (*Portugal*)

AKERBELTZ

Themes: Harvest; Charity; Health; Thankfulness; Beauty; Peace

Symbols: Rainbows; Health and Healing Amulets

About Akerbeltz: This Basque goddess attends the human body by protecting it from disease, encouraging health, and offering healing when needed, especially when we overdo summer activities! Being a goddess of earth and nature too, she sometimes appears as a rainbow, a bridge that takes us from being under the weather to overcoming circumstances.

To Do Today: The Tabuleiros has been celebrated for six hundred years in Portugal by honoring the harvest, giving thanks to the goddess for her providence, and making donations to charitable organizations. The highlight of the day is a parade in which people wear huge headdresses covered with bread, flowers, and doves—symbols of Akerbeltz's continued sustenance, beauty, and peace. These are retained by the wearer through the year to keep Akerbeltz close by, warding off sickness. A simpler approach for us might be to get a small rainbow refrigerator magnet or window piece that reflects this goddess's beauty throughout our home to keep everyone therein well and content.

Also, give a little something to someone in need today. Doing good deeds for others pleases Akerbeltz because it makes them healthier in spirit. She will bless you for your efforts with improved well-being, if only that of the heart.

July 19

Biding of the Wreaths (*Lithuania*)

LAIMA

Themes: Love; Unity; Blessing; Luck; Destiny; Magic

Symbols: Wreaths; Swans

About Laima: The Lithuanian goddess of fate, luck, beauty, and magic swoops into our lives in the form of a swan, reminding us of the transformative power of love. Traditionally, all Laima needs to change from one form to another is a swan feather, alluding to her nature as a shape-shifter who uses magical charms to manifest her will.

To Do Today: Around this time of year, young people in Lithuania gather in a temple at sunset, then go into the forest to harvest summer flowers. From these, circlets and strings are made to crown and bind lovers together in Laima's and nature's beauty. Then the young people dance together round a birch tree (rather like a Maypole) singing to the goddess and asking for her blessing. This is a lovely tradition that can be adapted by gathering summer flowers and holding hands around them at your family supper table. Allow Laima to renew your love and unity in a moment of silence before dinner. If you live alone, invite a close friend to join you instead.

Also, find a small rose-vine wreath at a craft shop. Adhere the image of a swan to this somehow (representing Laima), and hang it where you can easily see the wreath regularly. Each time you do, remind yourself that love is the most powerful of all the goddess's magic—and that includes loving yourself!

July 20

Moon Day (United States)

H I N A

Themes: Moon; Communication; Cycles; Mediation

Symbols: Lunar (silver/white items or any corresponding plants/stones); Coconut

About Hina: This Tahitian goddess is the Lady in the Moon who shines on us with her changing faces. As the dark moon, she presides over death. As the waxing moon, she is the creatrix who made people from clay and the moon, her home. As the full moon, she embodies a mature woman's warrior spirit. As the waning moon, she is the aging crone full of wisdom and insight.

According to tradition, coconuts were created from the body of Hina's lover, an eel god, after he was killed by superstitious locals. She also governs matters of honest communication, and when properly propitiated, Hina sometimes acts as an intermediary between humans and the gods.

To Do Today: On July 20 in 1969, American astronauts visited Hina in person, landing on the moon's surface and exploring it. In spiritual terms this means taking time to explore the magical nature of the moon today. If the moon is dark, it represents the need to rest from your labors. If it is waxing, start a new magic project and stick with it so the energy grows like the moon. If Hina's lunar sphere is full, turn a coin in your pocket three times, saying "prosperity" each time so your pocket remains full. If the moon is waning, start taking positive action to rid yourself of a nagging problem. Eat some coconut to help this along by internalizing Hina's transformative powers.

July 21

Mayan New Year (Central America)

ALAGHOM

Themes: Time; Destiny; Cycles; Magic

Symbols: Calendars

About Alaghom: In Mayan tradition, Alaghom created the human ability to think, reason, and mark time using those skills. She also designed the intangible parts of nature, which take us beyond concrete realities into the world of the goddess and her magic.

To Do Today: Mayans believed that each day and year had its own god or goddess, and that this being governed destiny during its time frame. So the new year was greeted with either joy or trepidation, depending on the divine persona in charge! For our purposes, this means invoking Alaghom's aid in making every moment of our lives count, making them magical, and filling them with goddess energy. Gather all your calendars and appointment books and place your hands, palms-down, over them. Then try this prayer:

> *Alaghom, today is but one day out of many, yet let me recognize the possibilities that lie within it. Give me the good judgment and sensibility to use my time wisely. Help me make every day on earth something truly magical and filled with your power. As I walk through this world, let me see beyond my eyes into the soul of creation. Let me appreciate the abundant spiritual power in every blade of grass and stone, and most important, within myself. So be it.*

July 22

La Fête de Madeline (France)

ISOLT

Themes: Love; Fertility; Sexuality

Symbols: White Items

About Isolt: Known throughout Western Europe as the lover of Tristan, Isolt of the White Hands is a Celtic goddess who encourages devoted love and improves sexual expression within a relationship. Close studies of her stories indicate three women who held this role, alluding to an ancient triple goddess whose role changed with time and bardic adaptations.

To Do Today: In France, this is a time for women to come to a cave in Provence thought to be an ancient dwelling of the goddess (later attributed to Mary Magdalene). They travel here from miles around seeking love and/or fertility, the cave acting like a creative womb in which the goddess's power grows. If you're fortunate to live in an area with caves, take a moment to visit one today. Sit inside and let Isolt hold you in her loving arms or fill you with an appetite for your partner. Otherwise, create a makeshift cave out of blankets draped over a table. Meditate inside, visualizing Isolt's white light filling your heart chakra until it all but bursts with devotion and fervor.

If you're seeking a mate, use this time to express your desires to Isolt, visualizing your ideal mate in as much detail as possible. Then get out and start socializing, so the goddess can open the path to love.

July 23

Leo Begins (*Various Locations*)

FREYJA

Themes: Devotion; Strength; Sun; Magic; Passion

Symbols: Lion; Strawberries

About Freyja: In Nordic tradition, Freyja's name means "lady." Generally speaking, it is her domain to care for matters of the heart. In mythology, Freyja is stunningly beautiful, a mistress to the gods, and she appears driving a chariot pulled by cats. When saddened, Freyja cries gold tears, and she wears a shining necklace (alluding to some solar associations). Many people in northern climes credit her for teaching magic to humankind.

To Do Today: In astrology, people born under the sign of Leo are energetic and filled with Freyja's solar aspect. And, like Freyja, they are ardent, dynamic lovers. If your love life needs a pick-me-up, Freyja's the goddess to call on. Start with a bowl of strawberries and melted chocolate that you feed your lover. Remember to nibble passionately while biting into Freyja's sacred food! This will digest Freyja's energy for lovemaking. If you're still single, eat a few berries at breakfast to internalize self-love so more loving opportunities will naturally come your way.

To improve love in other areas of your life (the love of friends, love for a job or project, etc.), wear gold-toned clothing or jewelry today to emphasize Freyja's solar powers. This will give you more tenacity, focus, and esteem for whatever you're putting your hands and heart into.

July 24

Nadam (Mongolia)

VATIAZ

Themes: Sports; Tradition; Strength; Excellence; Recreation

Symbols: Charms for Strength or Physical Well-Being

About Vatiaz: Vatiaz is the Mongolian goddess of physical prowess. Her name even means "woman of great strength." Now that summer is fully underway, we could use some of Vatiaz's endurance just to keep up!

To Do Today: The Nadam festival began in the thirteenth century with Marco Polo, who reported a gathering of ten thousand white horses with Mongolian leaders participating in numerous games of skill ranging from archery to wrestling. Today the tradition continues with sports, focused on exhibiting excellence and skill, followed by a community party to celebrate and revel in local customs. If there's a sports exposition or game that you enjoy, try to get out to the proverbial "ball park" today to honor Vatiaz and enjoy her excellence as exhibited through professional athletes.

For those who are not sports fans, making a Vatiaz charm for strength and vitality is just as welcome by the goddess and invokes her ongoing participation in your life. You'll need a bay leaf, a pinch of tea, and a pinch of marjoram (one herb each for body, mind, and spirit). Wrap these in a small swatch of cotton, saying,

> Health, strength, and vitality,
> Vatiaz, bring them to me!

Put the swatch in the bottom of your daily-vitamin jar to empower the vitamins with Vatiaz's well-being.

July 25

Tenjin (Japan)

TAMAYORIHIME

Themes: Cleansing; Health; Children; Water

Symbol: Water (especially moving water or saltwater)

About Tamayorihime: An ancient Japanese sea goddess, Tamayorihime rules not only moving water sources but also all matters of health. She also watches over birth waters to ensure a speedy, safe delivery for pregnant women.

To Do Today: This festival began in 949 C.E. as a way to get rid of summer maladies. If you've had a cold, the flu, or some other ailment, try an adaptation of Japanese custom. Take a piece of paper that you've left on your altar for a while and rub it on the area of your body that's afflicted. Drop the paper into moving water (like the toilet) to carry away sickness in Tamayorihime's power. Alternatively, burn the paper to purge the problem. Mingle the ashes with a few drops saltwater and carry them in a sealed container as a Tamayorihime amulet for health.

For personal cleansing and healing, soak in an Epsom-salt bath today. As you lie in the tub, stir the water clockwise with your hand to draw Tamayorihime's health to you, or counterclockwise so she can banish a malady. If time doesn't allow for this, add a very small pinch of salt to your beverages and stir them similarly throughout the day, while mentally or verbally reciting this invocation:

> *Health be quick, health be kind,*
> *within this cup the magic bind!*

Drink the beverage to internalize Tamayorihime's energy.

July 26

Feast of Saint Anne (Brittany, Canada)

ANNE

Themes: Miracles; Wishes; Kindness; Health

Symbols: Freshwater; Household Items

About Anne: Saint Anne is a freshwater goddess who helps us learn the value of abounding selflessness, and how to better tend to our household matters when the chaos of summer seems to have our attention elsewhere. In Canada she is also credited with miraculous healing powers.

To Do Today: Traditionally, supplicants come to Saint Anne wearing outfits from their cultures, kneeling, and speaking their requests. This is a little awkward in our workaday world. So, instead, quaff a full glass of springwater first thing in the morning so Saint Anne will stay with you all day, protecting you from the sniffles and encouraging a little domesticity.

If your house is cluttered, you can invoke Saint Anne and welcome her energy into your home simply by straightening up and using a little magical elbow grease as you go! Visualize white light filling your home, sing magical songs, burn some incense, and use plain water to wash the floors so Saint Anne's power can be absorbed into every nook and cranny. If you know of a person who's been laid up and unable to do such things for themselves, I also suggest offering a helping hand. This will draw Saint Anne's well-being to that individual and fill his or her living space with healthful energy. The act of kindness will also draw Saint Anne's blessings to you.

Niman: Hopi Kachina Dances
(Southwestern United States)

NUVAK'CHIN'MANA

Themes: Ghosts (Spirits); Blessings; Weather; Winter

Symbols: Cold Items; White; Moisture

About Nuvak'chin'Mana: This goddess's name means Snow Maiden. In the Niman festival, Nuvak'chin'Mana is a Kachina who appears to pray for the return of cold weather so the moisture in the earth gets replenished. In our lives, she comes to replenish the well of our spirits and cool any overheated tempers that erupt with summer's heat.

To Do Today: In Hopi tradition, Kachinas are spirits that help the tribe in all matters of life. Each year the Kachinas emerge around February to remind people of their blessings and to teach the sacred rituals that bring rain. Around this time of year, the Kachinas return to their rest, escorted out of the human realms by the Niman ritual.

To bring Nuvak'chin'Mana's coolheadedness and refreshing energy to your entire day, drink a glass of milk on the rocks at breakfast, lunch, and dinner (or anytime in between). It's very refreshing, and the appearance of the beverage honors the goddess. If your region has been suffering from a dry spell, pour out a little of the milk and ice on the ground as an offering to Nuvak'chin'Mana so she might carry your need for rain to the nature spirits.

Last, take a moment at some point during the day to thank the Powers for all your blessings. A grateful heart is one ready to give and receive more of the Goddess!

July 28

Sandcastle Days (*California*)

OLD WOMAN OF THE SEA

Themes: Water; Recreation; Rest; Art

Symbols: Sand; Saltwater; Sea Creatures

About the Old Woman of the Sea: Among the Native Americans of California, this simple designation says it all. This goddess is a primordial being whose essence and power is linked with the ocean and all that dwells within. Old Woman of the Sea washes into our lives today with waves of refreshment and relaxation. She is also a powerful helpmate for all water-related magic.

To Do Today: Sandcastle-building competitions began in Imperial Beach, California, in 1981. Many of the artistically crafted sculptures feature sea creatures and other water themes. Alongside the festival, all manner of community activities take place, including children's competitions, feasting, and live music. So, stop by a gardening store and get yourself a little sand! Mix up some saltwater to mold and shape it. As you do, listen to some watery music, and focus on the Old Woman of the Sea. Try to capture her image in the sand, and as you do, you will capture her magical power in your heart.

If you live anywhere near a beach, today's a perfect time to practice sand and water magic. Write a symbol in the sand describing what you hope to achieve, then let the tide carry it to the Old Woman for an answer. Or, step into the surf and let the goddess draw away your tension and anxiety into her watery depths.

July 29

Icelandic Festival

VOLUSPA

Themes: Foresight; History; Perspective; Divination; Time

Symbols: Stories or Storybooks

About Voluspa: This Nordic goddess was born before all things, with the knowledge of all time within her. When asked to tell a tale to the gods, she recounted history, including the gods' downfall. To commemorate this, wise women and seers in northern climes are still sometimes called Voluspa.

Voluspa teaches us the value of farsightedness and of remembering our history. We cannot know where we're going if we don't remember where we came from.

To Do Today: An old festival in Iceland known as the Islendingadagurinn preserves Voluspa's energy by recounting local heritage and custom in a public forum including theater, singing, writing, and costumes. For our adaptation, I suggest taking out or working on a family tree, or perhaps a personal journal. Read over the chronicles of people from your ethnic background, and honor their lives in some appropriate manner (perhaps by lighting a candle). Voluspa lives in these moments, and at any time that we give ourselves to commemorating the past.

Alternatively, get out some good storybooks and read! Turn off the TV for a while, and enrich your imagination with the words of bards who keep Voluspa's power alive in the world. Especially read to children, so they can learn of this goddess's wonders.

July 30

Dinosaur Days (Colorado)

TIAMAT

Themes: History; Change; Spirituality; Fertility; Birth; Creativity

Symbols: Reptiles; Seawater

About Tiamat: The personification of creative, fertile forces in Assyro-Babylonian traditions, Tiamat gave birth to the world. She is the inventive power of chaos, whose ever-changing energy hones the human soul and creates unending possibilities for its enlightenment. In later accounts, Tiamat took on the visage of a half-dinosaur or dragonlike creature, symbolizing the higher and lower self, which must work together for positive change and harmonious diversity.

To Do Today: Taking place at the Dinosaur National Monument, this festival celebrates the ancient, mysterious dinosaurs that speak of the earth's long-forgotten past—a past that Tiamat observed and nurtured. One fun activity to consider for today is getting an archaeology dinosaur kit at a local science shop and starting to "dig up" the past yourself! As you work, meditate on the meaning of Tiamat's energy in your life. The more of the bones you uncover, the more you'll understand and integrate her transformative energy.

Carry a fossil in your pocket today to help keep you connected to Tiamat and her spiritual inventiveness. Or, wash your hands with a little saltwater so that everything you touch is blessed with Tiamat's productive nature and cleansing.

July 31

Helena Blavatsky's Birthday (*Ukraine*)

THE NARUCNICI

Themes: Psychic Abilities; Spirituality; Destiny; Divination

Symbols: An Eye; All Symbols of Fate or Destiny

About the Narucnici: In Slavic regions, these are goddesses of fate who see each child's destiny at birth. At times they can be propitiated through prayers to alter one's destiny, especially when it's running headlong into disaster.

To Do Today: In 1831, the acclaimed mystic Helena Blavatsky was born under the watchful eye of the Narucnici, who must have predicted an impressive life for her. Helena grew up to establish the Theosophical Society, whose goal is to explore mystical phenomena, to better understand it, and to expose fraudulent dealings. To remember this remarkable woman and honor the Narucnici, focus on your own inherent magical potential. All of us have the Goddess's prophetic ability within; it's just a matter of activating that talent. One exercise that seems to help people is meditating on opening the chakra located in the middle of your forehead (the third eye). Close your physical eyes and visualize a purple-silver light pouring into your forehead from above. See it swirling clockwise, forming the image of an eye. Allow this eye to open, very slowly. Do you feel different as it opens? Can you sense things on the edge of your awareness you couldn't before? After the exercise, try your favorite divinatory tool and examine what new insights it offers now that you've cleared the path for that foresight a bit.

August

There are two theories as to how August got its name. Some historians say the designation honors the Roman emperor Augustus, a man renowned for his leadership skills and love of the arts. Others claim the name derives from Juno Augusta, an oracle in ancient times. In fact, Roman seers were often called "augurs," which gives some credence to the second interpretation.

In either case, August contains numerous music and art festivals and county fairs that continue in summer's high-energy cycle but also show signs of autumn's harvest theme. You will also begin to notice an increase in the number of festivals for the dead, now that the sun's light is waning.

In terms of magic, August accentuates kinship or community spirit through its gatherings. It is a time to enjoy the remaining warmth of the earth, celebrate the human spirit, and generally make yourself more aware of how you use your time. Remember, fall is just around the corner, so cast spells for energy and health, with a little happiness tossed in "just because"!

August 1

✧ ✧
✧

Lammas (*Various Locations*)

TAILTIU

Themes: The First Harvest; Excelling in a Craft or Sport

Symbol: Bread

About Tailtiu: The Irish goddess Tailtiu reconnects us with the earth's cycles and the spirit of excellence. Tailtiu was the foster mother to the god of light, Lugh, whom this date venerates. Lugh held her in such high regard that he created the Tailtean games, which took place during Lammas (rather like the Olympics). This honor may have also had something to do with Tailtiu's association as an earth goddess.

To Do Today: In Wiccan tradition, and in many others, today is a day for preparing food from early ripening fruits like apples. It is also a time for baking bread in honor of the harvest. Combining the two, make an applesauce bread. Stir the batter clockwise, focusing on any craft or sport in which you wish to excel. As you stir, chant,

> *Flour from grain, the spell begins, let the power rise within;*
> *Apples from trees, now impart, Tailtiu, bring _____ to my heart.*

Fill in the blank with a word that describes the area in which you want to encourage improvements or develop mastery. Eat the bread to internalize the energy.

Time-friendly alternatives here are buying frozen bread and adding diced apples to it, having toast with apple butter, or just enjoying a piece of bread and apple anytime during the day. Chant the incantation mentally. Then bite with conviction!

August 2

✧ ✧
✧

Day of the Dryads (*Macedonia*)

THE VEELAS

Themes: Fairies; Nature; Healing; Wealth; Abundance

Symbols: Sweet Bread; Sacred Fairy Plants (oak, ash, thorn, foxglove, etc.); Healing Herbs

About the Veelas: These Balkan goddesses preside over the woodlands and have the power to heal or harm, depending on the circumstances. The Veelas kindly treat humans who respect them and the earth, rewarding them with the knowledge of how to work harmoniously with the land, which, in turn, creates prosperity and abundance.

To Do Today: In ancient Macedonia, today was a time to appease the spirits of nature, called Drymiais. We can follow their customs by not harvesting any plants (especially vining ones), and not doing any cleaning (especially with water). If you must do one of these forbidden activities, carry iron to protect you from mischievous fairy folk.

If you live near any oak, ash, or thorn trees, leave under it a little gift of sweet bread for the Veelas. As you do, whisper a short request to the Veelas for renewed health and permission to gather some herbs associated with health and healing today. Afterward, look for an ash or oak leaf or some tansy flowers. These will act as an amulet for well-being whenever you carry them with you.

For prosperity and abundance, and to improve your connection with the earth, give the Veelas an offering of honey instead, and eat a bit yourself to consume the earth's sweetness.

August 3
✧ ✧
✧
Aomori Nebuta (Japan)

H U C H I

Themes: Harvest; Energy; Cleansing; Health

Symbols: Fire; Light; Energy Sources

About Huchi: This Japanese fire goddess keeps our internal fires burning to give us the energy necessary for completing whatever projects are at hand. She also uses her fires to cleanse the human body and protect it from disease

To Do Today: This ritual in Japan is designed to help farmers stay awake for longer intervals in order to complete their harvesting duties. By making an effigy of the sand figurine, they hope to appease the spirit of sleep and finish their tasks. So, when you need to keep a fire under a project or be a little more alert for the tasks at hand, turn on a light or ignite a candle. This activates Huchi's power in your living space.

Alternatively, get a little sand from a beach or a child's sandbox and empower it, saying,

Each pinch I take keeps me awake.

Keep this handy when you're working. Whenever you feel a little weary, release a pinch of the sand to the winds or the earth to refresh your energy.

For health-related matters, I suggest dressing warmly or taking a warm bath. As you do, meditate and visualize yourself in white, purifying flames that collect all your tensions or sickness and burn them away painlessly. Huchi lives in both the warmth and the fires of your vision.

Pilgrimage to Loch mo Naire (*Scotland*)

TRIDUANA

Themes: Banishing; Health; Protection

Symbols: Water; Oak

About Triduana: In Scotland, this goddess rules over sacred water sources, from which she selflessly gives of her elixir to all who ask in humility. Many of her wells are said to dwell beneath oak trees, ancient symbols of protection and well-being.

To Do Today: Since the 1800s, people have been coming to Loch mo Naire around this time of year to heal their body, mind, or spirit. People sip a bit of the water and bathe in it three times, giving an offering of silver coins to the generous water spirit there. For us this means drinking eight glasses of water today, as is often recommended by physicians for improved health. This helps flush our toxins and draws Triduana's healing energy into our bodies.

Another custom easily followed is that of taking off one's clothes and walking backward to banish sickness. Both of these actions symbolize a turning away or a change. If possible, choose clothing you don't need anymore, take it off, throw it out, then walk backward to a place where you can put on fresh clothing and don Triduana's blessings!

Interestingly enough, oak leaves have long been considered excellent health charms. If you can catch one before it touches the earth, you ensure yourself of Triduana's protection and a month without colds.

August 5

✿ ✿
✿

Fairhope Jubilee (Alabama)

DORIS

Themes: Abundance; Providence; Water

Symbols: Seawater, Plants, and Animals (especially fish)

About Doris: The daughter of Oceanus, this Grecian sea goddess is associated with the sea's gifts and its wealth. She joins in today's festivities by bringing an abundance of seafood to nourish the body, as well as spiritual sustenance to fulfill our souls.

To Do Today: The Fairhope Jubilee takes place in Mobile Bay, Alabama, sometime in August when there's an overcast sky, an easterly wind, and a rising tide. When these three factors are in place an odd phenomenon occurs: bottom-dwelling fish get trapped between the shore and low-oxygen water. So people rush out with any containers they can find and gather up Doris's plenty! For us, this equates to gathering up the sea's plenty figuratively, perhaps by having fish for dinner. Remember to thank Doris as you eat so that you internalize her providence.

To make a Doris charm that will draw abundance into any area of your life in need, find a seashell, a tumbled sea stone, or something similar that comes from the ocean. Place the token in seawater for three hours by a waxing moon so that abundance will grow like the moon. Bless it, saying,

> Doris, by this gift from your seas,
> draw abundance and wealth to me.
> Like a wave upon high tide,
> let your blessings here abide.

Carry the token regularly.

August 6

Hiroshima Peace Ceremony (*Japan*)

NAKISAWAME-NO-MIKOTO

Themes: Peace; Honor; History; Death; Forgiveness

Symbols: Trees

About Nakisawame-no-Mikoto: The goddess of mourning in Japan, Nakisawame-no-Mikoto weeps with the memories of the many innocent people who have died in wars throughout the ages. She comes into our hearts today in the hope that we will learn from our collective past.

According to tradition, Nakisawame-no-Mikoto lives in the base of trees, her roots holding firm to the earth and its history. This also speaks strongly of our family trees and the importance of kinship.

To Do Today: On August 6, 1945, the atom bomb landed in Hiroshima, resulting in the loss of thousands of lives and many years of radiation sickness. In the spirit of Nakisawame-no-Mikoto, today acts as a memorial to the people who died and a celebration of the peace that has since been maintained. Traditionally, tiny paper lanterns are floated on flowing waters as wishes for the dead. So, light a candle today for someone you know who died needlessly, or fighting for a just cause. The flame of the candle represents the goddess and the memory of that person whose efforts light the way for a better future

To encourage peace between yourself and someone else, plant a token that represents your desire beneath a tree so that this goddess can begin helping you achieve harmony.

August 7

✩ ✩
✩

Dog Days (*Various Locations*)

SOPDET

Themes: Fertility; Destiny; Time

Symbols: Stars; Dogs

About Sopdet: The reigning Egyptian Queen of the Constellations, Sopdet lives in Sirius, guiding the heavens and thereby human destiny. Sopdet is the foundation around which the Egyptian calendar system revolved, her star's appearance heralding the beginning of the fertile season. Some scholars believe that the Star card of the tarot is fashioned after this goddess and her attributes.

To Do Today: The long, hot days of summer are known as "dog days" because they coincide with the rising of the dog star, Sirius. In ancient Egypt this was a welcome time as the Nile rose, bringing enriching water to the land. So, go outside tonight and see if you can find Sirius. When you spy it, whisper a wish to Sopdet suited to her attributes and your needs. For example, if you need to be more timely or meet a deadline, she's the perfect goddess to keep things on track.

If you're curious about your destiny, watch that region of the sky and see if any shooting stars appear. If so, this is a message from Sopdet. A star moving on your right side is a positive omen; better days are ahead. Those on the left indicate the need for caution, and those straight ahead mean things will continue on an even keel for now. Nonetheless, seeing any shooting star means Sopdet has received your wish.

August 8

Teej (Nepal)

PARVARTI

Themes: Fertility; Femininity; Cleansing; Devotion

Symbols: Lotus; Elephant; Dance

About Parvarti: The celebrated Hindu goddess of women is the center of festivities in Nepal today. Parvarti's domain is that of faithful companionship and fertility, as she is the consort of Shiva. Art often shows Parvarti dancing, in the company of Shiva, or with an elephant's head.

To Do Today: Try following Nepalese custom. Wash your hands and feet with henna (or a henna-based soap product) for Parvarti's productive energy. Or, go out and swing on a swing set singing sacred songs; this draws Parvarti to you.

Another way to invoke Parvarti is by giving a special woman in your life (a friend, lover, relative, etc.) a gift in thankfulness for her companionship. The goddess exists within that friendship and will bless the relationship. Take a ritual bath to cleanse yourself of negativity and problems of the last year. Water offerings are also a suitable gift to this goddess. Pour out a little bit on the ground and then drink some to internalize any of her qualities that you need.

Wearing fine clothing and flowers is also customary, because all things of beauty please Parvarti. So get out your finery for your celebrations, and put on a boutonniere! Or wear something with a flower pattern to draw Parvarti close to your side.

Seven Sisters Festival (China)

ZHINU

Themes: Love; Relationships; Unity; Devotion; Divination

Symbols: Stars; Silver Items

About Zhinu: Zhinu is a stellar goddess in China, residing in the constellation of Lyre, a home from which she tends to harmony within relationships. According to legend, Zhinu came to earth to bathe with six friends, but a herdsman stole her dress. She could not return to the heavens this way, so she married him. Later, however, the gods called her back to the stars, and the herdsman followed her. On the seventh day of the seventh moon, the two are allowed to meet as husband and wife.

To Do Today: A similar celebration to the Seven Sisters Festival is the Weaving Festival in Japan (July 7), which commemorates the love between two stellar deities who meet in the silver river of the Milky Way one day out of the year.

Follow with custom and cover your altar with rice and melons, both of which can become offerings. Eat these as part of a meal later to internalize Zhinu's love and devotion. If you're single, offer her combs, mirrors, and paper flowers to draw a partner into your life.

Burning incense and reading one's future is also common today. Watch the smoke from the incense while thinking about a specific relationship. See if any shapes form in the clouds. A heart, for example, indicates adoration. A scale reveals a relationship with a healthy balance, and two interconnected rings indicate unity of mind and soul.

August 10

✿ ✿
✿

Saint Lawrence Day (Spain/Italy)

AUGE

Themes: Fire; Fertility

Symbols: Hearth; Fire; Stove; Cooking Utensils

About Auge: This Spanish goddess of heat and fertility helps us celebrate today's festivities by providing our cooking fire! Auge also inspires the warmth of passion so that fertility will flow in the relationship and on a physical level if desired.

To Do Today: In an odd turn of events, the same saint who was roasted alive because of his wit became the patron saint of the kitchen and cookery in Spain and Italy. In keeping with this theme, prepare grilled or roasted food today, invoking Auge simply by lighting the flames!

If weather permits, have a fire festival in your yard over the barbecue or hibachi, and bless your cooking utensils by placing them momentarily in the flames. As you do, add an incantation like this one:

> By the forge, by the fire, Auge build the power higher.
> Within these tools let there be an abundance of fertility!

Use these tools outside or in your kitchen whenever you need extra productivity. Should the weather not cooperate, this spell works perfectly on a gas stove, which gives off a flame in which Auge can dwell.

Finally, wear red or orange hues today (the colors of fire), and remember to light a candle to honor this goddess. Consider dabbing on some fiery aromas, too, like mint, orange, or ginger, for a little extra energy and affection.

August 11

Shooting Star Night (*Various Locations*)

WOHPE

Themes: Wishes; Peace; Beauty; Pleasure; Cycles; Time; Mediation

Symbols: Falling Stars; Sweetgrass; Peace Pipe

About Wohpe: This Lakota goddess's name literally means "meteor." Among the Lakota she is considered the most beautiful of all goddesses. She generates harmony and unity through the peace pipe, and pleasure from the smoke of sweetgrass. Stories also tell us that she measured time and created the seasons so people could know when to perform sacred rituals. When a meteor falls from the sky, it is Wohpe mediating on our behalf.

To Do Today: Go stargazing! At this time of year, meteors appear in the region of the Perseids, as they have since first spotted in A.D. 800. People around the world can see these (except for those who live at the South Pole). If you glimpse a shooting star, tell Wohpe what message you want her to take back to heaven for you.

To generate Wohpe's peace between yourself and another (or a group of people) get some sweetgrass (or lemon grass) and burn it on any safe fire source. As you do, visualize the person or people with whom you hope to create harmony. Blow the smoke in the direction where this person lives, saying,

> *Wohpe, bear my message sure; keep my intentions ever pure.*
> *Where anger dwells, let there be peace. May harmony never cease.*

Afterward, make an effort to get ahold of that person and reopen the lines of communication.

August 12

✡ ✡
✡

Fiesta de Santa Clara
(Southeastern United States)

S E L U

Themes: Harvest; Weather; Growth

Symbol: Corn

About Selu: This Southeastern Native American corn goddess planted her very heart so people wouldn't go hungry.
Corn sprouted from it. To this day, her spirit teaches us how
to refertilize the earth to bring us the sustenance we need.

To Do Today: In this primary festival among the Pueblo Indians,
Santa Clara replaced Selu, the spirit of the corn, when Christianity
took hold. For the Pueblo, corn is a staple, so as the sun reigns in
power they dance for rain and evoke the Corn Spirit for every portion of the crop's growth. Following this tradition, if it's raining
today, go outside and rejoice in Selu's growth-related energy. Dance
with a bit of corn (or eat some beforehand) to invoke her powers for
progress in any area of your life.

If your region has needed rain lately, try drumming for it while
scattering corn kernels mingled with pine needles on the ground.
The corn and needles act as a gift to the goddess, and the sound
they make is a kind of sympathetic magic to draw the rain.

Finally, carry corn in your pocket today. Beforehand, visualize a
specific characteristic you'd like to "harvest" within yourself. Each
time you think of the corn that day, visualize that goal again. Then,
at the end of the day, plant the kernel in the ground so Selu can start
it growing!

August 13

✿ ✿
✿

Mayan Calendar Begins (*Central America*)

XMUCANE

Themes: Time; Cycles; Creativity; Divination

Symbols: Calendars; Blue-Green Items; Light

About Xmucane: This Mayan goddess of time created time's calculation and the calendar along with her partner Xpiyacoc. She continues watching over all calendar functions and acts as a prophetess because she can see both past and future consecutively. Her folkloric titles include Day's Grandmother and Maker of the Blue-Green Bowl (likely the sky).

To Do Today: Mayans believe the universe began on this date in 3114 B.C.E. They also teach that time will end on December 23, 2012. Exactly what this means in terms of human evolution is left to the imagination. In either case, today is a time for fresh beginnings. Call upon Xmucane to bless your appointment book and help you make the most productive possible use of your time. Try this mini-ritual:

Light a blue-green candle secured in a bowl, and place it behind your calendar. Hold your hands palms-down over the datebook and say,

> Lady of time, see where I stand in your stream.
> Grant me the perspective with which to move forward confidently, using each day on this earth to
> grow and learn the ways of the Goddess. Inspire my
> efforts to transform every moment of my life with
> positive magic. Today, and tomorrow, and tomorrow, let my moments be filled with you. So be it.

Blow out the candle and keep it for other rites.

✿ ✿
✿

Obon (Japan)

INARI

Themes: Death; Kinship; Ghosts; Fertility; Love

Symbols: Fox; Rice; Red

About Inari: Among the Japanese, Inari is invoked to bring a long life, blood-red being her sacred hue. In death, she guides and protects faithful spirits. Portrayed as a vixen, Inari also has strong correlations with love, an emotion that survives even the grave. Rice is a common offering for Inari, as it is a crop to which she brings fertility.

To Do Today: The Obon is a festival for the dead in Japan, where people hold family reunions and religious rituals to honor their departed ancestors and dance to comfort the spirits. These observances are fairly easy to duplicate. Gather with friends or family, and include rice cakes and fruit as part of your menu planning. Leave out an extra platter of food both for the spirits of the departed and to please Inari.

To increase Inari's love in any relationship, or to draw a lover to you, make this charm: Find a red-colored stone (agate is a good choice), or any red-colored piece of clothing. Put this under the light of a full moon to charge it with emotional fulfillment. Then bless the item, saying,

> Inari be, ever with me.
> By this stone [cloth] of red, let love be fed.
> When at [on] my side, let love there abide.

Put the stone in your pocket (so it's at your side) and carry it when meeting with that special someone.

August 15

✿ ✿
✿

Khordad Sal (Persia)

ANAHITA

Themes: Honor; Love; Fertility; Pleasure; Cleansing

Symbols: Water; Lunar Objects and Colors; Green Branches

About Anahita: Anahita is the Zoroastrian moon goddess who shines upon the darkness in our lives, replacing loneliness with true love, barrenness with fertility, and impotence with pleasurable unions. She is the Lady of Heaven, the flowing force of the cosmos, whose name means "pure." A traditional offering for Anahita is green branches, which represent her life-giving power.

To Do Today: Today marks the birthday of Zoroaster, the founder of a religious sect that influenced the Maji of the Bible. Amidst Zoroaster's pantheon we find this goddess, radiating with the beautiful things of life, but only after a good "house cleaning." Honor her by washing your floors with pine-scented cleaner (i.e., green branches) so her energies can purify the sacred space of home. Afterward, light a white candle to represent Anahita's presence therein. Add a simple invocation like this one:

Lady of Purity, Lady of light, be welcome in my home and my heart.

Purify yourself, too, so that Anahita's passion can flow unhindered. Take a ritual bath, adding any woodsy aromatic to the water. As you wash up, say,

> *Anahita, carry the darkness away,*
> *so my body and spirit may revel in your pleasures,*
> *giving and receiving them equally.*

Then spend time with your loved one, letting nature take its course.

August 16
✡ ✡
✡

Ramadan (*Saudi Arabia*)

AL-LAT

Themes: Religious Devotion; Meditation; Purity; Home; Justice; Children

Symbols: Moon; Silver; White Stones

About Al-Lat: A Persian and Arabian moon goddess, Al-Lat is the feminine form of Allah. Post-Islamic writings banished her name from holy books, but her presence remained behind as a domestic guardian, the giver of children, and protectress of all good and just deeds.

To Do Today: Around this time of year, Muslims begin a time of abstinence to purify themselves and honor their sacred book, the Qu'ran. During this fast, people are instructed to look within and rededicate their hearts to the tenets of their faith. To do this and also honor Al-Lat, fast for this day if physically feasible. Or, just abstain from one well-loved food or beverage for the day, and study your own sacred text(s). Pray to Al-Lat for insight into the deeper meanings of the words. Write down any observations in a journal, so Al-Lat's presence will inspire good deeds and positive action for many years to come.

To attract Al-Lat's protective energies into your home, grasp four white items (coral and moonstone are excellent choices), saying,

> *Within these _____ of white,*
> *Al-Lat, place your protective light.*
> *Where'er these _____ s are placed around,*
> *your safety and presence shall abound.*

Put these as close as possible to the four directional points of the area that needs guardian power.

August 17

✦ ✦
✿

Festival of Diana (*Rome*)

DIANA

Themes: Fertility; Children; Providence; Abundance; Harvest

Symbols: Moon; Water; Forest Items; Sun

About Diana: This Roman goddess embodies the moon's fertility and watery aspects, along with the sun's protective and nurturing power over the forests and its creatures. On this day she was celebrated in Rome, and she will be remembered in our hearts as the huntress who helps us capture the spiritual "food" we need.

To Do Today: Starting on August 13, the Romans had a weeklong festival for Diana, praying to her for the harvest's bounty, and to turn damaging storms away. The traditional place to leave an offering of fruit or vines for her is in the forest, or at a crossroads. As you do, if any stone or leaf catches your eye, pick it up and carry it as a charm that will keep Diana's power with you that entire day. Come night, release the gift to flowing water or back to the earth with a prayer of thanks and a wish for one of Diana's attributes that you wish to develop in your life.

It is also customary to light some fire source to honor her on August 15 or anytime during the festivities. Afterward, to generate this goddess's physical or figurative fertility within you, follow Roman convention and wash your hair with specially prepared water (water to which just a little milk is added so that it looks white, like the moon). If you have children, doing this for them incurs Diana's protection over their lives.

August 18

✿ ✿
✿

Crow Fair (Montana)

GENETASKA

Themes: Tradition; Unity

Symbols: Amalgams (any item that mixes different components into a useful, harmonious blend)

About Genetaska: Since this festival has become a meeting ground for various tribes, we look to Genetaska to make the day productive and celebratory. As the Iroquois Mother of Nations, she not only created human diversity but also maintains the peace within it.

To Do Today: Since 1918, a great gathering of Native American tribes has taken place in Crow Agency, Montana. Here people meet, dance, and revel in native traditions. While the event is hosted by the Crow Tribe, others attend from tribes as diverse as Inuit and Aztec. In keeping with this theme, and to invoke Genetaska's harmony in your life, make peace with yourself or someone from whom you've been estranged. Ask Genetaska to help you find forgiveness in your heart.

Also, listen to some Native American music today, or maybe visit a museum that includes Native American exhibits to enjoy Genetaska's diversity. She lives within her people's artistic expressions of individuality and vision.

Finally, make a stew that includes squash and corn (two traditional Native American foods). Stir the stew clockwise and invoke Genetaska, saying,

Diversity and harmony, as I eat, abide in me!

The goddess will mix and mingle the food to magical perfection.

August 19

✿ ✿
✿

Eisteddfod (Wales)

OLWEN

Themes: Arts; Creativity; Excellence; Sun

Symbols: Late-blooming Flowers; Red or Gold Items; Rings

About Olwen: A Welsh sun goddess whose name means "golden wheel," Olwen overcame thirteen obstacles to obtain her true love (symbolic of thirteen lunar months), and she teaches us similar tenacity in obtaining our goals. Art portrays this goddess as having a red-gold collar, golden rings, and sun-colored hair that shines with pre-autumn splendor on today's celebrations.

To Do Today: Announced thirteen months in advance, this celebration preserves Welsh music and literature amid the dramatic backdrop of sacred stone circles. The Eisteddfod dates back to Druid times; it was originally an event that evaluated those wishing to obtain bardic status. Follow these hopeful bards' example and wear something green today to indicate your desire to grow beneath Olwen's warm light. Or, don something red or gold to generate the goddess's energy for excellence in any task.

You can make an Olwen creativity charm out of thirteen different flower petals. It is best to collect thirteen different ones, but any thirteen will do along with a red- or gold-colored cloth. Fold the cloth over the petals inward three times for body, mind, and spirit, saying with each fold,

Insight begin, bless me, Olwen.

Carry this with you, releasing one petal whenever you want a little extra inspiration.

August 20
✧ ✧
✧
Voyager 2 Launch (United States)

INANNA

Themes: Sky; Universal Awareness and Law; Movement; Peace; Unity; Love; Leadership

Symbols: Rose; Star; Lion; Wands Encrusted with Stones; Dates

About Inanna: The Sumerian Lady of the Heavens looks down upon the world, seeing it in wholeness and unity. Her gentle tears wash from heaven, putting out the emotional fires that keep people apart in this world, or anywhere in the Universe. Inanna oversees matters of love, divination, wine making, and leadership, just to name a few. In works of art she is depicted wearing a horned headdress and sprouting wings.

To Do Today: On August 20, 1977, *Voyager 2* was launched into space, bearing a message of peace and welcome to any alien life-forms that might find it. As it travels, we are reminded of what a truly big place the Universe is, and of the importance of making our part of it better under Inanna's guidance and care.

To make yourself an Inanna wand for directing magical energy designed to manifest peace, oneness, love, or leadership, take a large rose twig (or any fallen branch) and let it dry. Encrust this with an amethyst. During spells and rituals, point the crystal in the direction you want the energy to travel.

Finally, leave Inanna an offering of wine at dawn (she is the morning star) to attract her power to your day.

August 21

✧ ✧
✧

Ahes Festival (*Brittany*)

AHES

Themes: Water; Abundance; Fertility; Passion; Courage

Symbols: Seawater; Sea Creatures

About Ahes: This ancient pagan goddess symbolizes the sea's abundance, fertility, and passion. She also teaches us much about courage; she fought fervently against Christian influences to turn her into a monstrous figure akin to a siren.

To Do Today: Ahes was honored with a plethora of beautiful ceremonies around the end of summer. If you have a beech tree nearby, you can follow the custom of gathering beneath its bowers, or near a small pond. Here, wash any white cloth (perhaps an altar cloth). This brings Ahes's health and productivity to wherever you keep that fabric swatch. For those who can't find a beech tree or a pond, just add a little salt to your laundry today instead for a similar effect.

To engender this goddess's abundance, scent your hair with any earthy shampoo or cream rinse (the Bretons used moss). Definitely include some seafood in your diet today to partake of her courage. Flavoring the fish with borage flower, thyme, or a little black tea will accentuate brave energies. And, finally, if you have a seashell or bit of driftwood, find a way to release it back into Ahes's care today (for example, give it to a river or leave it in a well). This thanks the goddess for her providence and encourages her blessings in your life.

✦ ✦
✦

Virgo Begins (*Various Locations*)

ASTRAEA

Themes: Excellence; Learning; Purity; Justice; Knowledge; Reason; Innocence

Symbols: Stars

About Astraea: This Greek goddess motivates fairness and virtue within us. She empowers our ability to "fight the good fight" in both word and deed, especially when we feel inadequate to the task. According to lore, she left earth during the Golden Age because of man's inhumanity to man. She became the constellation Virgo.

To Do Today: In astrology, people born under this sign, like Astraea, strive endlessly for perfection within and without, sometimes naively overlooking the big picture because of their focus on detail. Astraea reestablishes that necessary perspective by showing us how to think more globally. To encourage this ability, draw a star on a piece of paper and put it in your shoe so that your quest for excellence is always balanced with moderation and sound pacing.

To meditate on this goddess's virtues and begin releasing them within, try using a bowl (or bath) full of soapsuds sprinkled with glitter (this looks like floating stars) as a focus. Light a candle nearby and watch the small points of light as they dance; each one represents a bit of magical energy and an aspect of Astraea. Tell the goddess your needs and your dreams, then float in her starry waters until you feel renewed and cleansed.

August 23

✿ ✿
✿

Vulcanalia (Rome)

JUTURNA

Themes: Fire; Water; Fate; Divination; Protection; Balance

Symbols: Fire; Water; Fountains

About Juturna: During the festival of Vulcan (the god of fire and the forge), Romans wisely invoked Juturna, a fountain goddess, to keep fire from damaging the land or homes. On another level, we can call upon her to put out emotional fires that have gotten out of control.

To Do Today: Historically, Vulcanalia was a time to divine using the smoke from incense (then put out the fire with Juturna's water). Choose your incense so it matches your question: rose or jasmine for love, mint for money-related matters, vanilla for health. The smoke may respond by creating a symbolic image or by moving in a particular direction. Movement toward your left is negative, to the right is positive, and smoke circling the incense stick reflects mingled fortunes or uncertain fates. When you're done scrying the smoke and have put the incense out, keep the mixture of ash and water. This symbolizes the balance between fire and water. Carry this with you in a sealed container, breaking it open amid aggravating situations. Releasing the contents invites Juturna's coolheadedness to keep anger reigned in.

To internalize Juturna's protective, balancing energies, simply stop at any water fountain today for a refreshing drink of her water. Whisper her name just before the water meets your lips to invoke her presence.

August 24
✿ ✿
✿

Shepherd's Fair (*Luxembourg*)

DAMONA

Themes: Animals; Health

Symbols: Sheep; Hot Water

About Damona: A Gaulish goddess who cares for all domestic animals, especially sheep and cows, Damona is sometimes portrayed as a hot spring, alluding to a healthful, warm quality. As fall nears, we can call on Damona to protect our pets, or to maintain the health of the animals who provide us with food.

To Do Today: As one might expect, this historical fair brought together sheep merchants to show their goods to interested parties, including a special parade of the animals bedecked in ribbons. The parade probably goes back to much earlier times when animals were taken into magic rituals that maintained health. One way to continue this tradition is by sprinkling a little warm water on your pet to invite Damona's protection (or brush it into the creature's fur—this works better with cats).

Wear woolen clothing (or wool blends) to don Damona's healthy aspect for your day. Or simply enjoy a cup of tea before the day gets busy; Damona abides in the warm water.

To ensure a healthful night's sleep and pleasant dreams, count sheep as you go to bed. Visualize each one jumping over Damona's waters and walking toward you. This brings Damona into your sleep cycle, where her energy can flow more easily to renew well-being.

August 25

✧ ✧
✧

Opiconsivia (Rome)

OPS

Themes: Opportunity; Wealth; Fertility; Growth

Symbols: Bread; Seeds; Soil

About Ops: This Italic goddess of fertile earth provides us with numerous "op-portunities" to make every day more productive. In stories, Ops motivates fruit bearing, not just in plants but also in our spirits. She also controls the wealth of the gods, making her a goddess of opulence! Works of art depict Ops with a loaf of bread in one hand, and the other outstretched, offering aid.

To Do Today: On this day, Ops was evoked by sitting on the earth itself, where she lives in body and spirit. So, weather permitting, take yourself on a picnic lunch today. Sit with Ops and enjoy any sesame or poppy breadstuff (bagel, roll, etc.)—both types of seeds are magically aligned with Ops's money-bringing power. If possible, keep a few of the seeds from the bread in your pocket or shoe so that after lunch, Ops's opportunities for financial improvements or personal growth can be with you no matter where you go. And don't forget to leave a few crumbs for the birds so they can take your magical wishes to the four corners of creation!

If the weather doesn't cooperate, invoke Ops by getting as close to the earth as you can (sit on your floor, go into the cellar). Alternatively, eat earthy foods like potatoes, root crops, or any fruit that comes from Ops's abundant storehouse.

August 26

✿ ✿
✿

Birthday of Krishna (India)

KAMALA

Themes: Spirituality; Love; Relationship; Passion; Pleasure

Symbols: Yellow; Lotus

About Kamala: The Hindu "lotus girl" of pleasure promotes ongoing faithfulness in our relationships inspired by mutual enjoyment and an abundance of love. Kamala also makes us aware of the spiritual dimensions in our physical exchanges that sometimes get overlooked.

To Do Today: In India, today is a time to celebrate the birth of Krishna, the most charming and kind incarnation of Vishnu. Kamala, as one of Lakshimi's incarnations, joins in this festivity as his lover and companion. To participate in the gala, eat Indian food, especially hot, spicy items that ignite passion (although you may want to follow this meal with breath mints and antacids). Anything that includes cinnamon, garlic, or saffron is a good alternative choice, as these items bear Kamala's lusty energy.

To improve your ability to give and receive love, including self-love, wear yellow-colored clothing today, especially an item that is worn near the heart chakra (a blouse, shirt, tie, bra, or perhaps a gold necklace or tie tack). As you don that item, say,

> Let pleasure flow freely from my heart;
> Kamala, abide there—your love impart.

Wear this same piece of clothing or jewelry again anytime you enact spells or rituals focused on sexuality or relationships.

✿ ✿
✿

Birthday of Mother Teresa (*Various Locations*)

DROL-MA

Themes: Kindness; Overcoming; Charity; Change

Symbol: Any Act of Kindness

About Drol-ma: This Nepalese goddess's name means "deliverer." So it is that Drol-ma visits us with compassion and transformative power, turning sadness into joy, poverty into wealth, and despair into hope.

To Do Today: On this day in 1910, the inspiring Mother Teresa was born. She received the Nobel Peace Prize in 1979 for her charitable works. To remember her and honor the spirit of Drol-ma that her life reflected so powerfully, do something nice for people today. Pick up a friend who normally has to take the bus, shop for someone who can't get out, baby-sit for a flustered mother, give a few bucks to a food bank, donate blood to the Red Cross, volunteer your time at a youth center. Drol-ma lives in all these selfless acts.

To help recognize an opportunity for kindness or charity, pray to Drol-ma before leaving the house today, using words like these:

> *Great Deliverer, she whose heart knows no limits,*
> *renew in me the spirit of benevolence that seeks*
> *not after its own reward but does good for good's*
> *sake. The world is a much lovelier place when*
> *your kindness flows through our hearts, reaching*
> *out to those in need. Take my hand, and guide my*
> *way. Let it begin today. Amen.*

Go out and keep your eyes and ears open!

August 28

✿ ✿
✿

Freeing the Insects (Japan)

SAKI-YAMA-HIME

Themes: Freedom; Luck; Prosperity; Wealth

Symbols: Insects; the Number Seven

About Saki-yama-hime: The Japanese goddess of fortune and abundance visits today's festivities with her lucky energy, especially for improving your finances. In the spirit of the moment, she also provides a little serendipity to help free you from any burdens weighing you down.

To Do Today: Throughout Japan, vendors line the streets around this time of year with small cages that house crickets and other insects. People purchase these, then take them to temples and free the insects, thereby ensuring luck and prosperity. This would be a fun activity for children who have a nearby park or woods where they can find a cricket. Alternatively, have them look for an ant on the sidewalk. Treat the insect kindly all day, giving it little bits of grass or a pinch of sugar. Then, come nightfall, release the creature back to the earth. It will tell the goddess about the human who took care of it! Saki-yama-hime can then respond by bringing more good fortune your way.

An adult version of this festival might simply entail not killing any insects today. Take spiders gently outside the home, try not to step on the creepy-crawlies on the walkways, and so on. Generally treat nature's citizens with respect so Saki-yama-hime can reward you with liberation and financial security.

August 29

✿ ✿
✿

Winegrower's Festival (France)

BRACIACA

Themes: Nature; Harvest; Abundance; Dreams; Summer; Fall

Symbols: Grapes; Vines; Wine; Grape Juice

About Braciaca: This Gaulish agricultural goddess has the pleasure of being a patroness of brewers, especially those who make ale. At this time of year Braciaca reflects late-summer and early-fall themes by abounding in rich grapes for wine-making or just eating fresh.

To Do Today: Since the sixteenth century, the winegrowers of Vevey, France, have gathered today with new wine to watch a parade that honors many of the agricultural gods and goddesses of the region. So decorate your altar, sacred space, or desktop with a bundle of fresh grapes, and nibble on them all day long. Internalize Braciaca's sweetness!

In the magical sense, grapes and grape wine have energy for profuseness, fertility, and visionary dreams. To inspire the latter, have a small glass of grape juice or wine before going to bed. Dab a bit on your forehead over your third eye, too, saying,

> Braciaca, spirit of the vine,
> inspire my dreams, bring visions with this wine.

Make sure to keep a dream diary near your bed tonight, or a tape recorder, so you can write down or record whatever messages the goddess brings.

If you enjoy home brewing, I heartily recommend making grape wine today and aging it to perfection. As the wine reaches maturity, Braciaca's abundance should show signs of manifesting in your life.

August 30

✫ ✫
✫

Summer Holiday (*United Kingdom*)

BON DAMMES

Themes: Rest; Pleasure; Fairies; Playfulness; Youthfulness

Symbols: Any Fairy Plants (Foxglove, Primrose, Oak, Thorn, Ash)

About the Bon Dammes: The Bon Dammes are devic goddesses in Brittany that appear much like fairies and often act with as much impishness. Having a kindly nature, the Bon Dammes inspire playful, youthful outlooks to take with us into early fall with childlike wonder in our hearts.

To Do Today: Follow the custom of all regions in the United Kingdom (except Scotland) and take a day off today. Enjoy family outings and a little leisure before the warm weather really starts to fade. Sleep in a bit, ask for a few hours off from work, get outside and play with the Bon Dammes. Leave them gifts of sparkling stones, honey, and sweet bread beneath any flower or tree that captures your eye and makes you smile. In return, the Bon Dammes will make sure your day is filled with pleasurable surprises.

Think about an activity you really enjoyed as a kid, and recapture that moment sometime today. Jump down a hopscotch board, play tag with the wind, climb a tree (carefully, please), pick buttercups, go berry picking, skinny-dip in a stream, or do whatever reinspires the Bon Dammes's youthfulness in your heart. You'll find that this moment refreshes your entire outlook and provides extra energy for the days ahead.

August 31
✿ ✿
✿
Obzinky (Slovak)

BABA YAGA

Themes: Harvest; Rest; Providence; Thankfulness; Cycles

Symbols: Corn Sheafs; Wreaths of Wheat, Corn, Rye, and Wild-flowers

About Baba Yaga: The Lithuanian/Russian goddess of regeneration, Baba Yaga is typically represented as the last sheaf of corn in today's festivities. As both young and old, she reawakens in us an awareness of time's ever-moving wheel, the seasons, and the significance of both to our goddess-centered magic.

To Do Today: Follow with tradition and make or buy a wreath or bundle of corn shucks or other harvest items. Keep this in your home to inspire Baba Yaga's providence and prosperity for everyone who lives there.

For breakfast, consume a multigrain cereal, rye bagels, or wheat toast. Keep a few pieces of the dried grains or toasted breads with you. This way you'll internalize Baba Yaga's timeliness for coping with your day more effectively and efficiently, and you'll carry her providence with you no matter the circumstances.

Feast on newly harvested foods, thanking Baba Yaga as the maker of your meal. Make sure to put aside one piece of corn that will not be consumed today, however. Dry it and hang it up to ensure a good harvest the next year, for your garden, pocketbook, or heart.

Finally, decorate your home or office with a handful of wild-flowers (even dandelions qualify). Baba Yaga's energy will follow them and you to where it's most needed.

September

September gets its name from the Latin word *septum*, meaning "seven," because it was originally the seventh month in the old calendar system. While the early portion of this month has many summery-feeling festivals, slowly we see a change in focus toward the fall and harvest celebrations. Children return to school, outdoor activities start to wane, and the Wheel of Time begins to paint the trees with color.

September's energy augments magic for prosperity and abundance, balanced with sensibility and a little frugality. It is especially a time for rituals that thank the Goddess for all her gifts throughout the year. Beyond this, start making amulets for health so that when the cooler winds come, you'll be magically fortified.

September 1

Odwira (*Ghana*)

ICHAR-TSIREW

Themes: Unity; Community; Justice; Spirituality; Purification; Home; Peace; Organization

Symbols: Water; Orderly Items; Peace Amulets

About Ichar-tsirew: In Ghana, this water goddess flows into people's lives, saturating them with peaceful intentions and tranquillity, especially in the home. She revels in good organization and any matters carried out in an orderly fashion.

To Do Today: Among the people of the Gold Coast, this festival is a time to honor their bonds as a nation and revel in the laws, beliefs, and customs established in the early 1600s (many of which are probably far older). One neat custom that can invoke Ichar-tsirew's organized attributes is that of burying a bundle of branches. This puts away any unnecessary negativity and banishes bad habits that somehow disrupt the orderly flow of your life.

When you find that the people in your living space have reached critical mass and you need to call a truce, Ichar-tsirew's waters can help. Go through the house (or building, if the "war zone" is your office) *before* talking to anyone, and sprinkle her peace in every nook possible (just a little is fine). As you go, repeat this incantation:

Negativity cease; by peace released!

Continue until the whole area is done. Now try reapproaching the people with whom tensions have been building, and let the goddess harness harmony.

September 2

Lost Days (Brittany)

HORAE

Themes: Time; Cycles

Symbols: Clocks; Hourglasses; Egg Timers

About the Horae: These are the Greek and Roman goddesses of time, ruling over the seasons and every hour of the day. They make sure that nature and life's order is kept, and they generally strengthen our awareness of time and the earth's cycles.

To Do Today: In the mid-1700s, Britain changed over from the Julian system to the Gregorian calendar. People went to sleep on Wednesday, September 2, and woke up Thursday, September 14, putting the Horae on notice that humans need help with scheduling! To evoke the Horae's promptness in your life, try blessing your watch by saying,

> By the minute, by the hour, instill in me a sense of time;
> by the season, by the year, renew the magic with this rhyme.

Repeat this phrase and touch your watch any time you have to be punctual, meet a deadline, or stay precisely on schedule for whatever reason. The Horae will then nudge you when you start to dilly-dally, lag behind, or get otherwise distracted.

For keeping up with everyday, mundane tasks, this spell works for alarm clocks, bakery timers, hourglasses, water clocks, and sundials. Bless the token using the same incantation. Then attach a schedule or "to do" list to any of these items in and around your home. This symbolically attaches the Horae's timeliness to those areas, enhancing your productivity levels.

September 3

Paryushana (India)

TRIPURA

Themes: Religious Devotion; Forgiveness; Relationships; Kindness; Truth; Spirituality; Patience; Restoration

Symbols: Gold; Silver; Iron

About Tripura: In Jainism, Tripura is the great mother who lives in three metallic cities (gold, silver, iron) that represent the heavens, the air, and the earth (or body, mind, and spirit). She unites these three powers within us for well-balanced spiritual living that reflects good morals and proper action.

To Do Today: Taking place between August and September, this Jaina festival focuses on the ten cardinal virtues of forgiveness, charity, simplicity, contentment, truthfulness, self-restraint, fasting, detachment, humility, and continence. It is also a time to restore relationships that have been damaged during the year and generally reassess one's life and perspectives, asking for Tripura's assistance during your daily meditations with words like this:

> *Great Heavenly Mother, create in me a temple*
> *that is strong and pure, a mind that seeks after*
> *truth, and a spirit that thirsts for enlightenment.*
> *Balance these parts of myself so I may walk along*
> *your path with harmony as my companion.*

Another way to generate Tripura's attributes within today is by wearing gold-, silver-, and iron-toned objects or clothing. If you can't find anything in an iron color, just iron your clothing using the magic of puns for power!

Horn Dance (England)

MAID MARIAN

Themes: Fertility; Youthfulness; Abundance; Energy; Beauty; Instinct

Symbols: Late-blossoming Flowers; Forest Plants

About Maid Marian: A predominant figure in the Robin Hood tales, Maid Marian is most certainly a remnant of the ancient youthful goddess, who blossoms with late summer's abundance, inspires fertility, reawakens our instincts, and exudes energy just when our resources seem all but gone.

To Do Today: The horn dance dates back to Norman times as a remnant of an ancient fertility and hunting festival. Today it remains as a reenactment of Robin Hood stories, complete with hobby horse and deer horn dancing for Maid Marian's fertility, rock candy for life's sweetness, and a little brandy to keep things warm! Should you want physical fertility, you can dance with a broom instead. Eat a bit of candy and drink brandy (brandy-flavored candy is also an option) to encourage sweet love and passion to flow in your life!

To draw Maid Marian's presence to any effort today, bring late-blossoming flowers into your home, office, or any place you visit. If you get organic ones, nibble on a rose. Digest the goddess's beauty within so it will manifest without.

Finally, wear shades of forest green, the traditional color for Robin Hood's clan, so you can figuratively accept a spot beside Maid Marian as an ally who fights against injustice and stands firm for good causes.

September 5

Labor Day (United States)

KA-BLEI-JEW-LEI-HAT

Themes: Work; Rest; Recreation; Prosperity

Symbols: All the Tools of Your Trade

About Ka-blei-jew-lei-ha: The Assam goddess of the marketplace and merchants takes a much-deserved rest from her labors today and focuses on rewarding tasks that have been well done throughout the last eight months.

To Do Today: For most folks in the United States, Labor Day represents a long weekend without normal workaday activities. From a magical perspective, this holiday offers us a chance to thank Ka-blei-jew-lei-ha for our jobs (which keep a roof overhead and food on the table) and ask for her blessing on the tools we use regularly. A secretary might empower his or her pen and steno pad; a musician can charge his or her instrument; a shopkeeper might anoint the cash register, a book clerk might burn specially chosen incense near goddess-centered books (and in the business section), and so forth.

Some potential herbal tinctures and oils to use for inspiring Ka-blei-jew-lei-ha's prosperity and watchfulness include cinnamon, clove, ginger, mint, orange, and pine. To partake of the goddess's abundance by energizing your skills with her magic, blend all of these (except pine) into a tea!

This goddess can help with job searches, too. Just tell her your need, then review the newspaper to see what companies catch your eye. Then get on the phone or get the resume out so Ka-blei-jew-lei-hat can open that doorway.

September 6

❀

Virgin of Remedies (Mexico)

TEMAZCALTECI

Themes: Health; Banishing (sickness)

Symbols: Medicinal Herbs; Health and Healing Amulets; Water

About Temazcalteci: This Aztec goddess's name means "grandmother of the sweet bath." It is she who teaches us how to use medicinal herbs to maintain our health or banish sickness as fall sets in (perhaps especially in teas, considering her name).

To Do Today: Follow the Mexican custom and rise at dawn, the time of renewed hope. Enjoy a hot cup of soothing, healthful tea to get your entire day off with Temazcalteci's energy for well-being.

Burning incense today is said to attract the goddess's favor and bring health and protection from fall maladies. Burn sage or cedar in every room, and wash your bedding or favorite clothing in sage tincture. This not only attracts the goddess's blessing but also decreases germs.

Dancing is another activity that promotes well-being today. Maybe try out a dance aerobics tape, and if you like it, stick with it! Boogie with the goddess every morning.

Don't forget to smudge your car with some healthful aromatics, too (like wintergreen or apple). Then drive over to the nearest health cooperative and get some good herbal supplements to add to your diet. This way you generate Temazcalteci's magic every day just by remembering to take the vitamin!

September 7

Festival of Durga (Hindu)

DURGA

Themes: Power over Evil and Negativity; Knowledge; Sustenance

Symbols: Fire; Yellow-colored Items; Lion; Rice Bowl and Spoon

About Durga: The Hindu warrior goddess Durga is typically depicted as a beautiful woman with ten arms that bear divine weapons to protect all that is sacred—including you. Her role in Indian mythology is so powerful that the national anthem sings her praises as a guardian. According to the stories, Durga overpowered the great demon who threatened to destroy not only the earth but the gods themselves.

To Do Today: Durga's festival comes during the early fall, when the skies are growing darker. As this happens, she offers to zealously defend goodness against any malevolence that dwells in those figurative shadows. If there is a special person or project that you want protected, pray for Durga's aid today. Light a yellow candle (or any candle) and say,

> Durga, protectress and guardian, watch over
> _____ [person, situation, or project] with all due
> diligence. Take the sword of truth, the power of
> justice, and the light of decency to stand guard
> against any storms that come. So be it.

Blow out the candle and relight it anytime you need safety.

To encourage Durga's providence, set out a bowl of rice on your altar with a spoon today. This is the symbol of Annapurna, an aspect of Durga who supplies daily food.

September 8

Festa da Serreta (*California*)

NOSSA SENHORA
DOS MILAGRES

Themes: Miracles; Wishes; Mediation

Symbol: Milk

About Nossa Senhora dos Milagres: "Our Lady of Miracles"
is likely a Christianized revamping of an earlier mother goddess, as implied by her sacred beverage, milk. Nossa Senhora
dos Milagres grants the heartfelt wishes of those who give
her small offerings (often coins). This particular goddess also
mediates on our behalf with the gods.

To Do Today: Today the catchphrase "got milk?" takes on whole
new meaning. It is customary to enjoy a banquet of milk and milk-
based foods today to honor the goddess and accept her miracles
into our lives. Get as creative as you want with this idea. For example, people having trouble with conception might request the miracle of fertility through an early morning eggnog. Those wishing
love can eat cheese. Those needing to get the budget under control
might make rice pudding! Someone suffering from illness can eat
ice cream with a blackberry garnish. All of these foods combine
milk into a symbolic substance that releases the goddess into the
area of your life where she's most needed.

To present a wish to this goddess, just put a coin under your
milk container in the refrigerator today and recite your desire. At
the end of the day, give the coin to a young child or person in need
so that the magic of happiness and kindness energizes your wish
and the goddess's answer.

Chrysanthemum Day (China/Japan)

LAN CAIHE

Themes: Longevity; Nature

Symbols: Flowers; Flute

Lan Caihe: The Buddhist patroness of florists or anyone who enjoys making things grow, this goddess often walked the streets playing flute music. Her name means "red-footed genius," alluding to a strong connection with the earth and rich soil.

To Do Today: Around this time of year, people in China drink chrysanthemum wine for longevity and wisdom, eat chrysanthemum petals in salads, and enjoy a plethora of flower displays throughout the land. If anyone in your neighborhood grows chrysanthemums, definitely try a few petals tossed with a green salad and lemon juice. Consume Lan Caihe's green thumb and internalize her awareness of earth directly!

Since it's September, take a leisurely walk today and enjoy people's gardening efforts. This honors Lan Caihe and allows you to revel in this goddess's artistry firsthand. If you can't walk around because of bad weather, send yourself a bouquet filled with Lan Caihe's abundance. When it arrives at work or home, it bears this goddess's energy within.

Finally, get out and work with the land in some way today. Plant a little hanging flower arrangement. Weed your lawn or garden. Lan Caihe will reward your efforts with a growing connection to earth and its greenery.

September 10

Dividing the Cheese (*Switzerland*)

MATRONA

Themes: Harvest; Providence; Health; Abundance; Autumn; Love

Symbols: Swiss Cheese; Water

About Matrona: This Teutonic mother goddess is the great provider of both food and refreshment, especially freshwater. A benevolent figure, she personifies the earth's abundance during the fall and offers to share of that wealth freely. Judging from artistic depictions of Matrona in the company of a dog, or carrying palm fronds, she may have also had a connection with the healing arts.

To Do Today: People in the Swiss Alps gather today to enjoy the fruits of their labors, specifically cheese that has been stored in cellars since grazing season in the summer. In many ways this is a harvest rite, rejoicing in Matrona's ongoing providence.

Consider enjoying a Swiss fondue today, complete with sliced harvest vegetables and breads from Matrona's storehouse. The melted cheese inspires warm, harmonious love. Matrona makes that love healthy and abundant. For physical well-being and self-love, simply add some sautéed garlic to this blend, or add other herbs known to combat any sickness with which you're currently coping.

Other ways to enjoy this goddess and invite her into your day? Have an omelet with cheese and harvest vegetables for breakfast, or grilled cheese and ice water at lunch. If you own a dog, share a bit of your healthful meal with it!

September 11

Coptic New Year (Egypt)

THE SPHINX

Themes: Harvest; Protection; Water; Beginnings; Fertility

Symbols: Water; Sand; Pyramids

About the Sphinx: This goddess is the Egyptian guardian of the
Pyramids, but she also has other important duties. She signals the beginning of the Nile's fertile flooding, the water
from which replenishes the soil at this time of year. This
abundant productivity and protection is what the Sphinx
offers us in preparation for autumn's harvests.

To Do Today: The Egyptian new year is celebrated in September to
correspond with the annual flood cycle of the Nile and to mark a new
planting season. The Sphinx joins in this celebration by producing
plenty wherever it's needed. To encourage this further, find a pyramid-
shaped object (like a fluorite crystal) and place a symbol of your need
beneath it (like a dollar for money). This puts your goal beneath the
Sphinx's watchful eye so she can attend to that matter diligently.

If you hold any type of ritual today, use sand to mark the magic
circle, along with this invocation to the goddess (you can change
the words boldfaced here to reflect more personal requirements:

> Great watcher, Lady of the Pyramids, I sprinkle your sands to the
>   wind—
> let the magic begin.
> Sand to the east for abundant hope;
> sand to the south for fiery energy; sand to the west for flowing love;
> sand to the north for firm foundations;
> and sand in the center to bind the powers together. So be it.

September 12

Pumpkin Festival (France)

MENG JIANGNU

Themes: Harvest; Children; Unity; Kinship; Community

Symbols: Pumpkin; Squash

About Meng Jiangnu: In the true spirit of a global culture, Meng Jiangnu is "imported" for today's festivities from China, being a pumpkin girl born from the vines of two different households. Her birth united the two families and brought them harmony where strife had once been. Today she continues to offer us unity with those we love, plus a profusion of positive feelings.

To Do Today: Around this time of year in France, people gather in central markets looking for the Mother of all Pumpkins, which actually gets enthroned for the festivities! This is later made into a communal soup, so those who eat it are magically partaking of Meng Jiangnu's energy. Eating of this soup reaffirms community spirit and ensures a good pumpkin harvest the next year. So definitely make pumpkin or squash a part of your menu today. Consider pumpkin bread for breakfast with a friend or family member to encourage good feelings toward each other throughout the day. At lunch, a warm buttered squash side dish keeps love warm. Last of all, don't forget some pie for dessert after dinner to bring sweetness to your relationships!

Carve a pumpkin or squash with a symbol of any pressing need you have in a relationship. Put a candle inside and light it up so the pumpkin girl can shine her energy into that situation and begin the healing process.

September 13

All Soul's Day (Egypt)

NEPTHYS

Themes: Death; Spirits; Rebirth

Symbols: Fire; Basket; Myrrh

About Nepthys: This Egyptian funerary goddess has a hawk for a sacred animal. Together they guide and watch the souls of our loved ones in the afterlife. In Egyptian tradition, Nepthys lives in the east, where she can receive the rising sun, a symbol of the hopefulness she can instill and of resurrection.

To Do Today: Today was Nepthys's festival day in ancient Egypt. As with other festivals for the dead, it was a time not only to propitiate the goddess with offerings of aromatic incense like myrrh but also to satisfy any wandering spirits. If someone you care about passed away during the last year, burn some incense for this goddess and leave a small basket filled with a token for her on your altar. This acts as a prayer to Nepthys to keep a watchful eye on that soul and grant them peace.

If you find your sense of hopefulness waning under everyday pressures, light a candle honoring Nepthys today, and every day, until you sense a difference in attitude. Try to choose a candle whose color represents hope and change to you (sprout green is one good choice). Inscribe the candle with a symbol of what you most need to turn things around so that this goddess can shine dawn's revitalizing light into your heart and begin lifting some of that heaviness.

September 14

Keiro no Hi (Japan)

AME NO UZUME

Themes: Honor; Longevity; Wisdom; Psychic Abilities; Prosperity; Protection; Kinship

Symbols: Antique Items; Aged Wines or Cheeses (anything that grows better over time); Sacred Dances

About Ame no Uzume: A Japanese ancestral goddess, Ame no Uzume's magic is that of generating a long, happy life for her followers. Shinto festivals in her honor include special dances that invoke the goddess's favor for longevity, honor, prosperity, protection, and a close-knit family. In some areas, people also turn to her for foresight, considering Ame no Uzume the patroness of psychic mediums.

To Do Today: Join with people in Japan and celebrate the wisdom that longevity brings in this festival for the aged. If there is an elder in your family or magic community who has influenced your life positively, pray to Ame no Uzume for that person's ongoing health and protection. Go see that individual and say thank you. The gesture greatly pleases this goddess, who will shower blessings on you, too!

To gain Ame no Uzume's insight in your psychic efforts, find an antique item that you can wear during readings, like a skeleton key (to "fit" any psychic doorway). Empower this token, saying,

> *Ame no Uzume, open my inner eyes, help me to see!*
> *Let nothing be hidden that needs to be known, whene'er I speak*
>   *this magical poem.*

Touch the key and recite your power phrase, the incantation, before reading.

September 15

†

Birthday of the Moon (China)

CH'ANGO

Themes: Moon; Relationships; Purity; Devotion; Instinct; Growth; Manifestation

Symbols: All Lunar Symbols or Items

About Ch'ango: This Chinese moon goddess is stunningly beautiful, shining on our lives with all the best energies of the moon. On this, her birthday, she reaches out to embrace the earth and its people, inspiring pure, devoted relationships, stirring long-forgotten insights, and sharing energy for growth and manifestation in nearly any area of our lives.

To Do Today: This festival in honor of the moon goddess is a national event in China, and the traditions are easily adapted to our efforts. Begin by gathering with family or friends and exchanging moon gifts (anything that represents the moon and meets a magical need for the person to whom it's intended). After the gift exchange, enjoy some moon-shaped cookies or cakes, as well as other foods that invoke Ch'ango's favor, like dumplings shaped like a crescent moon (dim sum) and grapefruit slices.

Don't forget to go moongazing (if the weather is poor, use a poster or book images). Hold hands with your companions and bask in the silvery glow. Moonlight is said to enliven creativity, romance, and other positive emotions today. Additionally, looking upon Ch'ango's visage draws the goddess's blessing and protection.

September 16

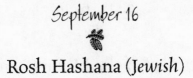

Rosh Hashana (*Jewish*)

MALKUTH

Themes: Forgiveness; Cleansing; Health; Peace; Earth; Balance

Symbols: Yellow-colored Items; Quartz; Cereals and Grains; the Number Ten

About Malkuth: Malkuth is the goddess of the tenth *sephira* in the Cabalistic Tree of Life. Here she reminds us of the need for positive actions on the physical plane, not simply good thoughts or lofty words, to bring about change. Malkuth also counsels us to always balance our goddess spirituality with real life and to keep peace with the earth, which she personifies.

To Do Today: This is the Jewish new year and typically a time for prayer, introspection, and healing the emotional wounds that keep people apart. Take ten minutes out of your morning routine and pray to the goddess or meditate on recent months. This will give you time to begin integrating all the lessons and changes that have occurred.

Jumping into or over water today liberates you from sin and negativity, as does naming a handful of grain after your problems and tossing it in water. Eating a round loaf of bread dipped in honey brings longevity, and eating apples dipped in honey brings the sweetness of Malkuth's health.

To encourage Malkuth's balance and harmony throughout your day, wear something yellow or carry a yellow-colored stone or a piece of quartz with you. The quartz in particular engenders better communication skills and an improved connection with the earth/physical plane.

September 17

The Month of Hathor (Egypt)

HATHOR

Themes: Joy; Love; Arts; Femininity; Beauty; Sexuality; Sky

Symbols: Mirrors; Cow; Sandalwood and Rose Incense; Rattles

About Hathor: One of the most beloved sky goddesses in Egypt, Hathor brings happiness, romance, and an appreciation for musical arts into our lives. Sacred or erotic dances are a welcome offering for Hathor, as is any effort to beautify the body. As the patroness of the toilette, she also protects women and embodies the pinnacle of feminine qualities. Her favorite musical instrument, the sistrum (a kind of rattle), was said to banish evil wherever it was played.

To Do Today: From September 17 until October 16, Hathor reigned in Egypt. To honor this goddess, make an effort to make yourself as physically appealing as possible, then spend some time with a significant other or in a social setting. In the first case, Hathor's favor will increase love and passion; in the second, she'll improve your chances of finding a bed partner.

To fill your living space with Hathor's energy, take rice or beans and put them in a plastic container (this creates a makeshift rattle). Play some lusty music and dance clockwise around every room of the home shaking the rattle. Perhaps add a verbal charm like this one:

> *Love, passion and bliss,*
> *by Hathor's power kissed!*

This drives away negativity, generates joyful vibrations, promotes artistic awareness, and increases love each time you kiss someone in your home.

September 18

White Horse Festival (Britain)

RHIANNON

Themes: Movement; Communication; Rest; Ghosts; Fertility; Leadership

Symbols: White; Horses; Moon

About Rhiannon: This Celtic horse goddess rides into our festival calendar today on a white mare bearing fertility, leadership, and a means to get things moving where they may have stagnated. Some historians believe the swiftness of her steed (which is white, a lunar color) alludes to a lunar goddess. In stories, Rhiannon commands singing birds that can wake spirits or grant sleep to mortals.

To Do Today: In Britain, people come to Berkshire hillside today to scour the white horse that adorns the grasses here. This ancient galloping steed is created from pale clay, and this ritual keeps it, and Rhiannon's memory, vibrant. So, if you have any images of horses (magazines, statuary, paintings) around, dust them off and put them in a place of honor today.

Since this was a festival for horses, you might consider tending to your own "horse," be it a car or a bicycle! Give it a tune-up or oil change, then take a ride! As you go, visualize yourself on the back of Rhiannon's horse moving swiftly toward attaining productivity or improved authority wherever you need it. Alternatively, wear something silver or white so that Rhiannon's lunar energies can begin filtering into your day through the color's vibrations.

September 19

Harvest Moon Day (*Various Locations*)

PAPA

Themes: Providence; Thankfulness; Abundance; Earth; Fertility; Weather; Grounding; Harvest; Moon

Symbols: Moon; Harvested Foods; Rainwater; Rocks

About Papa: Polynesians summon Papa to help in all earthly matters. She is, in fact, the earth mother who gave birth to all things by making love to the sky. To this day, the earth and sky remain lovers, the sky giving its beloved rain for fertilization. Papa is sometimes known by the alternative title Papa Raharaha, "supporting rock," through which she provides foundations and sustenance for our body, mind, and spirit.

To Do Today: Harvest moon festivals take place during the full moon closest to the autumnal equinox. The full moon here represents the earth (Papa) in all its abundance and the crop's maturity. If it's raining today, skip an umbrella for a moment and enjoy a little of the sky's love for Papa. Gather a little of the water and drink it to encourage more self-love.

Carry any crystal or stone with you today to manifest Papa's firm foundations in all your endeavors. And definitely integrate harvested foods into your menu. Some that have lunar affiliations include cauliflower, cabbage, cucumber, grapes, lettuce, potatoes, and turnips. Thank Papa for her providence before you eat, then ingest whatever lunar qualities you need for that day or for the rest of the year.

September 20

Spring Equinox (Incan)

MAMA KILYA

Themes: Fire; Sun; Cycles; Spring; Time; Divination; Health; Prosperity

Symbols: Fire; Golden/yellow Items

About Mama Kilya: In Incan tradition, Mama Kilya regulates the festival calendar and all matters of time. She is also a prophetic goddess, often warning of impending danger through eclipses. When these occur, one should make as much noise as possible to frighten away evil influences.

To Do Today: Because they live south of the equator, Incans consider today, which for them is the spring equinox, the sun's birthday. Follow with tradition and rise early today to catch the first rays of the sun as they come over the horizon. These rays hold the goddess's blessing for health, prosperity, and timeliness.

Another customary practice today was that of sun and fire divinations. If the sun is shining, sit beneath a tree and watch the patterns it creates in the shadows and light. Keep a question in mind as you watch, and see what images Mama Kilya creates in response. Make note of these and look them up in dream symbol books or any guide to imagery for potential interpretive values. Should the weather prove poor, place any yellow-colored herbs on a fire source and watch what happens. Popping and flying indicates lots of energy and a positive response. Smoldering indicates anger and an iffy response. Finally, flames dying out completely is a negative—definitely don't move forward on this one.

September 21

Wings and Water Festival (New Jersey)

NINGAL

Themes: Ecology; Nature; Abundance; Earth; Water

Symbols: Water; Maritime Art; Seafood; Reeds; Marsh Plants

About Ningal: This ancient Mesopotamian goddess abides in regions filled with reeds or marshes, which she also vehemently protects. She is also considered an earth and vegetation goddess who visits us with abundance during the autumn.

To Do Today: This festival takes place over two days during the third weekend in September. It's dedicated to fund-raising for Ningal's endangered wetlands in southern New Jersey and educating the public on the tremendous value of these regions to the local ecology. To honor this effort and the spirit of Ningal, consider making a donation to a group that strives to protect wetlands (please investigate them first), and perhaps enjoy a nice seafood chowder as New Englanders do today. This meal reconnects you with the water element and Ningal's fertility.

For tokens that bear Ningal's power into your home, look to cattails, lily pads, mosses, indoor water fountains, or art that depicts these types of things. First thing in the morning, don dark greens, mossy browns, or clothing that depicts reeds or marshy scenes. Also drink plenty of water or take a cool bath to create a stronger connection to this element's power and to commemorate Ningal's dwelling place.

September 22

Autumn Equinox (*Various Locations*)

AUTUMNUS

Themes: Harvest; Abundance; Thankfulness; Balance; Wisdom; Foresight; Autumn

Symbols: Fall Leaves; Harvested Items

About Autumnus: This is the Roman personification of the autumn season. While the actual gender of this being is often left to the imagination, the strong connection with the harvest, wines, and fruits intimates a powerful earth goddess, blossoming with her seasonal array.

To Do Today: In magic traditions, today is a time to appreciate the earth's abundance somewhat cautiously. After this festival, the daylight hours will begin to wane, meaning wise prudence is called for. So while we reap Autumnus's bounty from the sowing season, we also begin prudently planning.

Decorate your dining table or sacred space with colorful autumn leaves today. Enjoy as many harvested fruits and vegetables (perhaps from a farmer's market) as possible today to internalize Autumnus's prosperous, wise energy. Leave out a libation of wine or grape juice for the goddess to please her and to encourage continuing providence when her stores begin to wane.

For children, today is a perfect time to have a leaf-raking party in which they figuratively gather what they need from the goddess, then play happily in her energy afterward by jumping in the piles.

Libra Begins (*Various Locations*)

TULA

Themes: Balance; Justice; Peace

Symbols: Scales; Balanced Items

About Tula: This Hindu goddess is represented by the constellation Libra, her name even meaning "balance." In all things, Tula teaches us how to harmonize the diverse nature of our hectic lives and reintegrate goddess-centered ideology within that framework.

To Do Today: People born under the sign of Libra seem to integrate Tula's characteristics of harmony and balance, especially in aesthetic sense. They cultivate relationships carefully and enjoy fighting for just causes. When those of us not born under this sign would like to do similarly, we can call on Tula for aid. Stand on the bathroom scale first thing in the morning and invoke her, saying,

> *Tula, instill in me a growing sense of harmony.*
> *Between sound and silence let serenity dance;*
> *between the shadow and the light, let peace prance.*
> *Where'er injustice dwells, let equity swell;*
> *in my heart, in my life, bring an end to all strife*

Afterward, try to dress in balanced tones of clothing (like a white shirt and black pants) and spend the rest of the day monitoring your personal balance—your sense of equilibrium—maintaining your temper, pacing your steps, being aware of your center of gravity. In all these things, Tula's equitable energy abides.

September 24

❧

Festival of Poets (Japan)

IZANAMI-NO-KAMI

Themes: Art; Creativity; Excellence

Symbol: Poetry

About Izanami-no-kami: In Japan, this creative goddess is considered to have made all things, and she inspires similar inventiveness within us. Traditionally, she is honored through artistic displays, including dance, song, music, and poetry reading.

To Do Today: Every September, poets from across Japan come to the imperial palace to compose verses. Upon receiving a cup of sake floated down the river, each poet must create an impromptu verse. The winner becomes the nation's poet laureate. In keeping with this idea, concentrate on trying your own hand at a little sacred poetry today, perhaps even a haiku. Traditional haiku contains seven syllables in the first line, five syllables in the second line, and seven or five in the last; each line evokes an image or feeling in the reader's mind. Here's one example:

> *Izanami-no-kami*
> *paints the universe*
> *radiant—eternity*

If poetry isn't your forte, engage in another art form through which Izanami-no-kami's imaginative spirit can shine. Ask for her assistance and inspiration before you begin, and see what wonders her nudge can arouse in you. Or, visit an art gallery, making notes of the things that really strike a harmonious chord in your spirit.

September 25

Doll Memorial (Japan/China)

SUNG TZU NIANG NIANG

Themes: Prayer; Kindness; Children; Fertility; Offering

Symbols: Dolls

About Sung Tzu Niang Niang: Called "she who brings children" in the Far East, this goddess has abundant energy that not only generates fertility but also instills a kinder, gentler heart within us. Sung Tzu Niang Niang is said to always listen to and answer prayers addressed to her with compassion.

To Do Today: Traditionally, childless couples bring an offering of a special doll to this goddess today and pray for physical fertility. For couples wishing for natural or adopted children, this ritual is still perfectly suitable. Find any small doll and dress it in swatches of your old clothing, or bind a piece of both partners' hair to it. Place this before your goddess figure and pray, in heartfelt words, to Sung Tzu Niang Niang for her assistance.

On a spiritual level, you can make any artistic representation of areas where you need productivity or abundance and give it to the goddess. In magic terms, these little images are called poppets. For example, stitch scraps of any natural silver or gold cloth together (maybe making it circular like a coin) and fill it with alfalfa sprouts. Leave this before the goddess until more money manifests. Then, give the poppet to the earth (bury it) so that Sung Tzu Niang Niang's blessings will continue to grow.

September 26

Miwok Acorn Festival (*California*)

CHUP

Themes: Harvest; Reason; Weather; Providence

Symbols: Acorns; Oak; Rainwater; Fire

About Chup: As a Native American goddess of food, Chup is the founder of our feast today. She oversees nature's energies, specifically those of wind, rain, and fire, and teaches people to use a combination of reason and their emotions to solve difficult problems.

To Do Today: This is an event of the Miwok Indians, who gather today as they have for thousands of years to celebrate the harvest through ritual and feasting. Acorns get made into breads and soups, having been a regional staple for early peoples. Therefore, I advocate finding some creative uses for acorns, perhaps making them into runes or using them to mark the sacred circle in the east, west, or south (the elemental regions that correspond to Chup).

To increase your reasoning skills, especially for a pressing situation, try this Chup spell: The next time it rains, gather the rainwater and warm it, gently blowing over the top of the pan three times and saying,

> *By Chup's sensible winds, let this magic begin.*
> *Within this water I bind keenness of mind.*
> *By the fire actuate, all confusion abates.*

To this water add some spearmint leaves and a pinch of rosemary to augment conscious thought, then drink the tea to start the transformation process.

September 27

Aloha Festival (Hawaii)

HAWUMEA

Themes: History; Tradition; Energy; Restoration

Symbols: Leis; Fresh Flowers; Polynesian Foodstuffs

About Hawumea: Hawaiian stories tell us that Hawumea is the mother of Hawaii, having created it, the Hawaiian people, and all edible vegetation on the islands. Today she offers us renewed energy with which to restore or protect our traditions and rejoice in their beauty.

To Do Today: In Hawaii this marks the beginning of a weeklong celebration of local custom and history complete with dances, parades, and sports competitions. For us this translates to reveling in our own local cultures, including foods, crafts, and the like. Hawumea lives in those customs and revels in your enjoyment of them.

If any historical site or tradition is slowly fading out due to "progress," today also provides an excellent opportunity to try to draw some attention to that situation. Ask Hawumea for her help, then write letters to local officials, contact preservation or historical groups in the region, and see what you can do to keep that treasure alive.

For personal restoration or improved energy, I suggest eating some traditional Hawaiian foods today, as they are part of Hawumea's bounty and blessings. Have pineapple at breakfast, some macadamia nuts for a snack, and Kona coffee at work, and maybe even create a luau-style dinner in the evening for family and friends to bless them, too.

September 28

Festival of Themis (*Greece*)

THEMIS

Themes: Justice; Equity; Reason; Morality; Organization; Foresight; Karma; Truth

Symbols: Balanced Items; Scales

About Themis: In Greek tradition, Themis personifies the law in both spirit and deed. She regulates karmic order in the cosmos and presides over matters of moral judgment. Today, Themis strengthens the voice of consciousness and the gift of foresight within us, becoming a sound counselor in difficult decisions and offering balanced perspectives.

To Do Today: Bearing in mind Themis's legal theme, tend to any pressing legal matters today. If a court matter is pending, check on it. If you need to catch up on past-due parking tickets, do so. Themis will help resolve any matter of law in the most equitable manner possible. Should you actually have to go to court today, carry an image of a scale or any balanced geometric figure in your pocket to invite her assistance.

Themis lives in just actions and orderliness, so just by treating people fairly and organizing your day, you invoke her presence. Throughout the day, take an extra moment to consider the repercussions of your actions, both mundanely and spiritually. Consider this a time to balance your karmic checkbook and make right some wrongs in your life. Also, be honest in your words and thoughts today. This honors and pleases this goddess greatly.

September 29

Quarter Days (England/Scotland)

NISKAI

Themes: Cycles; Time; Luck; Home; Success

Symbols: A Quarter; Calendars; Water

About Niskai: This Western European water goddess has a threefold nature, exemplifying the full movement of time's wheel from birth and maturity to death and rebirth. She instills in us a respect for each season and the ability to use time wisely so that all our goddess-centered efforts will be more successful.

To Do Today: Throughout England, Ireland, Wales, and Scotland, Quarter Days mark the four quarters of the year. It is traditionally a time to pay one's bills in Niskai's timely fashion so that prosperity stays with you. Also, this is a very propitious time to move into a new residence; it brings luck!

To keep Niskai's promptness with you and augment your awareness of the cycles in your life, try this spell. Begin with a quarter (which is round, representing the Wheel of Time). Place the token in moonlight for three hours and sunlight for three hours to charge it. Then bless it, saying,

> To everything, there is a season;
> to every moment, a reason.
> For Niskai's timeliness I pray,
> every hour of every day.

Carry this in your wallet or purse. If, for some reason, you start running late, touch the quarter and recite the incantation again. Then use the quarter to call folks so they don't worry!

September 30

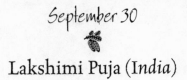

Lakshimi Puja (India)

LAKSHIMI

Themes: Devotion; Luck; Wealth; Relationships; Prosperity; Love; Harvest; Autumn

Symbols: Lotus; Rice; Coins; Basil

About Lakshimi: A favorite goddess in the Hindu pantheon, Lakshimi brings devoted love into our lives, along with a little luck and extra pocket change to help things along. When called upon, Lakshimi opens the floodgates of heaven to meet our heart's or budget's needs.

To Do Today: This annual festival celebrates Lakshimi and honors her ongoing goodness, which manifests in an abundant autumn harvest.

If you are a merchant or store owner, it's customary to appeal to Lakshimi today for the ongoing success of your business. You can do this by placing a few grains of rice, some basil, or a coin in your daily tally sheets. This neatly tucks Lakshimi's fortunate nature into your finances.

For those wishing for Lakshimi's luck in love, gather a handful of rice cooked in basil water (the cooking process adds energy and emotional warmth). Sprinkle this on the walkway leading up to your home and your preferred vehicle, saying,

> Lakshimi, let true love find its way to my home;
> let me carry luck with me wherever I roam.

Keep a pinch of this in an airtight container, and carry it with you into social situations. It will act as a charm to improve your chances of meeting potential mates.

October

Following the pattern started in September, October gets its name from *octo*, meaning eight, as it is the eighth month on the old calendar system. Throughout the month, festivals for the dead increase with the waning light, and late harvest festivals continue. The latter often include propitiation to ensure that the Goddess's abundance will keep people whole through harsh or barren times.

Magical efforts accentuated by October's characteristics include clearing away old, unnecessary things or habits so that our mind, body, and spirit are prepared for winter. Any spells for memory, especially commemorating loved ones, are apt. Beyond this, metaphysical efforts for health, luck, and debt paying seem common, ensuring that winter, the season of rest and death, will come and go with the least negative effect.

October 1

Reunion with the Goddess
(Southeastern United States)

CHEROKEE FIRST WOMAN

Themes: Spirituality; Universal Truth; Unity; Cleansing; Abundance

Symbols: All Animals and Plants

About Cherokee First Woman: This goddess appears in Cherokee myths as an ancestress to the tribe and creatrix of all animals and plants. After the world was first inhabited, Cherokee First Woman continued to give birth to one child a year (this child may have symbolized the new year). Additionally, she motivates the earth's bounty and generates abundance to sustain us through the months ahead.

To Do Today: Around this time of year, Cherokee tribes often hold a festival of offerings meant to celebrate their unity with the Sacred Parent and reunite them with this power. One custom easy to follow is that of exchanging clothes with a loved one; this symbolizes oneness among humans, the gods, and each other.

Washing in running water today (shower or tap) will cleanse away any barrier that stands between you and the goddess. If you hold a formal ritual today, place a bowl of water near the circle where each participant can rinse their hands to invoke Cherokee First Woman's blessing and purification.

Finally, drink a tall glass of springwater today to release this goddess's spiritual nature, rejuvenation, and abundance into every cell.

October 2

❦

Guardian Angel Day (Spain/Europe)

ENNOIA

Themes: Mediation; Communication; Magic; Knowledge

Symbols: Angels

About Ennoia: In Gnostic tradition, Ennoia is the goddess of knowledge, intention, and thought. Through her all things were designed and manifested, including the angels. Through Ennoia we can learn the art of magic and how to communicate with angels as mediators between us and the gods.

To Do Today: Today is a time to give thanks to the angels in our lives—those powers and people who protect, inspire, and watch over us. One easily adapted tradition from Spain is that of wearing scarves and bells. These represent the beauty and music angels are said to bear into human life.

Second, take a moment to give back to the people in your life who have been like earthly angels (you know, the folks who bring soup when you're sick, or offer money when funds are tight). Do something really nice for them, or minimally, light a candle on their behalf asking for angelic blessings in their lives.

Finally, try to connect with your guiding guardian angel(s). During your daily prayers or meditation, ask that power to reveal itself in words comfortable to you. Wait, watch, and listen. The angel may reveal itself as the sound of bells or quiet music, with radiant light, or in other manifestations. If the being speaks with you, write down the words and ponder them in the days ahead.

October 3

❦

Tangun (Korea)

BEAR GODDESS

Themes: Change; Peace; Devotion; Inspiration; Patience

Symbols: Bears; Wormwood; Garlic

About Bear Goddess: Korean myth recounts the tale of two friends, a bear and a tiger, who wished to be human. To receive this transformation, the two had to stay in a cave eating wormwood and garlic for one hundred days. Unfortunately, the tiger lacked patience, found this too difficult, and left. The bear, however, stayed determined. After one hundred days, she transformed into a beautiful human woman and then bore a son who founded Korea, naming it "the land of morning calm." This quiet peacefulness and devotion is what the Bear Goddess inspires, especially for personal transformation.

To Do Today: In Korean tradition, today is National Foundation Day, the time when Bear Goddess's son founded the country. To commemorate this and strengthen your connection with Bear Goddess, include garlic in your diet today (or, if you're a really devoted garlic fan, add it to one meal a day for one hundred days)!

Should you need improved tranquillity, try visualizing yourself in a deep cave (this is Bear Goddess's womb). Stay here as long as you wish in your meditations until the quiet solitude saturates your inner self.

Finally, for any personal transformation you need to undertake, carry any image of a bear with you. This will inspire Bear Goddess's tenacity for success.

October 4

Saint Francis Day (Italy)

HYBLA

Themes: Earth; Ecology; Nature; Animals

Symbols: All Natural Objects

About Hybla: This Sicilian goddess presides over earth and nature, tending to all its needs. She also gave birth to humanity and inspires greater earth awareness within us.

To Do Today: Saint Francis of Assisi's life is celebrated today because of his gentle relationship with nature, which he considered a family member (often calling animals "brothers and sisters"). This is why he became the patron of many environmentalists. To remember him and honor Hybla's spirit, which he so powerfully displayed, say a prayer for the earth today. Invoke Hybla's nurturing energy with words like these:

> Earth Mother, look upon your child. Look upon
> the plants—restore the earth's greenery. Look upon
> the animals and protect them from more harm.
> Look upon the waters and purify each drop. Look
> upon the winds, and cleanse the air. Take the
> world gently in your caring arms, and love it back
> into wholeness once more. Amen.

Tuck a flower petal or leaf in your pocket or shoe today to keep Hybla's earth awareness close by. And, if you have pets, today is the perfect time to bless them. Give them special foods, find nonchemical pest repellents, and pamper them with extra love. Remember, life is a network: showing kindness to one strand extends that energy outward to the web.

October 5

❦

Carnival of Flowers (Australia)

RAINBOW SNAKE

Themes: Beauty; Life; Joy; Fertility; Tradition; Children; Health

Symbols: Flowers; Rainbows; Rainwater; Pearls

About the Rainbow Snake: This Aborigine goddess, also sometimes called Julunggul, represents the fertile rains and the waters in the seas. According to tradition, she flows into people's lives, bringing children, joy, the knowledge of magical healing arts, and protection for sacred traditions.

To Do Today: The city of Queensland, Australia, blossoms around this time of year in a colorful array of flowers. This carnival honors the joy of living, something the Rainbow Snake embodies. If you have floral prints, definitely wear them today to inspire the Rainbow Snake's ability to flow and adapt, using beauty and happiness as a powerful coping mechanism.

If it rains today it is a sign of this goddess's blessing. Release your inner child and dance in the downpour. Jump in puddles and let her fertile, productive energy splash freely all over your life and everything around you.

To internalize a little of the Rainbow Snake's attributes, collect rainwater in a clean pan on or around this date, then steep some edible flower petals (like roses) in the water. Drink or cook with this today so her power can blossom in your heart.

October 6

❦

Whole Enchilada Festival (New Mexico)

ÇHICOMECOATL

Themes: Fire; Providence; Energy; Community; Abundance; Fertility; Strength

Symbols: Hot Spices (especially chili peppers); Corn; Fire

About Çhicomecoatl: In Mexico, this goddess presides over maize and all matters of plenty during this time of harvest. Çhicomecoatl is also the hearth goddess and provides warmth, energy, and fertility to those in need. Her fiery, strong character is depicted vibrantly in artistic renderings, in which Çhicomecoatl bears the sun as a shield.

To Do Today: Around this time of year, people in New Mexico enjoy a day of taste-testing a ten-foot-long enchilada in a communal atmosphere, and you might like to follow suit. The hot spices in enchiladas (or other Mexican foods you like) motivate Çhicomecoatl's fire within for physical and emotional warmth. If you're sensitive to hot peppers, add corn to your diet today instead. This invokes the goddess's strength and fertility.

More simply still, Çhicomecoatl abides in any fire source. So, light a candle first thing in the morning to welcome her into your home today. For portable magic, carry matches or put a lighter in your pocket. Throughout the day, light a match or the lighter whenever you need a boost of energy or vitality, or when you need to improve your communications with those around you. This action also draws Çhicomecoatl's attention to your financial needs.

October 7

❦

Kermeese (Germany)

WEIBEN FRAUEN

Themes: Banishing; Blessing; Joy; Protection; Fertility; Divination

Symbols: Any Sacred Symbol; Forest Items; White

About Weiben Frauen: Known as "White Woman" of the German forests, this goddess is said to have been worshiped by ancient pagans and witches where she lived—in the woods. In later times, people looked to her to predict the future, help with matters of fertility, and protect the land.

To Do Today: This unique festival dates back to pagan worship of the grove goddess (and pagan gatherings in the woodlands). Traditionally, some type of sacred symbol is dug up and carried around town to renew blessings and happiness in all who see it. The ritual also banishes evil influences. To follow this custom, plant a white stone or token in a flowerpot, garden, or lawn this year, and next year dig it up temporarily to release White Woman's power. At the end of the day, return the token to the earth so she can protect your home or land and fill every corner of it with magic. Repeat this annually to continue the cycle!

Wear something white today to invite Weiben Frauen's protection on the figurative land of your spirit, and spend some time in the company of trees at some point. Meditate on the pagans, who weaved magic in such places, and on this goddess, who empowered the spells. As you do, listen closely to the voices of the trees and see if they have a message for you.

October 8

❧✦❧

Festival of High Places (China)

BIXIA YUANJIN

Themes: Air; Protection; Luck; Freedom; Birth; Movement

Symbols: Wind; Clouds; Kites; Chrysanthemum Petals

About Bixia Yuanjin: A weather goddess who lives in cloudy high places, Bixia Yuanjin attends each person's birth to bestow good health and luck upon the child. She is also a wind deity, helping to liberate and motivate us with fall's gently nudging winds.

To Do Today: During midautumn, the Chinese take to nearby hills and fly kites to commemorate a sage, Huan Ching, who saved villagers from disaster by instructing them to take to high places, thereby protecting them from a mysterious plague. So, consider doing likewise today, even if it means just climbing a ladder! Move up off the ground, breath deeply of Bixia Yuanjin's fresh airs, and discover renewed wellness.

If you feel adventurous, chrysanthemum wine and cakes are traditional feast fare for longevity and good fortune. An alternative is steeping chrysanthemum petals in water and then adding the strained water to any soups, juices, or other water-based foods and beverages for a similar effect.

Should the winds be with you, fly a kite named after a burden and liberate yourself in the winds. Also, carefully observe the shapes in the clouds today. If you have a pressing question on your heart, Bixia Yuanjin can answer it through these, her messengers.

October 9

❧

Grandparents' Day (*Massachusetts*)

HOLDA

Themes: Longevity; Wisdom; Kinship; Magic; Destiny; Karma

Symbols: White Items; Aged Items

About Holda: Among the Teutons, Holda is known as the White Lady, an appellation that alludes to the color of her hair. This goddess is the wise, ancient crone, who has learned the lessons of destiny and karma from a long, well-lived life and who bears the knowledge of magic's deeper mysteries to us with patience and time.

To Do Today: In Massachusetts, the first Sunday in October is set aside to honor grandparents and their vital role in families. Customarily, grandparents (or "adopted" ones) are invited for dinner and showered with attention. I think this is a lovely tradition as it stands, honoring Holda's wisdom through the elders in our community. Go to a nearby nursing home and spend half an hour or more cheering up someone. Listen to people's stories of days gone by, and let their insights inspire you.

To improve your own awareness of karmic law, or to increase your magical insights, wear Holda's white (a scarf on your head would be good) or carry a white stone with you to represent her (coral is ideal, being a stone of wisdom). Alternatively, eat some aged cheese or drink aged wine to remind yourself that "old" doesn't mean outmoded. People can become better with time and with Holda's guidance, if we remember to appreciate the years and the people who have gone before us on this path.

October 10

※※※

White Sunday (*Samoa*)

RA'I RA'I

Themes: Children; Youthfulness; Recreation; Play; Joy; Fairies

Symbols: Sunlight; White or Pastel-Yellow Items

About Ra'i Ra'i: In Polynesia, Ra'i Ra'i is the goddess of unbridled happiness and sunshine, lighting the way for truly joyful living. When Rai Rai came to earth to mother the first humans, she brought with her tiny frolicsome fairies who lived in the elements, often playing with people and watching over nature.

To Do Today: Follow Samoan tradition and wear white to inspire your inner child, then go enjoy the children in and around your life. In this part of the world, the entire day today is dedicated to children and activities to promote their delight.

Go for a nature walk and look for signs of Ra'i Ra'i's fairy friends. Small circles of mushrooms, a ring of trees, the sound of tiny bells all indicate the fey are nearby watching you!

Get outside and allow this goddess's warm light into your body through the sun today. If the weather isn't cooperating, wear any golden or pastel-yellow items today as a type of color therapy to inspire Ra'i Ra'i's youthful energy within.

Definitely take time to do something frisky today. If there's a recreational activity you enjoy, go play! This invokes Ra'i Ra'i's happiness and pleases this goddess greatly.

October 11

Han'gul day (Korea)

TI CHIH HSING CHUN

Themes: Learning; Communication; Karma; History

Symbols: All Alphabets; Paper and Pen or Pencil

About Ti Chih Hsing Chun: This goddess is record keeper of heaven in this part of the world, making detailed notes of all good and evil deeds. As such, she makes us more aware of the importance of effective communication and keeping accurate histories. Ti Chih Hsing Chun also reminds us of how our actions (or inaction) affect all things, helping us get our karma back in balance.

To Do Today: This day commemorates the origination of the Korean alphabet, which became the official writing system and heralded a new age of development for the Korean people. Koreans traditionally practice handwriting (or calligraphy) on this day, which for us translates into carefully tending to your personal journal or book of shadows (your personal spell and ritual collection). As you write, invoke the goddess's aid for accuracy. Also review the notes you've made thus far this year. Ti Chih Hsing Chun lives in those words and will show you how much your spirit has grown toward true goddess-centered living. This awareness inspires hope, which in turn will energize your efforts through the next two months.

Finally, consider learning a new alphabet type today, such as the runes. These magical sigils provide all types of symbols to empower your spells, and they can become useful tools in expressing ideas not easily communicated with words.

October 12

❦

Festival of Fortuna Redux (Rome)

FORTUNA REDUX

Themes: Travel; Good Fortune; Success; Fate

Symbols: Chamomile; Oak

About Fortuna Redux: This aspect of Fortuna specifically watches over all travelers, especially now that the weather might make for unsafe conditions. Whenever you travel, she goes with you to make a happier, luckier journey filled with success. She can also give you predictions about what to expect during your travels.

To Do Today: If you've been thinking about planning a trip, today is the perfect time to start. Fortuna Redux will make sure you get good connections, directions, hotels, or whatever you need so your journey will go off without a hitch.

No matter where you have to go today, you can take this goddess's blessing with you simply by carrying some chamomile tea bags or placing an oak leaf in your shoe. This invokes her protection on your car, the bus, train, or any other mode of transportation to help you avoid mishaps and traffic jams en route! Better still, if the day gets hectic, you can drink the tea for improved luck!

To see what the future holds in terms of travel, try sprinkling some loose chamomile over a damp surface (ideally your car's hood). Look to see what patterns emerge. If the flowers form an octagon, for example (the shape of a stop sign), this might be a message to stop your plans temporarily. If they form a wheel, the pattern could be interpreted as an omen to travel by car or bus.

October 13

Fountanalia (Rome)

FONS

Themes: Water; Wishes; Thankfulness; Healing

Symbols: Fountains; Water Sources

About Fons: This Roman goddess of fountains holds a special place in today's festivities, when people gather around her in the spirit of community gratitude for the refreshment that Fons provides in all seasons.

To Do Today: This ancient Roman festival gives thanks for fresh drinking water, and many of its traditions are easily assimilated. For example, customarily, fresh flowers were tossed in flowing water sources to thank the spirit of Fons that abides therein. So, toss a flower into your hose water, a stream, or a fountain. Or, float a flower atop a beverage today to honor Fons as part of that drink.

Fons's waters are also known for healing, cleansing, and wish granting. To generate well-being, include as many water-based foods and beverages in your diet today as possible. This allows you to partake of Fons's healing powers. For wishes, give the goddess a token (like a coin or flower petals) and whisper your desire to her waters. For cleansing, take a hot bath or shower so her waters will carry away your tensions.

Finally, you might want to focus on improving your water supply today. Buy a water filter, get some bottled water, bless your water jugs, or do something else along these lines so that Fons can cleanse and purify everyone in your home.

October 14

❧

Interplanetary Confederation Day
(United States)

HINE TURAMA

Themes: Unity; Cooperation; Universal Law; Sky

Symbols: Stars; Spaceships (or artistic depictions of space)

About Hine Turama: The Maori of New Zealand believed that this goddess created the stars that fill our night skies with such beauty. Today we look to her to expand our awareness of the universe and its wonders and possibilities.

To Do Today: For UFO enthusiasts, this is a festival for looking outward with hope and appreciation. Within Hine Turama's Milky Way alone, the earth shares space with numerous other planets with the potential for life. So, celebrate the potentials in the universe! Read a book by Carl Sagan or watch *Star Trek* or another science-fiction program or movie tonight, then go outside and look up! Count Hine Turama's stars; each one represents an aspect of human potential. Reach outward and upward, letting her silvery light fill you with hopefulness. Make a wish on the first star you see for improved awareness and unity among people no matter their place of origin.

During the day, wear silver- or white-toned clothing and jewelry to strengthen your connection to this sky goddess. If you hold a ritual today, consider covering a black robe with glow-in-the-dark stars (you can buy these at nature shops inexpensively)—it makes a really neat effect when you dance in a circle. You then become the center of swirling stars and Hine Turama's energy!

October 15

🪶

Thanksgiving (Canada)

GAIA

Themes: Abundance; Providence; Thankfulness; Nature; Divination; Promises; Earth

Symbols: Harvested Foods (especially fruit and grain); Soil

About Gaia: In Greek tradition, Gaia stretched out at the beginning of time, becoming the earth's land. In this form, she continues to give life and sustenance to all things that dwell in and on the planet, even when the cold weather tries to steal away that life. So sacred are Gaia's soils that any promise made with one hand on the earth is irrevocable. The oracle at Delphi belonged to Gaia before Apollo took over, giving her the additional attribute of prophesy.

To Do Today: The thanksgiving theme among Canadians is much the same as in the United States; it's a time of expressing gratitude to the earth and the heavens for their ongoing providence. Enjoy a robust feast of harvested edibles today to internalize Gaia's blessings and foresight. Remember to give thanks to the creatrix of your feast before eating! Also consider following Greek custom by leaving Gaia an offering of barley, honey, or cakes in an opening in the earth. This show of gratitude inspires Gaia's fertility in the coming months and years.

To help keep yourself true to a promise, carry a few pinches of soil with you in a sealed container today. If you sense your resolve waning, release a little back to Gaia. This invokes her strength and sense of duty.

October 16

🐝

World Food Day (United Nations)

ANNAPURNA

Themes: Providence; Prosperity; Charity

Symbols: Corn; Grain

About Annapurna: This Indian grain goddess is kind and charitable, providing food to those in need. According to tradition, Annapurna watches over the world's storehouses when supplies wane, and over the storehouse of our soul when our spirits hunger.

To Do Today: The United Nations created this holiday to draw public attention to the world's food problems and promote cooperation among people to battle hunger and poverty.

Today is an excellent time to give some canned goods to a local food pantry or shelter, especially corn or grain products. The canning process preserves Annapurna's energy for providence to help those less fortunate turn their lives around in powerful ways, or at least to reclaim some sense of dignity. Say a brief prayer over the goods before giving them away so the goddess's blessing will inspire renewal for those in need.

To keep Annapurna's providence in your home, take any grain product and sprinkle it around the outside perimeter of the dwelling. The birds will carry your need to the goddess. If you must perform this spell indoors, sweep up the grain in a clockwise manner and keep it in an airtight container to preserve its positive energy. Release a pinch of this to a northerly wind any time you need money quickly.

October 17

✦

Buchmesse (Germany)

NAT

Themes: Learning; Knowledge; Communication

Symbols: Books; Writing Utensils; Stars

About Nat: A Teutonic goddess of the night sky, Nat generates artistic inspiration and knowledge. She refreshes those suffering from creative blockages and arouses new visions for any endeavor, especially when fall's declining energies get the best of us. Myths portray Nat as bearing the silver-studded night sky like a blanket across the dusk. Her chariot bears a frost mare, alluding to the moon.

To Do Today: Buchmesse is the world's largest book fair for the publishing industry, featuring exhibitors from over ninety countries and attended by over two hundred thousand people. In this region of the world, book fairs have been around for over eight hundred years, making Germany one of the centers of world literacy.

For writers, today is the perfect time to ask for Nat's blessing on your efforts. Submit a poem, article, or manuscript to potential publishers. Write in your journal. Draft a meaningful ritual for improved creativity, and let Nat's energy guide your hand. Alternatively, read a favorite poem or book—Nat's power is beneath those words—or make a book donation to the local library to honor this goddess's contribution to human civilization.

Finally, gather all your pens and pencils in a basket and empower them for all your writing tasks by saying,

> Nat, inspire creativity;
> when taken to hand, the magic is freed!

October 18

Festival of Lights (Brazil)

PERIMBO

Themes: Forgiveness; Religious Devotion; Banishing; Justice; Karma

Symbols: Light; Lunar Emblems

About Perimbo: This Brazilian goddess is the creatrix of all things. From her home in the moon, Perimbo gently guides human life in benevolent ways. Balancing this kindness, she is also a goddess of justice, meting out karmic punishment to teach important lessons when necessary.

To Do Today: During mid-October, the city of Belem in Brazil holds a parade in which people go barefoot, carrying weights and lights to banish evil, sin, and negativity from their lives. To adapt this in a simple way and draw Perimbo's benevolence into your living space, take a flashlight, candle, or long-stemmed match clockwise around your house, saying,

> Perimbo, shine the light of fairness and devotion throughout my home.

Try to make sure the light reaches as many nooks and crannies as possible, symbolically banishing the shadows that hide there.

For a portable Perimbo charm to inspire equity in all your dealings, find a glow-in-the-dark image of the moon. Charge it up for several hours using sunlight or the flashlight from the previous spell, saying instead,

> Perimbo, shine the light of fairness and devotion throughout my life.

Carry this in your pocket to radiate the goddess's power no matter where you may be.

October 19

❦

Bettar-tchi (Japan)

YAMA-NO-SHINBO

Themes: Luck; Wealth; Prosperity; Protection; Joy

Symbols: Good-Luck Charms

About Yama-no-Shinbo: This Japanese goddess of prosperity and good fortune joins in today's festivities by blessing all efforts to improve our luck. Her name means "mother of the mountain," which, in feng shui (the art of placement in accordance with a region's energy patterns for the most beneficial result), represents a protective, ancient power that brings happiness and wealth to those within its shadow.

To Do Today: This annual festival takes place near the shrine of Ebisu to encourage good luck. Sticky items are among the favored tokens carried today, to encourage good fortune to literally stick to the participants. For our purposes this might translate into using double-sided tape inside a piece of clothing so that the outside can gather Yama-no-Shinbo's fortunate energy. Alternatively, put a symbol of an area of your life that needs better luck (such as a dollar bill for money) on the refrigerator with a magnet, while whispering a brief prayer to the goddess. This action symbolizes prosperity sticking with you (and attracting right energy).

Take out any tokens or objects around your home that you value for their lucky energy. Clean them off, and ask Yama-no-Shinbo to energize them anew for protection. Put your hands over the tops of these, visualize a personally lucky–colored light filling them, and say,

> *Goddess of fortune, fill this charm;*
> *keep me ever safe from harm.*

October 20

❦

Boomerang Festival (*Virginia*)

SRINMO

Themes: Karma; Universal Law; Excellence; Sports; Cycles

Symbols: Wheel; Boomerang

About Srinmo: In Tibet, this goddess holds the Great Round, a cosmic wheel upon which the movement of human life is recorded with each thought, word, and deed. Srinmo's demonic visage represents the human fear of death and reminds that one should strive for good in this life for the beauty it brings now and in our next incarnation.

To Do Today: In Virginia, this is a competitive festival of skill centering on the ancient boomerangs believed to have been used originally by the Egyptians.

Metaphysically speaking, the boomerang's movement represents the threefold law and Srinmo's karmic balance (i.e., everything you send out returns to you thrice). To give yourself a greater understanding of this principle, or to recognize the cycles in your life that may need changing, carry any round object today, such as a coin. Put it in your pocket, saying,

> *What goes around comes around.*

Pay particular attention to your routine and the way you interact with people all day, and see what Srinmo reveals to you.

For aiding the quest for enlightenment, and generally improving karma through light-filled living, try this little incantation in the car each time you make a right-hand turn today:

> *As I turn to the right,*
> *I move closer to the Light!*

October 21

✥

Misisi Beer Festival (Uganda)

MEME

Themes: Ghosts; Joy; Health; Offerings; Longevity; Harvest

Symbols: Beer; Corn

About Meme: The Ugandan creatrix of life, Meme was also the first woman of the region. In her human form she taught shamans the art of healing, and she continues to be called upon to aid in all matters of health and well-being.

To Do Today: This festival takes place right after the millet harvest, with a plethora of beer, maize, plantain, bullock, and chicken. Any of these foods can be added to your diet today in thankfulness for Meme's providence.

Follow Ugandan custom and join with your family or friends. The eldest member of the gathering should pour a libation to the ground in Meme's name and then offer the rest to those gathered. This mini-ritual ensures long life and unity for everyone. It also ensures a good harvest the next year (of a literal or figurative nature).

To inspire Meme's health or request her aid in overcoming a specific fall malady, carry a corn kernel with you today, and consume corn during your dinner meal. Bless the corn beforehand to ingest this goddess's vitality. Alternatively, take a small bowl of beer and place a finger into it. Channel your negativity and illness into the beer (visualize this as dark, muddy water leaving your body), then pour it out to disperse that negative energy and give it into the goddess's care.

October 22

❦

Hi Matsuri (Japan)

IZU NO ME MO KAMI

Themes: Mediation; Health; Cleansing

Symbols: Fire or Water

About Izu no me mo Kami: A goddess of purification, Izu no me mo Kami helps us prepare for the sacred festivals of late fall and early winter with her cleansing power. While she was born in water, this goddess's energy exists in any rites for purification, including those centered on fire.

To Do Today: This is a fire festival in Japan designed to welcome and help people commune with the native deities who come to earth this day. People carry light sources like candles and torches, which offer Izu no me mo Kami's purifying energies to the meeting. In this part of the world it is considered unseemly to go before the gods spiritually or physically dirty.

In keeping with this theme, take a ritual bath today before your daily prayers or meditations. Add cleansing herbs like pine needles, bay leaves, fennel, lemon rind, or mint. Alternatively, drop in a few herbal tea bags (like peppermint or chamomile) to keep the dried items from clogging the drain. Before getting in, stir the water counterclockwise, saying,

> Goddess of cleansing power, purify me this sacred hour.
> Remove all guilt, all blame or shame.
> I ask this by invoking your name: Izu no me mo Kami.

Keep whispering the goddess's name at regular intervals until you get out of the tub. Then enter your prayers and meditations with a purified mind, heart, and spirit.

October 23

❦

Scorpio Begins (*Various Locations*)

ISARA

Themes: Creativity; Sexuality; Passion; Instinct; Fire; Energy

Symbols: Scorpion (or any stinging, hot items)

About Isara: An ancient Mesopotamian goddess, Isara is known for her fiery nature. The Syrians specifically worshiped her in the form of a scorpion when they wished to improve sexual prowess or passion. In other traditions, Isara judges human affairs fairly but firmly, and all oaths made in her name are sacred.

To Do Today: In astrology, people born under the sign of Scorpio are said to be creative, tenacious, sturdy, and sensuous, often internalizing Isara's fire in their sign for personal energy. To do likewise, enjoy any hot beverages (such as coffee with a touch of cinnamon for vitality) first thing in the morning. This will give you some of Isara's fire to help you face your day, both mentally and physically.

For those wishing to improve interest or performance in the bedroom, today is a good time to focus on foods for passion and fecundity. Look to bananas or avocados in the morning, olives, dill pickles, radishes, or licorice sticks as a snack, beans as a dinner side dish, and shellfish as a main platter. Remember to invoke Isara's blessing before you eat. And, if you can find one, put the image of a scorpion under your bed so that Isara's lusty nature will abide in the region and you can tap into it during lovemaking.

October 24

✦

United Nations Day (*Various Locations*)

EURYNOME

Themes: Unity; Peace; Balance

Symbol: Sacred Dancing

About Eurynome: This ancient Greek goddess reached out to the chaos at the beginning of time, embraced it, and made order in the world. Through her sacred dance, the winds were born, from her womb came the land and stars, and then she created rulers for the poles (one male, one female) so that balance would forever be maintained.

To Do Today: On October 24, 1945, the peace-keeping United Nations was formally established in the orderly spirit of Eurynome to stress the need for understanding between people and the power of working for a unified cause. To honor this occasion and uplift Eurynome's positive energies, gather today with any group that you work with regularly. Do something together that focuses on your power as a group to really make a difference in one another, your community, or the world.

To bring Eurynome's organization and balance into your home, take a small bowl filled with water and three drops each of one male-oriented herbal oil (like cedar, clove, lavender, mint, or pine) and one female-oriented oil (like apple, coconut, jasmine, lemon, or vanilla). Put on some inspiring music, dance joyfully around your living space, and sprinkle this water as you go to draw Eurynome's blessing to you.

October 25

Sweetest Day (United States)

FELICITAS

Themes: Kindness; Charity; Love; Romance; Joy; Success; Luck

Symbols: Greetings (greeting cards)

About Felicitas: This Roman goddess brings happiness, success, and good fortune whenever someone salutes another with good words or amiable deeds. She comes to us today to energize late fall and early winter with the transformational power of kindness.

To Do Today: While Sweetest Day seems to be focused on lovers these days, in earlier years it represented an opportunity to shower anyone and everyone with cheerful trinkets, kind acts, and gentle words to lift people's spirits. By looking to Felicitas for help, we can return this holiday to its original form and bring joy to people who might otherwise be feeling a case of autumn blues. Look for, or make, some humorous greeting cards to send to folks you know would appreciate the thought. Lay your hands on them and invoke Felicitas's blessing in any way that feels right.

To improve the effect further, anoint the cards with rejuvenating aromatic oils that match the recipient's needs (such as pine for money, rose for love or peace, cinnamon for luck, sandalwood for health, and lavender to combat depression). This way, when they open that card, the magic and the aroma will be released together to bless, energize, and bear Felicitas's greetings along with your heartfelt wishes!

October 26

Birthday of the Earth (*Various Locations*)

TELLUS MATER

Themes: Earth; Ecology; Promises; Abundance; Prosperity; Fertility

Symbols: Globe; Soil; Grain

About Tellus Mater: The Roman earth mother celebrates today's festivities by sharing of her abundance, being a goddess of vegetation, reproduction, and increase. In regional stories, Tellus Mater gave birth to humans, which is why bodies are returned to the soil at death—so they can be reborn from her womb anew.

To Do Today: According to James Ussher, a seventeenth-century Anglican archbishop, God created the earth on October 26, 4004 B.C.E. While this date is uncertain at best, it gives us a good excuse to honor Tellus Mater and hold a birthday party on her behalf. Make a special cake for the earth mother out of natural fertilizers. Take this to a natural setting (don't forget the candle). Light the candle and make a wish for the earth's renewal, then blow it out, remove the candle, and bury your gift for Tellus Mater in the soil, where it can begin manifesting your good wishes!

While you're outside, pick up a pinch of soil, a stone, or any natural object that strikes your eye and keep it close. This is a part of Tellus Mater, and it will maintain her power for abundance wherever you go today. It will also help you stay close to the earth mother and honor the living spirit of earth in word and deed.

October 27

Allan Apple Day (England)

I D U N A

Themes: Love; Divination; Dreams; Longevity

Symbols: Apples

About Iduna: This Teutonic goddess of longevity and love was born of flowers and lives in Asgard, protecting the magical apples of immortality. The wife of Braggi, a poetic god, she joins in today's festival with her apples and Braggi's kind words to ensure lasting love.

To Do Today: Follow Cornwall customs. Polish an apple today, sleep with it under your pillow, and ask Iduna to bring you sweet dreams of love. At dawn, rise without speaking to anyone and go outside. The first person you see is said to be a future spouse (or friend, for those who are already married).

All types of apple magic are suited to this day. Peel an apple while thinking of a question and toss it over your shoulder. Whatever symbol or letter the peel forms represents your answer. Eat the apple, then try composing some love poems for that special someone in your life!

Drink apple juice first thing in the morning, blessing it in Iduna's name, to improve your communications with all your loved ones. Enjoy a slice of apple pie at lunch to bring sweetness to your relationships and improve self-love. Come dinner, how about a side of applesauce to keep relationships smooth and empowered by Iduna's staying power?

October 28

Saffron Rose Festival (Spain)

EOS

Themes: Wealth; Love; Joy; Health; Fertility; Leadership; Passion; Beauty

Symbol: Saffron

About Eos: In Indo-European tradition, Eos is a sky goddess who offers us dawn's hopeful, renewing energy. Greek stories tell of Eos's intense beauty, which inspires passion. As a faithful consort and fertile divinity, she also ensures us of productivity and devoted love.

To Do Today: Saffron is the world's most expensive herb, and on the last Sunday in October, people in Consuegra, Spain, honor the crop with folk dances and pageantry. Magically speaking, saffron embodies Eos's loving, joyful, healthy, and fertile powers, which is why it was sacred to her. So, consider getting up at dawn and adding a few strands of saffron to your morning tea to bring renewed hope.

Later in the day, consume saffron rice to internalize any of Eos's attributes. Or, carry a container of saffron as a charm to manifest passion, inspire inner beauty, and motivate positive financial improvements.

The ancients also used saffron to dye the robes of kings, giving it associations with leadership. So, if you need to improve your sense of control or authority in any situation, integrate something with a saffron hue into your wardrobe today. The color's vibrations strengthen self-confidence and generate the administrative skills you need.

October 29

Kartika Snan (India)

ARAMATI

Themes: Cleansing; Religious Devotion; Offering; Beauty; Banishing; Meditation; Prayer

Symbols: Water; Fire; All Acts of Veneration

About Aramati: Translated, Aramati's name means "piety." So it is that this Indian goddess embodies the attributes of religious devotion and selflessness through which a person reaches higher states of awareness and returns to oneness with the Sacred Parent. According to tradition, Aramati protects people during worship.

To Do Today: Kartika is the Hindu name for the period between October and November, and it is considered a sacred month in which acts of piety will be rewarded. Bathing in streams, wells, or any running water source early this morning brings Aramati's purification and inner beauty. Afterward, it's customary to pray and meditate for the goddess's blessings and assistance in being faithful to one's religious studies and goals.

If you hold any rituals today, or cast spells, consider asking Aramati to safeguard your working area from unwanted influences and to guide the magic for the greatest good. Finally, keeping lamps burning today drives away evil influences that may hinder or trip up your path. Perhaps leave one lit near your altar, religious tools, or any goddess image. This action honors Aramati and invokes her ongoing protection in your sacred space of home.

October 30

Angelitos Day (Mexico)

TONACACIHUATL

Themes: Ghosts; Death; Hope

Symbols: Flowers; All Symbols of Death

About Tonacacihuatl: In Mexico this goddess's name means "Our Lady of Flesh." Tonacacihuatl is a creatrix who gives life to all things and to whom the spirits of children return at death.

To Do Today: Part of a weeklong festival for the dead, Angelitos Day is specifically focused on departed children. If there is a child who has passed over and who was special to you somehow, make cakes or foods that feature symbols of death and leave them in a special spot. This invites Tonacacihuatl to release that child's spirit for the day and welcomes the souls of the departed to the festival.

Put out the child's picture in a place of honor with a candle nearby to help light their way. Cook and eat the young one's favorite foods, leave a lamp lit near your threshold, and strew flowers (especially marigolds or dandelions) on the walkway to guide the child's spirit back home.

According to tradition, eating hen or chicken today ensures a visitation by ghosts, because then the bird can't crow loudly and frighten away the spirits! In all due caution, however, you might want to keep a little salt, violet petals, sage, or ginseng handy to banish any unwanted ghostly guests.

October 31

Halloween (*Various Locations*)

NICNEVEN

Themes: Protection; Ghosts; Divination; Peace; Winter

Symbols: Pumpkins; Gourds; Traditional Halloween Fare

About Nicneven: In Scotland, Nicneven is the crone goddess of Samhain, which is the predecessor of modern Halloween festivals. Nicneven governs the realms of magic and witchcraft and also represents the imminent onset of winter.

To Do Today: In magic and Celtic traditions, this is the new year—a time when the veil between worlds grows thin and spirits can communicate with the living. Follow the usual customs of carving a pumpkin or turnip for protection and to illuminate the way for family spirits to join you in today's celebrations.

In druidical tradition, Samhain was a time to rectify any matters causing dissent. Nicneven provides the magical glue for this purpose. Take a white piece of paper on which you've written the reason for anger in a relationship, then burn it in any hallowed fire source (the pumpkin candle, or ritual fires). As you do, ask Nicneven to empower the spell and destroy the negativity completely.

To inspire Nicneven's wisdom or magical aptitude within, enjoy traditional Halloween fare—apple pie, for example, brings sagacity. Sparkling apple cider tickles magical energy. And root crops provide solid foundations and protection while magical creatures are afoot!

November

While November is the eleventh month on modern calendars, it was once the ninth, as evidenced by the Latin number *novem*. In the United States, November contains one of the oldest national holidays—Thanksgiving. Actually, festivals of gratitude combine with late harvest festivals in many parts of the world; at this time people pray for divine providence and give thanks for the earth's bounty. Other predominant festivals during early winter months include commemorative rites for the dead and rituals that protect individuals or whole communities from evil influences.

For people living in four-season climates, the snows begin to accumulate and winter winds decorate the windows with frosty reminders of the outside chill. Because of this, magic for continued health is fitting during November, as are spells and charms for protection. Wintery months also seem to be a time for introspection—to use divination tools for foresight and preparation, to seek guidance within, and to ask the Goddess for a special spiritual vision to carry us through the last months of the year.

November 1

❋

Author's Day (United States)

NISABA

Themes: Creativity; Communication; Excellence; Inspiration; Universal Law; Divination; Dreams

Symbols: Pens; Computers; Books; Snakes (her sacred animal)

About Nisaba: In Sumerian tradition, this goddess's name means "she who teaches the decrees," referring specifically to imparting divine laws to humankind. In order to communicate these matters effectively, Nisaba invented literacy, and she uses creative energy to inspire scribes. Besides this, Nisaba is an oracular goddess, well gifted in dream interpretation.

To Do Today: Since 1928, this day has been observed as a time to honor authors who have contributed to American literature and encourage new writers in their talents. If you're an aspiring author, today's definitely the time to submit a poem, article, or manuscript, invoking Nisaba's blessing on it before sending it out. Also take a moment to ask Nisaba to empower all your pens, pencils, resource books, computer, and so on, so that all your future writing efforts will be more successful and fulfilling.

For those who don't consider authorship a forte, you can ask Nisaba to give you a symbolic dream instead. Put a marigold, rose, or onion peel under your pillow to help with this, and keep a dream journal or tape recorder handy. Immediately upon waking, record any dream you recall. Then go to a favored dream guide (such as my *Language of Dreams*), and whisper the goddess's name before looking up interpretations.

November 2

All Soul's Day (*Various Locations*)

NEPHTHYS

Themes: Death; Ghosts; Rebirth; Devotion

Symbols: Sunset; Hawk (her sacred animal)

About Nephthys: Just as Isis embodies life's energies in Egypt, her sister Nephthys is the force of death and reincarnation. Traditionally, Nephthys dwells in tombs, guiding and welcoming spirits into the afterlife. Her name means "death which is not eternal," referencing the Egyptian belief in the soul's rebirth to a new existence.

To Do Today: Following on the heels of Hallows and All Saints' Day, this festival honors the faithful departed. In early times children would go "souling," collecting small cakes believed to rescue souls from purgatory. In keeping with this idea, go out at sunset to honor Nephthys with a small cake or cracker. Leave this in a natural location and ask the goddess to bring peace to any restless souls in her care.

Oddly enough, Romans announced engagements today (likely as a way of stressing life's continuance). So if you've been thinking of deepening a relationship, or making a commitment to a beloved project, this is one date that might suit the occasion. Again, go outside at sunset, and as the sun slips behind the horizon pray to the goddess. Tell her your goal or speak your pledges in her name. Ask her to rejuvenate your determination so that tomorrow you might be born anew to your task or relationship.

November 3

※

Inuit Autumn Festival (Alaska)

THREE KADLU SISTERS

Themes: Summer; Winter; Weather; Banishing

Symbols: Lightning; Thunder

About the Three Kadlu Sisters: Among the Inuit and several other northern tribes, these divine sisters rule the weather, so watch today's ritual closely to see what winter will be like! Children's stories claim that when the goddesses play together they make thunder and lightning.

To Do Today: Around this time of year, people in Alaska have a playful tug-of-war between winter and summer. Those born in winter take winter's side—those born in summer stand opposite. If the summer side winds, winter will be mild and goodness will prevail. This activity is fun for children, and it reinforces the idea of seasonal cycles. Place a ribbon in the middle of the tug rope with the name of these sisters painted upon it. When the game is over, see which side the goddess landed upon to know what the weather will be like!

If it rains today, it's a sign of the goddesses playing together, so get outside and join them (even if cold weather keeps this brief)! Thunder on your right tells of better days ahead. Thunder on your left warns that caution is prudent. Lightning stretching across the sky symbolizes your ability to likewise stretch and grow. Lightning in front of you represents your ability to go forward boldly with your plans, knowing these goddesses light your way.

Turning Devil's Boulder (England)

HENWEN

Themes: Peace; Prosperity; Fertility; Harvest

Symbols: Sow; Grain; Honey; Eagle; Wolf

About Henwen: This fertile British goddess appears in the form of a pregnant sow who births abundance in our lives. In mythology she wandered the countryside mothering grains, bees, cats, eagles, and wolves as she traveled. Henwen also presides over all physical and magical agricultural efforts.

To Do Today: In Devon village, England, there lies an old stone called the Devil's boulder. Legend says that during a battle, Satan flung this stone into the village. To keep peace and prosperity in the town and ensure continued good harvests, the stone must be turned annually. For us, this might translate into an annual furniture rearrangement, leaving one piece of grain in each piece to invoke Henwen's ongoing providence for your home.

To partake of Henwen's abundance and encourage your own nurturing nature, try eating a whole-grain toast for breakfast with honey (which comes from the goddess's bees!). Or enjoy a BLT for lunch and pork roast for dinner. Since the sow is Henwen's sacred animal, eating its meat symbolically allows you to "take in" this goddess's essence.

If you have indoor plants, ask Henwen to keep them green and growing by putting a piece of grain or small dab of honey in each pot. This will become part of the soil, nourishing the plant with Henwen's power.

✳

World Community Day (United States)

AXTIS

Themes: Peace; Justice; Victory

Symbols: White Items; Peace Sign; Charms; Tokens

About Axtis: This Iranian goddess's name means "victorious peace"—peace with ourselves, each other, and the world. The victory here comes from finding the right opportunity to create symmetry where only discord once dwelled.

To Do Today: Celebrated by Church Women United, this celebration encourages world peace and justice through proactive community service. Axtis's spirit permeates this festival and provides heartfelt comfort before winter moves into full swing.

To honor this idea and Axtis, do something in your area to likewise engender harmony. Help two warring neighbors take the first steps toward understanding. Get involved in a community campaign to improve local laws so they're equitable. Make a donation to any organization dedicated to fostering international peace. Meditate to find Axtis's peace within yourself; then extend that power outward to transform everything and everyone you touch.

Wear white today (the color of truce) and carry an amethyst, carnelian, or sodalite stone with you to generate harmony wherever you go. Keep your words serene today (try to keep your cool no matter what). This extends Axtis's gentle nature to others. You'll be surprised at how potent quiet discourse can be.

November 6

✳

Stewardship Sunday (United States/Canada)

VASUDHARA

Themes: Religious Devotion; Charity; Thankfulness; Abundance

Symbols: Cow; Golden Items

About Vasudhara: In India, this golden-breasted earth goddess provides us with enough abundance to be able to give back freely of what we receive. Vasudhara's golden color alludes to some solar attributes, including manifesting financial prosperity for those who call upon her. In her wealth-giving aspect, Vasudhara sometimes appears as a cow.

To Do Today: Around this date, many churches in the United States and Canada begin their annual fund-raising campaign by asking parishioners to give back a little of what the divine has given them. While many New Age practitioners don't belong to a church, this idea still holds merit and would please Vasudhara greatly. Donate a little money to a pagan defense fund, for example. Put on something gold to draw the goddess's prosperity back to you, then buy some good magic books for your library. The proceeds indirectly "give back" to the teachers whom you admire through royalties!

If your schedule allows, stop in at your favorite New Age store and volunteer an hour of your time to give back to the community. Write thank-you letters to people who have somehow touched your life deeply. Should any of these people live nearby, help them with chores or bring them a special dish for dinner. These acts of kindness are a type of stewardship that reflects Vasudhara's spirit by blessing others.

November 7

Sadie Hawkins Day (United States)

AHNT KAI

Themes: Balance; Femininity; Freedom; Protection; Fertility; Overcoming

Symbols: Fish; Sacred Music and Dancing

About Ahnt Kai: In Mexico this goddess of women and children taught them how to freely dance and sing, expressing the beauty within and liberating them from societal constraints. In myths of the Seris, Ahnt Kai specifically teaches the fish dance, alluding to fertility.

To Do Today: Sometime around the 1930s a comic-strip artist captured the image of Sadie Hawkins optimistically stepping outside the usual boundaries of "womanhood" to ask a man for a date. The custom continued through special dances for many decades, as people reveled in Ahnt Kai's liberating atmosphere. Thus, for both women and men, today is a time to free yourself from any restricting, stereotypical, negative, or outmoded images that originate with yourself, others, the media, or the public. Ahnt Kai's counsel today is to remember that true comeliness, true beauty, is not measured by externals—it begins within as we reunite ourselves with the goddess and learn to love ourselves just as we are.

Add fish to your diet today (maybe a tuna sandwich) to internalize self-love and begin the process of personal liberation. Name the meal after an attribute needed to overcome your constraints. Ask the goddess to bless your food, then eat with anticipation and self-confidence!

November 8

Festival of the Kitchen Goddess (Japan)

OKI TSU HIME

Themes: Fire; Providence; Kinship; Health

Symbols: All Fire Sources (especially those cooked upon); Boiling Water

About Oki Tsu Hime: Oki Tsu Hime is the Shinto goddess of kitchens in Japan. Here she watches over all foods prepared and over family interactions to keep health and emotional warmth in the home. Traditionally, any pot of boiling water represents this goddess's activity.

To Do Today: As in Japan, today is the perfect time to honor those people who prepare your food (even if it's *you!*). Give your kitchen goddess the day off and go out to eat. Or, alternatively, uplift the kitchen goddess's talents by preparing a truly sumptuous meal of all your family favorites. Leave a small portion of each course on or near your stove as an offering to Oki Tsu Hime. Later, put these tidbits in the compost, or outside for the birds, so the goddess's blessings will continue to generate good things.

Light a candle today, and get out some cleaning utensils to scrub the stove, toaster oven, or microwave so that Oki Tsu Hime's energy can really shine in the area where you prepare most of your meals. Symbolically, the cleaning process washes away sickness and negativity. Afterward, light or turn on that appliance for a moment to draw the kitchen goddess back to her honored place of residence.

November 9

※

Loy Krathog (Thailand)

PHRA NARET

Themes: Water; Wishes; Abundance; Wealth; Prosperity; Beauty; Luck

Symbols: Candles; Boats; Water

About Phra Naret: In Thailand (formerly Siam), Phra Naret is the goddess of good fortune, prosperity, and beauty. Having been born of water, she flows into today's festivities with fertility, abundance, and wealth.

To Do Today: This charming festival includes the launching of small boats filled with candles, incense, coins, and gardenias on a nearby river. According to tradition, should the candle stay lit until it flows out of sight, the launcher's wish will come true. You can re-create this by using a stream of hose water, a raft of popsicle sticks or plywood, and whatever tokens you want to give to Phra Naret to generate her luck in manifesting your wish. Just make sure you choose biodegradable items, since you need to let the raft flow out of your site so the magic can release itself. Anyone finding the wish boat will also be blessed with a wish and a little of Phra Naret's prosperity.

Drink plenty of fresh water to internalize Phra Naret's positive attributes today, and wash your floors with plain water so that her abundance and fertility will be absorbed into every part of your home. If you have plants, remember to give them a little water today too, so they can grow with this goddess's profusion.

Celebration of the Goddess of Reason (France)

THE GODDESS OF REASON

Themes: Logic; Reasoning; Learning; the Conscious Mind

Symbol: A Crown of Oak Leaves (representing the seat of the divine)

About the Goddess of Reason: While this lady had no other specific designation other than the Goddess of Reason, she dispenses the power of knowledge to those who seek her. The French honored this goddess with celebrations at Notre Dame, the world's most acclaimed center of scholarship. Traditionally, the woman depicting her wore a blue robe and red cap, then was crowned in laurel at the end of a processional.

To Do Today: To improve conscious awareness and logical abilities, tuck a bay leaf in your shoe today so the Goddess of Reason walks with you. Or, wear any garment with predominantly blue or red coloring to invoke her powers through color therapy!

Today is an excellent day to take up any course of study you've been considering. Burn incense blended from dried sage (for wisdom), rosemary (for memory improvement), and mint (for alertness). If possible, pre-prepare the incense at noon to accent conscious awareness and the rational self. Move your study tools through the smoke of the incense, saying,

> *Goddess of Reason, see my desire.*
> *Ignite in me knowledge's fire!*

Finally, wax an oak leaf (press it in waxed paper with an iron) and keep it in a book that you're studying. This keeps reason with you while you read.

November 11

✳

Lunantishees (Ireland)

OONAGH

Themes: Fairies; Nature; Devotion; Relationships

Symbols: All Fairy Plants; Silver; Dew

About Oonagh: This ancient Irish Queen of the Fairies is also a potent goddess of magic. In Irish legends, Oonagh is a faithful wife and the most beautiful of all goddesses, having long, silky hair and a robe of silver and dew. Today she brings the fey into our lives to remind us of the unseen worlds and to awaken the child within each of us that dares to dream and wish.

To Do Today: Sometime in November, the people of ancient Ireland celebrated a day for the "wee folk"—a time to revel in fairy folklore and superstition. We can honor Oonagh and her children by following suit. Today wear green, which is a favorite fairy color. Don some pleasant-sounding bells that tinkle lightly when you walk. Fairies love this sound. Or, carry a staurolite stone, also known as the fairy cross. This stone not only brings luck but also helps in controlling elemental beings such as the fey.

To see fairies today, find a four-leafed clover and lay seven kernels of grain beneath it. Or go to an area where oak, ash, and thorn trees grow together. This is said to be sacred ground for both the fey and Oonagh.

If you're concerned about fairy mischief, wear red for protection. Or, carry some flint as the Irish did to keep fairies at arm's length.

November 12

✳

Tesque Feast (Southeastern United States)

YELLOW WOMAN

Themes: Nature; Providence; Animals

Symbols: Yellow Items; Green Items; Embroidered Items

About Yellow Woman: This Pueblo goddess of magic, agriculture, and the hunt is also the heroine of many local stories, having taught humans important sacred ceremonies. Today she helps us remember these rituals and reintegrate them into our lives.

Art depicts Yellow Woman wearing an embroidered blanketdress, a green mask (revealing her connection to nature), and a white mantle. Sometimes she appears as a corn goddess and other times as a witch, bear, or ogress.

To Do Today: This is the time of the Buffalo Dance, which honors nature and mimes, an ancient hunting ritual thought to ensure a successful hunt. This dance is a type of sympathetic magic that also appeases the souls of the animals about to be captured. For our purposes, this equates to a kind of ritual mime in which we enact our hopes as realized, asking Yellow Woman to guide our movements so they will manifest in magic. For example, to improve self-love, give yourself a hug so you receive that energy. For relationships, open your arms wide so they await the right person (figuratively receiving a "good catch," which is in Yellow Woman's dominion too!).

To improve your awareness of the significance of ritual, eat corn today or wear yellow, white, and/or green clothing. Embroidered items also please this goddess.

November 13

✳

Ludi Plebeli (Rome)

FERONIA

Themes: Fertility; Abundance; Earth; Freedom; Sports; Recreation

Symbols: Fire; Coals

About Feronia: This Roman fire goddess provides fertility and abundance during even the harshest of times. When boredom sets in, she arrives with arms bearing festive energies and earth's riches as a "pick-me-up." According to Roman tradition, she is also the patroness and liberator of slaves, or of anything that allegorically enslaves us.

To Do Today: Every November 13, the Plebian games opened in Rome with all manner of sports competitions. This festival also honored the goddess Feronia and her liberating nature. Mirroring this theme, get outside and do something physical to release any anger or tension you bear. Give it into Feronia's care so she can transform it into healthful energy.

Carry a piece of coal today to generate a little of Feronia's abundance in all your efforts. Keeping this near your stove (or any fire source, like the heater) maintains this goddess's energy in your home year-round. If a day comes when you have a really pressing need, burn the coal in Feronia's liberating flames to release the magic for fast manifestation.

If you find your inner reserves waning with the winter's darkness, light a candle sometime today to invoke Feronia's vitality. Better still, light it for a few minutes each day until you feel your energy returning.

November 14

Asking Festival (*Alaska*)

PUKKEENEGAK

Themes: Kinship; Community; Thankfulness; Charity; Kindness

Symbols: Tattoos

About Pukkeenegak: This Inuit goddess presides over all household and community affairs. As a mother figure, she watches kindly over her children, making sure we have clothing and food. Art shows her with a tattooed face, boots, and a lovely dress befitting the patroness of seamstresses.

To Do Today: Among the Inuit, this is a time when youths go door to door gathering foods for a huge community feast. Afterward, people petition one another for gifts—exchanging the entire community's goods in the spirit of thanksgiving. So, orchestrate a gathering of people of a like mind for a potluck dinner at which Pukkeenegak is the guest of honor (leave a place setting for her).

Wear special clothing today that reflects the goddess's gift with needle and thread. Or organize a clothing drive so people can donate items they no longer need to a charitable cause. This way the goddess can bless each person who receives one of those garments with her providence!

If you've found your home or heart tense lately, invoke Pukkeenegak's unifying, steadying energy by drawing an emblem of peace over your heart chakra or on the back of your hand (use nontoxic markers or body paint). Leave it there until it naturally wears off, by which time the magic should show signs of manifesting.

Shich-go-San (Japan)

TATSU TA HIME

Themes: Children; Health; Luck; Thankfulness; Autumn; Blessing; Abundance; Protection

Symbols: Fall Leaves

About Tatsu ta Hime: This windy Japanese goddess blows into our lives today offering blessings and abundance for all our efforts. Tradition tells us that she weaves the fall leaves into a montage of color, then sweeps them away along with any late-fall maladies. Sailors often wear an amulet bearing her name to weather difficult storms at sea safely.

To Do Today: Also known as the 7–5–3 festival in Japan, this is a huge birthday celebration for children who have reached these ages. Parents take their young ones to local shrines for the goddesses' and gods' blessings. Here they receive a gift of rice for prosperity, and a bit of pink hard candy for a long life. If you have children, by all means follow this custom to draw Tatsu ta Hime's protective energies into their lives. Place some rice, a piece of pink candy, and a strand of the child's hair in a little sealed box. Write the goddess's name somewhere on the box to keep her blessing intact. Put this in the child's room or on the family altar.

To manifest this goddess's health and well-being, take several swatches of fabric bearing her name and sew them into various items of clothing, or carry one in your pocket. Should your day prove emotionally stormy, this little charm will keep you centered, calm, and "on course."

November 16

Dwali (India)

DHARANI

Themes: Luck; Abundance; Wealth; Beginnings

Symbols: Baskets (filled); Basil (sacred plant); Rice; Seedlings

About Dharani: In Indian mythology, Dharani is the wealth-providing, luck-bringing, abundant aspect of Lakshimi. This prosperity, which she freely offers to us when our storehouses grow scant, is potently portrayed in artistic renderings, which show her with an overflowing basket of rice or seedlings.

To Do Today: Around this time of year, people in India celebrate a festival of lights, which is the beginning of the Hindu new year. This festival also venerates Dharani in the hopes of getting the new year off to a really good start.

To invoke Dharani's good fortune, wash your floors, car, shoes, pets, and/or clothing with basil water to rid yourself of any lingering bad luck. Since basil is Dharani's sacred herb, it banishes any energy of which the goddess doesn't approve!

Light candles carved with your personal good-luck emblems so that the shadows in your life will flee. When the flame melts the image, Dharani's magic for good fortune is released (if you like, anoint that image with a little basil oil, too).

Finally, to bless anyone visiting your home or desk today, fill a basket with rice cakes, offering some to any passersby. This way you share the wealth and allow the goddess to bring her prosperity to many more lives.

Western Lights (China)

DOU MOU

Themes: Death; Ghosts; Divination; Health

Symbols: Sun; Moon; Star

About Dou Mou: Dou Mou is the Chinese goddess of the north star. To this day, people invoke Dou Mou to protect spirits of departed loved ones and to safeguard the living from sickness. From her heavenly domain between the sun and the moon, Dou Mou records each birth and death, and she is the patroness of fortune-tellers.

To Do Today: In mid-November, the Chinese celebrate the last of three festivals for the dead. Today they burn clothing for departed loved ones to keep them from death's chill, along with money and other gifts that the smoke delivers. If there's someone you'd like to send a message to on the other side, burn it. Dou Mou will transport it to their attention.

Because of today's focus on death and divination, you might wish to go to a medium today or try a fortune-telling method that uses spirits guides (like the Ouija). The only caution here is to invoke Dou Mou before you proceed, so only spirits that have your best interests at heart will respond. Just as you wouldn't leave your front door open to strangers, let the goddess stand firmly between you and the spirit realm.

To generate Dou Mou's protection for your health, wear silver and gold or white and yellow items today (representing the sun and the moon). Or dab yourself with lemon and lime juice for a similar effect.

Makahiki (Hawaii)

MATARIKI

Themes: Stars; Harvest; Peace

Symbols: Stars; the Number Seven

About Matariki: In Polynesian tradition, this goddess and her six children became the Pleiades, and they continue to help humans by showing us when to begin harvesting the labors of hand or heart.

To Do Today: From mid- to late November the people of Hawaii take part in special rituals to celebrate the appearance of the Pleiades in the skies, which is the beginning of harvest season. In reverence for this occasion, all war is forbidden. It makes one wish that Matariki and her children appeared around the world all the time!

To encourage similar peacefulness in your own life, and harmony with those around you, carry seven stars in your pocket, wallet, or purse today. You can draw these on paper, use seven typed asterisks, get the marshmallow kind out of a cereal box, or collect seven noodles from a chicken 'n' stars can. If you use edible items, eat them at the end of the day to bring serenity to your spirit.

If there's something you've been working on that seems to be taking forever, look to Matariki to show you how to begin effectively manifesting your efforts. Pray, meditate, and watch for unique openings throughout the day, especially after the stars appear in the sky, representing her power.

November 19

Equal Opportunity Day (*United States*)

T E N G A

Themes: Balance; Justice; Morality; Freedom

Symbol: Soil

About Tenga: Among the Mossi of Senegal, Tenga is a potent earth goddess who presides over all matters of justice and morality. Today she joins our celebration by offering to right wrongs and restore the balance in any area of our life that's gotten out of kilter.

To Do Today: This holiday commemorates Abraham Lincoln's Gettysburg Address and the liberating energy it created for all people. Tenga had to be pleased by Mr. Lincoln's efforts, and we should honor both him and this goddess today by reconsidering any prejudices that cloud the way we look at other people or situations.

One way of doing this is through visualization. Hold a handful of soil as you mentally review the last week of your life and the way you handled certain individuals or circumstances. Consider: Did you go into a meeting with negativity, anticipating the worst? Did you overlook an opportunity, or close the door on a relationship because of a bad experience in the past? These are the negative patterns that Tenga helps us to attack and transform with honest candidness (including being honest with yourself about shortcomings). You may not like what she shows you, but the results will be worth it. Tenga improves your awareness of the Goddess in all things and all people.

November 20

✳

Rights of the Child Day (*United Nations*)

STRENIA

Theme: Children; Protection

Symbols: Bay; Palm; Figs; Honey; Youthful Images

About Strenia: While this goddess's traditional festival date in Italy was January 1, she joins in our holiday observances today to extend her protective care to children. Among the Sabines and Romans, Strenia safeguarded the youth by providing health and strength. Traditional offerings for this goddess include burning bay leaves and leaving out sweet breads mixed with dates or figs.

To Do Today: On this day in 1959, Strenia was likely standing by and applauding as the United Nations adopted the Declaration of the Rights of the Child to encourage proper treatment of our youth and inspire their future. So, take time with the children in your life today. Teach them in the "way they should grow" and revel in their innocent trust and love. Invoke Strenia's blessings and health for that young one by sharing fig cookies (heck, eat a few yourself for strength!). Or, make the child a small power pouch that includes a bay leaf and a dried crumb of sweet bread. This way they can carry the goddess with them even when you're not around.

For those without children, try volunteering at a youth shelter or orphanage today. Take one of those kids out for lunch or to the zoo. Through your efforts, Strenia can gather that child in arms of warmth and comfort.

November 21

✳

Tori no Ichi (Japan)

OKAME

Themes: Luck; Kindness

Symbols: Masks; Good-luck Charms

About Okame: In Japanese art, Okame is portrayed as simple and somewhat homely, yet her domain is the beautiful energy of good fortune and kind acts. In this form, Okame gently reminds us that true beauty really does come from within. Local lore claims that any area that bears a mask of Okame's likeness is blessed with her lucky nature.

To Do Today: Late in November, just preceding the new year in Japan, this is a day for rituals to improve one's wealth and luck. Following the Japanese tradition, begin by finding any lawn rake (or broom), and attach as many personal good-luck charms to it as you can find. Take this token clockwise around your home, raking or brooming inward, to gather up Okame's fortunate energies. As you go through your house, add verbal incantations like the following:

[In the kitchen] *Okame, in my kitchen shine, so that good luck will be mine!*

[Dining room] *Okame, at this table where we eat, let good fortune take a seat!*

[Living room] *In this room where people lounge, let your fortuity come around!*

[Bathroom] *Clean negativity and problems away; let my good luck start today!*

To encourage Okame's serendipity even further, you can burn orange, rose, heather, violet, or allspice incense or potpourri as you go.

November 22

*

Sagittarius Begins (*Various Locations*)

LEUCOTHEA

Themes: Creativity; Energy; Communication; Balance; Harmony; Change

Symbols: Bow and Arrow; White Items; Milk; Seawater

About Leucothea: In Greek tradition, this woman gave birth to the centaurs and was a wet nurse to Dionysus. Her name translates as "milk-white goddess," alluding to a strong maternal nature. In later times she became a sea goddess, bearing the visage of a mermaid. Through this transformation we see the mingling of the spiritual nature (water) with that of the earth (half-human appearance) to create Sagittarius's customary energies.

To Do Today: In astrology, Sagittarius is the centurion archer who represents a harmonious mingling of physical and spiritual living. Those born under this sign tend toward idealism, upbeat outlooks, and confidence. Like Leucothea, Saggitarians seem to have a strong drive for justice, especially for those people under their care.

To consume a bit of Leucothea's maternal nature or invoke her spiritual balance in your life, make sure to include milk or milk products in your diet today. Or, wear something white to figuratively don her power.

For help with personal transformations, especially those that encourage personal comfort and tranquillity, soak in a nice, long saltwater or milk bath today. As you do, ask Leucothea to show you the right steps to take next.

November 23

Tellabration (Connecticut)

CALLIOPE

Themes: Arts; Communication; History

Symbols: Stories; Books; Pens and Pencils; Quill

About Calliope: A member of the Thracian muses, Calliope is the goddess of epic poetry and eloquence, whose symbol is that of a stylus and tablets. Greek stories claim that this goddess is the mother of all poets and musicians.

To Do Today: This national storytelling festival began in 1988 as a way of preserving and perpetuating oral traditions and the bardic art of telling "tall tales" and good stories, which Calliope inspires. Today she joins our celebration to motivate creativity in all areas of our lives, especially written and spoken words.

In today's hurry-up world we often forget how powerful a word or phrase can be. To honor this goddess, slow down a little all day long, and really consider how you're communicating your ideas. As the old saying goes, be sure your brain is in gear before shifting your tongue to high. During those moments of contemplation, Calliope will flow through you and give you the words you need.

During a break, take out a beloved book and start reading it again (*Walden* is my choice). Calliope will help you find something new and wonderful in those pages to inspire you even further in any task you undertake today. And perhaps go out and buy yourself a special pen and pencil and bless them to use for important missives.

November 24

Thanksgiving (United States)

SPES

Themes: Thankfulness; Hope; Abundance; Harvest

Symbols: A Bouquet of Flowers

About Spes: In Roman tradition, this goddess's name means "hope." She joins us today to celebrate the successful harvest and keep our hearts hopeful as the earth's plenty wanes. In art, Spes often appears as a simple bundle of flowers whose beauty inspires the most distraught of spirits.

To Do Today: Follow pilgrim tradition and set aside time today to thank the goddess for her blessings in any way that seems suited to your path and vision. For example, give Spes an offering of the first slice of holiday bread, share food with those in need, or perhaps treat the birds and squirrels in your neighborhood to some bread and nuts.

Locally we invite any friends who have no family nearby to join with us in a delightful symbolic meal. I serve round rye bread and dill dip for unity and kinship, sweet potatoes for life's sweetness and Spes's harvest energies, cranberries mixed with oranges to keep our energy and health intact, vegetables for firm foundations, and pumpkin pie with magical sigils carved in the crust for the goddess's protective spark. If you look at your own traditional menu, I'll bet you will find many other foods and beverages that have similar symbolism to bring meaning and Spes's magic to your table for this holiday. As you eat, remember to pass all the food and beverages clockwise to invoke Spes's ongoing providence.

November 29

✳

Saint Catherine of Alexandria's Day (Europe)

ARIANRHOD

Themes: Arts; Magic; Manifestation; Rebirth

Symbols: A Silver Wheel (spinning tools: shuttle, yarn)

About Arianrhod: In Welsh tradition, this is the goddess of the "silver wheel" upon which magic is braided and bound together into a tapestry of manifestation. Stories tell us that Arianrhod abides in a star where souls wait for rebirth (the wheel here becomes the wheel of life, death, and rebirth).

To Do Today: Known as Catherine of the Wheel, this saint oversees spinsters (literally and figuratively). Like Arianrhod, she is a patroness for lace makers and seamstresses. In keeping with this theme, today is an excellent time to try your hand at making a special pouch for housing some of your magical tools or trinkets. Begin with two rectangles of natural-fiber cloth one inch larger than the item you wish to house within. Put the right sides together and stitch three edges, leaving a three-quarters of an inch opening at the top for a drawstring or finished edge. Turn the pouch right side out. Repeat the goddess's name to bind Arianrhod's power in each stitch. Fold over the top hem twice so it won't unravel, and stitch that with silver thread for the goddess's protection.

If time doesn't allow for this, a favored beverage to inspire this goddess's blessings is ale or cider with an apple slice or caraway bread and tea. Pour a little of this out as a libation, then drink it fully to awaken and energize Arianrhod's magical potential within you.

November 26

☀

Gujeswari Jatra (Nepal)

GUJESWARI

Themes: Earth; Water; Abundance; Offering; Prayer

Symbol: A Bowl of Water

About Gujeswari: Gujeswari is a potent Nepalese goddess of earth and all its bounty, and today is her festival day. In many temples, the goddess's presence is represented by a simple bowl of water, the life-giving substance and purifier of body, mind, and spirit.

To Do Today: Buddhists and Hindus in this region honor the mother goddess Gujeswari today by giving her offerings, usually preceded by fasting and prayer. Follow this example, and put a bowl of fresh water on your altar or a special place where it won't be disturbed for the day. If physically feasible, abstain from eating one meal today to honor the earth and Gujeswari's goodness by returning (or preserving) some of that bounty. Otherwise, simply abstain from a favorite food for the day as a kind of sacred sacrifice.

At the end of the day, just before you go to bed, sprinkle the water from the bowl around your living space. First, go counterclockwise to banish negative energy that hinders free-flowing blessings. Then go clockwise, allowing Gujeswari's water to cleanse and renew the ambiance in every room. If you have some left over, sprinkle your pets (for health), your car (for safety in travel), and children's beds (to protect them from nightmares), and dab some on mechanical objects to keep them working smoothly.

November 27

Shalako (Southeastern United States)

MINA KOYA

Themes: Weather; Health; Ghosts; Blessing

Symbol: Salt

About Mina Koya: The salt goddess of the Pueblo Indians, Mina Koya is often venerated during autumn festivals for her power to cleanse, protect, and preserve things, including our homes and traditions. Her healing power becomes all the more important as winter's chilly hold gets stronger.

To Do Today: A New Mexican festival, Shalako is an all-night ritual of dancing and chanting to bless homes, commemorate the dead, bring good weather, and improve health for all participants. One tradition that honors Mina Koya and draws her well-being into the sacred space of home is that of noise making. Take a flat-bottomed pan and sprinkle salt on it. Bang this once in every room of the house (so some of the salt shakes off). This banishes negativity and evil, replacing it with Mina Koya's blessing. To improve the effect, chant and dance afterward, sweeping up the salt and keeping it for the weather charm that follows. Or, flush the salt down the toilet to flush out any maladies.

If it's been wet or snowy and you need a reprieve, bind a little salt in a white cloth and bury it. The weather should change temporarily soon thereafter. This bundle will also protect your home and its residents from damage by harsh weather for as long as it stays in the ground nearby.

November 28

✳

Festival of Lights (New York)

CHIU-RANG-GURU

Themes: Water; Beauty; Overcoming; Victory

Symbols: Rough Water; Light

About Chiu-rang-guru: This grouping of goddesses includes those who dwell in rapids, rough water, or waterfalls, and they can guide us through any rough waters that our lives face. Their name literally means "senders down of the current." Thanks to water spirits like these, Niagara Falls has become a favorite tourist attraction, especially during this festival.

To Do Today: This breathtaking festival takes place nearly in my backyard. At this time of the year, Niagara Falls is bedecked with hundreds of lights, including colored floodlights that adorn the falls in potent beauty, accented by these goddesses' vibrant power.

If you find yourself facing difficult times right now, know that the Chiu-rang-guru can ease the flow of problems. One way to magically mimic this is by using a freestanding Jacuzzi in the tub turned on high. Immerse yourself in this torrent, then speak the goddesses' name and turn it down slowly. When you've reached the last setting, turn off the machine and pull the plug in the tub, letting those problems literally flow down the drain. The effect of this activity can be accentuated by using a black light in the bathroom, glitter in the water, and candles. This turns your tub into a light show in which you can wrap yourself in Chiu-rang-guru's spirit and be renewed.

November 29

Stir-up Sunday (*England*)

HESTIA

Themes: Religious Devotion; Home; Wishes; Manifestation; Kinship; Unity; Beginnings

Symbols: Fire (ovens); Sparks

About Hestia: The Greek goddess of household affairs, Hestia watches over our cookery today to help manifest family unity and ensure tasty outcomes. As a hearth goddess, she provides the spiritual energy necessary to keep our faith sure and the inner fires burning bright. Greek art did not try to portray this goddess, because she was considered the beginning—the source from which all else was ignited and set in motion.

To Do Today: Getting its name from the annual Yule-pudding making that takes place in many homes around this time of year, Stir-up Sunday is also a time in the Christian Church to motivate determined faith. So why not blend the best of both worlds? Invoke Hestia's blessing in your kitchen and make some pudding for the whole family (or a gathering of friends). Have each person present stir the pudding clockwise for a few minutes as they focus on a wish. By next year at this time, the wish should manifest.

Light a candle this morning to welcome Hestia's unity and energy into your home. Or, carry matches in your pocket so the spark of this goddess can ignite in any situation where it's needed. Throughout the day, when you need more commitment to your beliefs, just light one match to invoke Hestia's aid.

November 30

※

Zibelemarit (Switzerland)

AINE

Themes: Protection; Healing; Divination; Luck; Earth; Moon

Symbols: Moon (lunar items); Silver and White Items; Meadowsweet

About Aine: This Celtic goddess of the moon shines on today's celebration, her name meaning "bright." Aine has strong connections with the land. Her blessing ensures fertile fields. She also gives luck to mortals and keeps us healthy.

To Do Today: Dating back to the 1400s, this onion festival takes place in Bern. It includes several parades with intricate mechanical figurines and a huge harvest festival with—you guessed it—tons of onions! Magically speaking, onions are closely related to Aine because of their lunar appearance. According to metaphysical traditions, carrying or growing onions grants safety and banishes negativity.

A freshly cut onion rubbed on sores, bug bites, or scratches restores Aine's healthy energy by gathering the problem and taking it away. Bury or burn this slice to dispel the problem altogether.

One great (and tasty) way to invoke Aine, improve well-being, and improve your lunar attributes is by making and eating onion soup (or any other onion dish) today. Use red, Spanish, white, and cooking onions along with chives. By heating and blending them, you mix the magic to perfection. Stir clockwise, whispering Aine's name into the soup so she abides in each vitality-laden sip.

December

In the Julian calendar, this month came tenth in succession; thus the name for December comes from *decem*, meaning "ten" (hence the name for our modern decimal system). During this month the nights continue to get longer, and the weather often turns wet and cold. Many people find themselves struggling with the blues because of the lack of sunlight. This was probably the case for our predecessors too, so its not surprising to find, scattered throughout the month, many rituals of light (like Yule), or those that give strength to the sun. These inspire extra inner light to keep things warm emotionally and physically.

Metaphysically, December is a good time to look within, meditate, and regroup before the new year. Focus on magic that purifies, heals, banishes depression, improves endurance, and increases your personal vitality. Also extend a little of this energy to the earth and sky, so that the Wheel of the Year will turn toward the light once more, and with it your spirit.

December 1

Kencha-sai (*Japan*)

UNCHI-AHCHI

Themes: Spirituality; Universal Law; Mediation

Symbols: Tea; Teapots and Cups

About Unchi-ahchi: Presiding dutifully over the family stove is this Japanese goddess, whose name means "grandmother hearth." From this position in the home she joins today's festivities to warm the tea and to mediate on our behalf with the other gods and goddesses. Afterward, she returns to our homes and lives with important insights about the meaning of sacred ritual.

To Do Today: In Japan, today is a time to go to Kyoto temple and watch or participate in the ancient tea ceremony. In this culture, each movement and ingredient in the tea ceremony represents a spiritual principle or truth—all mingled into a simple, satisfying cup. This is a lovely tradition, so share a cup of tea with a friend or family member today. Invoke Unchi-ahchi simply by lighting the stove. Use the stove to ignite a candle, and take the candle to wherever you're sitting to carry the goddess's energy to that spot. Discuss spiritual ideas, allowing this goddess to give you new insights. To increase the significance of your tea ceremony, choose the tea's flavor according to the topic of conversation or something needed in that relationship. If discussing divination or alternative health, for example, use orange or mint, respectively. To deepen love or friendship, use lemon.

December 2

♆

Pan-American Health Day (United States)

NINA

Themes: Health; Cooperation; Dreams; Magic; Mediation

Symbols: Lions; Fish; Serpent (her sacred animals)

About Nina: A very ancient mother goddess figure in Mesopotamia, Nina has many powers, including healing, herb magic, mediation, dream interpretation, and helping civilization along when needed. Today we will be focusing on her healthful attributes and knowledge of herbs to improve well-being for the winter months.

To Do Today: Pan-American Health Day focuses on worldwide cooperation in the public health field. On the home front, do everything possible to make your home and body healthy and strong. Beginning in your living space, wash the floors using sage water, and burn a sage smudge stick. This herb decreases germ infestation and is magically aligned with Nina's energy. As you go through your home, carry a small bell and add this incantation:

> Nina, come and make us well;
> banish sickness with the ringing of this bell.

Ring the bell in each room at the end of the incantation. In many religious traditions, bells are considered to scare away the evil influences that cause sickness.

To overcome a troublesome malady, put a picture of one of Nina's sacred animals under your pillow to invoke a healing dream. This tradition is very old and sometimes results in healthful energy being conveyed through your dream, or in a dream that shows you what to do for a cure.

⚜

Hungarian Wedding

BOLDOGASSZONY

Themes: Winter; Love; Romance; Relationships; Devotion; Purity; Fertility

Symbol: Milk

About Boldogasszony: This Hungarian mother and guardian goddess watches diligently over her children, wanting only the best for them, as any mother would. Her sacred beverage, milk, is also considered a suitable libation when asking for this goddess's blessing.

To Do Today: Hungarian wedding festivals often take place in winter, after the harvest season and meat preparation. The traditions here are laden with magic we can "borrow" for building strong personal relationships, asking for Boldogasszony's blessing by having a cup of milk present at any activity. For example, cutting a rope that is attached to your home symbolizes your release from the old ways and freedom to enter into a commitment. Stepping across birch wood purifies intentions and ensures a fertile, happy union.

Lighting a torch (or candle) represents vigilant devotion in a relationship. Do this at the time of your engagement, as you recite vows, or as you both enter a new residence for the first time so that commitment will stay with you. Wherever you are, eating off each other's plates and drinking from one cup deepens harmony (include a milk product like cheese). Finally, dancing with kitchen utensils ensures that the home fires will always stay warm.

Mevlana (Turkey)

ISTUSTAYA

Themes: Divination; Communication (with the divine); Destiny

Symbols: Sacred Dance; Circles; Mirror; Thread

About Istustaya: In Anatolia this goddess rules over all matters of fate and is an adept diviner, often using a mirror for descrying so she can share insights into our future. Besides this, she personally weaves the thread of life for each person born, patterning his or her destiny.

To Do Today: The Mevlana is celebrated by the Whirling Dervishes in Turkey as a ritual dance through which the devout attain oneness with the divine, often for the purpose of fortune-telling. The festival includes chanting while dancers twirl around, effectively becoming the center of a magical circle formed by their skirts. So, if you hold a ritual today, use yarn or thread to mark the sacred space, with a mirror and your preferred divinatory tool on the altar to honor Istustaya. Dance clockwise around the circle, or your home, before attempting any divinatory effort. This draws the goddess's vision into your spirit.

If you want to try mirror descrying specifically to venerate Istustaya, sit somewhere comfortable with a candle behind the mirror. Dab a little sandalwood oil on the surface, rubbing it clockwise. Let your eyes unfocus and wait to see what images appear in the reflected light and oil. These may be symbolic or literal in nature. A dream interpretation guide may help in figuring out the meaning.

December 5

♨

Walt Disney's Birthday (*United States*)

CASTALIA

Themes: Art; Creativity; Joy; Children; Inspiration

Symbols: Cartoon Characters; Fountains

About Castalia: In Greek tradition, this goddess embodies the force of artistic inspiration. Her power is so profuse that art often depicts her simply as an ever-flowing fountain from which we can drink when our motivation wanes.

To Do Today: On this day in 1901, the legendary Walt Disney was born. During his life, Disney inspired millions of children with a Castalia-rich imagination and well-beloved cartoon characters. To remember this man and uplift Castalia's childlike ability to awaken the artist within, watch a favorite Walt Disney film today, reveling in the wonder of it. Then get out and do something creative! Try drawing your own magical cartoon (this is just for you and the goddess, so don't worry about a lack of skill—the keynote today is having *fun* with your fancy).

To quaff this goddess's inspiration for any task you're undertaking, find a water fountain and drink fully of it. Visualize the water filled with a color of light that, to you, represents creativity. Also fill a small container with a secure top with some of this water and keep it with you. Carry Castalia's power into the situation in which you need inspiration. Pour a little out before your meeting, artistic effort, or speech to release her power. Or sip a bit of it to wet your whistle and renew the magic.

December 6

Kashim (Alaska)

TAKANAKAPSALUK

Themes: Providence; Purification; Strength; Thankfulness; Luck; Health

Symbols: Saltwater; Arctic Animals

About Takanakapsaluk: This Arctic sea goddess rules over the successful catching of game and over personal health. Takanakapsaluk lives far beneath the cold waters, where she also receives the spirits of the dead and cares for them.

To Do Today: Among Inuit hunters, this is the time of year when special rituals propitiate the spirits of Takanakapsaluk's animals, who give themselves for the tribe's food. Specifically, all the bladders of seals, whales, and polar bears are returned to her icy waters in thankfulness. In a similar spirit, go to any open body of water and toss in a small biodegradable offering to the goddess in thanks for your food. Consider abstaining from meat today, or from some other beloved food, as a way of showing appreciation for the goddess's bounty.

The Kashim traditionally includes ritual fire jumping and sweat baths for purification. Try this yourself by jumping a small candle (carefully, please) or taking a steamy shower (the goddess is part of that water). Additionally, any show of physical prowess today brings continued strength. So, add a little exercise to your day. Take a brisk walk, do some jumping jacks. As you do, think of Takanakapsaluk filling you with revitalizing health.

December 7

♆

La Quema del Diablo (*Guatemala*)

IX CHEBEL YAX

Themes: Protection; Banishing; Health; Providence; Home

Symbols: Lunar Emblems; Spinning Tools; Baskets

About Ix Chebel Yax: In Guatemala, this goddess bears a striking resemblance to Ix Chel (see May 7) in that she teaches spinning, weaving, and basketry to humans. More important, she is a mother figure who watches over all household concerns from the moon, her home.

To Do Today: Part of the Guatemalan advent season, this festival finds people burning bundles of garbage in ritual fires to banish the spirit of evil, negativity, and sin from their midst, especially from the home. Doing so also purifies the people, keeping them healthy and staving off hunger. Considering that winter is in full swing, this isn't a bad idea. Go through your living space and gather up any garbage (including items that have been waiting for a trip to the secondhand shop). Find one item that can be safely burned, and snip a swatch off of it. Release it to any fire source to burn away any tensions or sickness troubling your home.

Afterward, clean as much of your house or apartment as time will allow. Invoke Ix Chebel Yax's blessing by placing a spool of thread in the room where you're working (white or green thread are good choices for peace and health, respectively). Carry this spool from room to room, then put it in your pocket for the day to keep the goddess and her providence close by.

December 8

♆

Hari Kuyo (Japan)

NARU KAMI

Themes: Offerings; Excellence; Arts

Symbols: Needles; Thunder and Lightning; Trees

About Naru Kami: In Japan this goddess embodies the odd combination of weather magic and artistic inspiration. Perhaps this is how we come by the phrase "struck by lightning" to describe a flash of creativity. In local tradition, any place hit by lightning is thereafter sacred to Naru Kami. She is also the protectress of trees.

To Do Today: Participants in this festival, known as the Mass for Broken Needles, honor the ancient art of sewing by bringing broken or bent needles into temples and later consigning them to the sea with thankfulness.

We can translate this observance into a blessing for any creative tool, be it a paintbrush, clay, a musical instrument, or even a computer! Take the item and wrap it in green paper (which comes from this goddess's sacred trees). Leave it on your altar or in your workroom for the day so Naru Kami can fill it with her inspiring energy.

For those who sew, crochet, or knit, definitely take out your needles today and leave them in a special spot with an offering for the goddess, cakes or tofu being customary. At the end of the day, take these up and use them in your craft to honor Naru Kami and commemorate this holiday with your skills.

December 9

⚜

Tonatzin (Mexico)

TONATZIN

Themes: Religious Devotion; Blessing

Symbols: Soil; Light

About Tonatzin: An ancient mother figure who nurtures people and all that dwells in the land, Tonatzin is the life and light of the world. Today she joins our festival as the originator of this holiday.

To Do Today: Juan Diego, an Indian convert, was surprised when this goddess appeared to him in 1531 in an ancient site of pagan worship and requested that the temple be rebuilt. Juan Diego believed this apparition was Mary, and therefore he did as she commanded. To this day, people come here at this time of the year for the goddess's blessing.

While most of us cannot travel to Mexico just to implore Tonatzin, there is nothing that says we can't honor and invoke her at home. Light a candle or lamp and place before it a potted plant or bowl of soil. This configuration represents Tonatzin's presence in your home throughout that day. From here she can illuminate the shadows and generate the light of hope and joy for all those who live there.

Carry a seed and some soil wrapped in a green cloth with you today. Name the seed after any earth quality you want to develop in your life, such as strong foundations or emotional stability. When you get home, put the seed and soil in a planter or your garden. Tonatzin's magic is there to manifest growth for the seed and your spirit!

December 10

♆

Nobel Day (*Various Locations*)

SAMJNA

Themes: Knowledge; Learning; Excellence; Reason

Symbol: Walnut (the mind)

About Samjna: In Hindu tradition, this goddess is the source of all conscious thought and action. Her name even means "consciousness," and she is the patroness of learning, reason, logic, and knowledge.

To Do Today: Every year at this time, the Nobel Prize is awarded for mastery in chemistry, medicine, literature, and peace keeping. It is a time to revel in humankind's achievements and limitless potential for good, motivated by Samjna's gentle leadings.

To honor this goddess and the people who have achieved the pinnacle of what she represents, spend time enriching your mind today. For instance, you might read field manuals applicable to your career to advance your knowledge; watch educational television; go to a library, and perhaps donate to its shelves some old books that you no longer read; organize a local reading group for improved literary appreciation; or turn off the television and engage in intelligent conversation for mutual edification. The options here are limitless.

For a Samjna charm that improves conscious awareness and your reasoning powers, carry a shelled walnut today. The shape of this nut equates to the mind. Eat this at the end of the day to internalize her power for thoughtful actions.

December 11

♆

Blowing the Midwinter Horn (Netherlands)

SKADI

Themes: Protection; Banishing; Communication; Insight; Winter

Symbols: Snow; Wind (cold or northerly); White Crystals or Clothing

About Skadi: In Northern tradition, Skadi is the spirit of the north wind, who is blowing powerfully over the earth now. She is the goddess of winter and wears white fur, crystal armor, and a bow and arrow for hunting. Hers is the power of communication—of announcing new insights and perceptions as they awaken within.

To Do Today: In this festival, which dates back two thousand years, farmers around the country take out birchwood horns today and blow them to scare away evil influences and announce Skadi's presence. To encourage her communicative powers in your own life, stand outside and breathe deeply of a cool, northerly wind today, letting the air empower your speech. Or, carry a pumice stone wrapped in white cloth with you throughout the day (if you can't find one, cut out a white paper snowflake instead and write Skadi's name on it). This keeps the goddess with you in all your discourse.

At home, find a horn (perhaps a kazoo or noise maker). Follow the Dutch custom of blowing this once in all four cardinal directions to send protection throughout your living space. Afterward, put four white decorations (candles, stones) close to the directional points. This welcomes Skadi's insight and open discussions therein.

December 12

♆

Sada (Persia)

BAMYA

Themes: Victory; Banishing; Protection; Overcoming

Symbols: Light; Fire

About Bamya: In Zoroastrian tradition, this goddess guides the sun god Mithra's vehicle through the sky. More important, as the goddess of twilight, her presence signals the beginning of today's festival.

To Do Today: As the sun sets in Iran today, a huge bonfire will be ignited near a water source to symbolize the power of light to overcome darkness and the power of good over evil. For us this means accepting our power and potential to overcome any obstacles that life may bring in any season.

Too often our lives seem overwhelmed with obligations, and we find ourselves feeling lost in the seething sea of humanity. Bamya's counsel today is to learn how to swim in that sea by recognizing the ability of one person to truly make a difference—be it within yourself, in the life of another, in a specific situation, or in the world.

At sunset today, light an orange candle (or another one the color of twilight) and greet Bamya with this prayer:

> Lady of gentle twilight, I welcome you. As the sun
> sets on this day, let things from the past that I no
> longer need to bear also fade away. Teach me to
> leave them behind as easily as you leave behind
> the daylight. As darkness falls, grant rest to my
> unsettled spirit so that I can rise tomorrow
> renewed and whole. Bamya be with me. Amen.

December 13

⚜

Saint Lucy's Day (Sweden)

LUCINA

Themes: Banishing; Kindness; Charity; Health; Protection

Symbols: Candles (light sources)

About Lucina: Lucina means light, and judging by her description and attributes, it is very likely that this Swedish goddess was the prototype for Saint Lucy. Lucina is a mother and guardian, offering fertility, protection, and well-being. In worship, Lucina is often represented by a simple, lit candle.

To Do Today: To chase away winter's oppression and darkness, Saint Lucy's festival is one of lights and charitable acts. Saint Lucy is the patroness who protects against winter throat infections, and commemorating her (or Lucina) today keeps one healthy.

Begin the day in Swedish tradition by lighting a candle to represent the goddess's presence. After this a breakfast of coffee, saffron buns, and ginger cookies is traditional fare. Coffee provides energy to give of yourself, saffron is often used in healing spells, and ginger promotes success in all your endeavors today.

To manifest Lucina's energy and keep the goddess close by today, carry luminescent stones like moonstone or cat's eye with you, then visit hospitals or elder homes in the spirit of giving of yourself. Lucina will bless those you visit, and you, with well-being, productivity, and safety.

December 14

Soyal (Southwestern United States)

SAKWA MANA

Themes: Prayer; Communication; Cycles; Harvest; Health; Joy; Providence

Symbols: The Color Blue; Corn; Prayer Sticks; Pine

About Sakwa Mana: The Hopi Blue Corn Maiden, this goddess participates in the Soyal festival by carrying a tray of blue corn and spruce bows, both of which represent the goddess's ongoing providence, no matter the season.

To Do Today: The Hopi gather in kivas today to comfort and bring happiness to the old year so that the new one will be filled with earth's and Sakwa Mana's bounty. Several customary activities today are fun to try. First, offer the gift of a feather to a friend. This ensures them of a new year filled with health and joy. To invoke Sakwa Mana's blessing on the gift, pack it with a few pine needles. Over time, the feather will absorb the goddess's aroma and disperse her power each time it's fanned in ritual.

Making a sun shield brings victory in your life over any darkness holding you back. To create a simple one, cut out a round piece of paper and decorate it with your creative vision of the sun. Either keep this with you or put it in a predominant spot in your home. When success comes, burn the paper with a thankful heart.

Finally, find a fallen pine twig outside and attach a small feather to it. This represents both the goddess and your wish for a gentle voice in prayer.

December 15

♆

Faunalia (Rome)

FAUNA

Themes: Fertility; Nature; Divination

Symbols: All Forest Items

About Fauna: In Roman mythology, Fauna is the consort to Faunus, whom this date venerates. With Faunus, she protects the woodlands and plants that live there. While her role in stories seems minor, Fauna's power lives on in botanical terminology, her name having been given to vegetation.

To Do Today: Faunus was a woodland god like Pan, who sends messages through the forests for those who know nature's omens and signs. If at all possible, go to a natural location today (even a park or a quiet tree in your neighborhood will do) with a small libation of wine or milk, both of which are customary. Pour this on the ground, focusing on your intention to learn more about nature's messages to us. Then spend at least twenty minutes observing. Take notes as you do. Do the trees' leaves seem to talk? Do they move in a specific way? Are birds taking flight? Where do they go? Do any drop feathers on the ground? Do any animals appear unexpectedly? If so, what does the creature do, and where does it go? All of these things, and other similar experiences, can carry a sign meant to help you today or in the days ahead. To interpret what you see, consult any good folklore or superstition collection, like my book *Victorian Grimoire*, or another of my books, *Futuretelling*, which discusses natural harbingers.

December 16

♆

Saint Hildegard Dies (Germany)

HEXE

Themes: Health; Banishing; Magic

Symbols: Healing Herbs and Charms

About Hexe: This ancient Germanic witch's goddess rules over health, banishing curses, and teaching people the effective use of spells, charms, and other mystical procedures for improving well-being. Thus we come by the old phrase "hex doctor."

To Do Today: Living in the 1100s, Saint Hildegard was a renowned Benedictine nun living in Bingen and ministering to people with herbal preparations received in visions. Many of these had magical overtones, perhaps guided by Hexe's influence. In any case, today's theme is learning the art of weaving "Hexes" for physical, mental, and spiritual health.

On the physical level, take a natural object like a cut potato and rub it against an inflicted area. Bury the potato to "bury" the malady and decompose it. Or carry a jet stone to absorb the problem, then cleanse the rock in saltwater to wash the bad energy away. For mental well-being, enjoy a soothing cup of mint tea stirred counterclockwise so tensions and negativity will wane. Or, carry a fluorite stone with you throughout the day to strengthen your mental powers. For spiritual health, sprinkle nutmeg-laden water clockwise throughout your aura to empower your psychic self. Or, carry a lapis or amethyst stone to draw goddess-centered thinking and action into your day.

December 17

Hanukkah (Jewish)

SEPHIRA

Themes: Miracles; Victory; Success; Overcoming

Symbol: Light

About Sephira: This ancient Cabalistic goddess embodies divine light—the active, energetic power that flows through the Universe in all directions. Thus, it is no coincidence that the ten spheres on the Tree of Life are called Sephirah, for this goddess guides our way and path with her radiance.

To Do Today: This festival commemorates the rebellion of the Jews against the Syrians, in which a miracle took place. A small bottle of oil stayed lit for eight days, keeping the temple consecrated until more oil could be brought.

Since Sephira is the light of miracles, today's a good time to focus on seemingly impossible goals or situations that you may have set aside or left behind in discouragement. Revisit those dreams; reconsider the logistics of those circumstances. If there is a better way to approach things, Sephira will illuminate that path or options for you in your meditations.

Make sure to turn on light sources today, and open curtains to let natural light into your home. Symbolically, this welcomes Sephira's active power into your spiritual life and quest. Also consider following with Jewish tradition and giving coins to friends or family. These tokens draw financial security. Or, eat potato pancakes for providence.

December 18

Mesa de Gallo (*Philippines*)

IKAPATI

Themes: Prayer; Harvest; Thanksgiving; Luck; Protection; Banishing; Health; Energy; Providence

Symbols: Harvested Foods

About Ikapati: In the language of the Philippines, this goddess's name literally means "giver of food," making her the provider of today's feast! She diligently promotes abundance of fields and crops, and she protects farm animals from disease.

To Do Today: When the sun begins to rise today, people take to the streets with all manner of noise makers to invoke Ikapati's protection and to banish evil influences that might hinder next year's crops. Effectively, even in more Christianized forms, this is a lavish harvest festival in which Filipinos thank the divine for their fortune and food, which is always a worthy endeavor.

We can join the festivities today by eating the customary rice cakes to internalize Ikapati's providence and drinking ginger tea for health and energy. It is traditional during this meal to invite the goddess to join you at the table. Just leave her a plate and cup filled with a portion of whatever you have. Tonight, consign this offering to the earth, where Ikapati dwells (or to your compost heap), and whisper a wish for improved luck to the soil. The goddess will then accept the gift and turn it into positive energy for the planet and your life.

December 19

Pongol (India)

MAKARA SANKRANTI

Themes: Blessing; Offering; Mediation; Earth; Sun; Thankfulness; Love, Passion; Abundance

Symbols: Water; Light; Soil; Caves

About Makara Sankranti: This is Makara Sankranti's festival day. After many months of slumber, this mother goddess awakens from the earth's womb to restore love, abundance, and passion in our lives through sacred rituals, over which she presides.

To Do Today: Pongol is a three-day harvest celebration with several "borrowable" traditions that venerate both Makara Sankranti and the holiday. Begin with a ritual cleansing and blessings for your home in any manner suited to your tradition. This keeps relationships strong and banishes sickness. Bathing sacred cows today also brings prosperity. This might translate into washing the image of a cow, your images of the goddess, or even a special coin to improve financial stability.

In terms of an offering for the goddess, sweet rice is customary, followed by an afternoon of kite flying so that the burdens in your life will become as light as the wind! For people in four-season climates, it might be too cold for kite flying today, so just release a little of the goddess's soil to the wind and ask her to take your problems away, replacing them with solid relationships and success.

December 20

Chinese Winter Solstice (*China*)

XI HOU

Themes: Kinship; Longevity; Unity; Divination; Weather

Symbols: Sunlight; Gold Dragons

About Xi Hou: As the Chinese mother of the sun, this goddess joins our festivities today to celebrate her child's rebirth. Each morning, Xi Hou diligently bathes one of ten suns in the lake of creation so it can shine in purity, and then she puts it on top of the trees, where it's received by a dragon chariot that moves the sun across the sky.

To Do Today: Consider following Chinese custom, and rejoice in the solstice by gathering in the kitchen with your housemates and leaving offerings of chopsticks, oranges, incense, and candles for unity and long life for all those gathered. Open a curtain to let the sunlight flood in, then thank Xi Hou for her child and its warmth. Also, at some point during the day, enjoy some Oriental-style dumplings (dim sum) for kinship.

Among the favorite activities today are weather prophecies. Go outside and see what direction the wind is coming from. An east wind portends trouble, west winds indicate the ripening of an effort or a good grain crop, south winds counsel watching your money, as the harvest will be poor (don't invest in crop shares!), and north winds foretell bounty. Red clouds reveal that your personal energy will wane and droughts may follow, black clouds predict floods, yellow clouds precede prosperity and abundant crops, and white clouds reveal arguments or wars.

Capricorn Begins (*Various Locations*)

AMALTHEIA

Themes: Success; Humor; Reason; Devotion; Providence

Symbols: Goat; Cornucopia; Stars

About Amaltheia: In Greek mythology, this she-goat goddess nourished Zeus as an infant. In later years, Zeus broke off one of her horns, which became the cornucopia, providing sustenance for all earth's creatures. For her diligence and service, Amaltheia was transformed into the constellation Capricorn, where she remains.

To Do Today: This astrological sign begins on the first day of winter with the power of logic and reason to guide action, balanced by a keen sense of humor when the going gets tough. Those born under this sign strive tenaciously for success, like the stubborn goat they are.

To improve your personal tenacity, make a paper horn filled with fruit. From now until the end of the year, eat a piece of fruit each day named after the area of your life in which you need Amaltheia's diligence. Take that energy with you each day so that by the end of the year you will achieve success. Other ways of emphasizing Amaltheia's power include keeping the image of a goat (perhaps cut out of a magazine, or one made of stone) on your altar or in another place of honor today, carrying fortitude-inspiring herbs like gingerroot and carnation, or tucking in your pocket for the day stones that inspire victory (like marble).

December 22

⚕

Winter Solstice (*Various Locations*)

CAILLEACH BHEUR

Themes: Balance; Cycles; Rebirth; Overcoming; Winter

Symbols: Snow; Blue Items

About Cailleach Bheur: In Scottish tradition, this is a blue-faced crone goddess who blusters with power throughout the winter months. She brings the snow and cold until the wheel of time turns toward spring on Beltane (May Day).

To Do Today: Just as darkness seems to be winning, the Crone goddess stirs in the earth's womb and inspires hope. She knows that the time for her rebirth as a young woman will come in spring, when she will fertilize the earth. For now, however, the first step is renewing the sun, whose light will begin to get stronger.

Since this goddess is one of cold honesty, wear something blue today to encourage personal reserve, control, and truth with yourself throughout the day.

In keeping with the themes of this celebration, try this mini-ritual: In the morning, cover your altar or a table with a yellow cloth (maybe a napkin or placemat) to represent the sun. Place a blue candle in a central location on the table, along with a bowl of snow to represent Cailleach Bheur and winter. As the candle burns with the light of the sun, the wax shrinks and this goddess's snows melt, giving way once more to the power of warmth and light. Keep the remnant wax and remelt it for any spells in which you need a cooler head. Pour the water from the snow outside to rejoin the goddess.

December 23

Larentalia (Rome)

LARUNDA

Themes: Earth; Home; Ghosts

Symbols: Stove or Oven; Soil or Clay

About Larunda: Lara is one of the Roman goddesses of earth and the home. She is also the mother and guardian to ghosts, or *lares*, who reside in the hearth and protect the family. Traditionally, today is her festival day.

To Do Today: In Rome, this day was a time to say prayers for the dead and the nation, as well as to bring joy to one's home. In keeping with this tradition, convey words like these to Larunda:

> *Larunda, hear my words. Bless the spirits of those*
> *who have gone on before me, and grant them*
> *serenity. Bless also my nation, that it may know*
> *peace and prosperity this year and always. Finally,*
> *bless my home with your happiness, prosperity,*
> *and love. Let all who visit or dwell within feel*
> *your presence and protection surrounding them.*
> *Thank you for these blessings. Amen.*

To invoke both Larunda's and the *lares*' blessing on your residence, leave a small jar of soil somewhere near your oven, microwave, toaster, or heater, and say,

> *Larunda, lares, this house bless, with your warmth and gentleness.*

Whenever tensions in the house reach a boiling point, take a pinch of the soil outside and dispose of it. This releases the magic and symbolically gets rid of the problems. Don't look back.

December 24

♆

Mother Night (*Europe*)

E G U S K I

Themes: Femininity; Birth; Renewal

Symbols: Dawn; Daylight

About Eguski: In Basque tradition, this daughter of the earth is the solar disk and the eye of God, being beautiful, warm, and welcoming. Eguski continues to embrace her mother in golden arms each day, gathering us in the glow.

To Do Today: The night before Christmas was Mother Night, when the goddess prepares once more to give birth to Eguski and growing daylight. It is traditionally a time to enjoy the goddess's energy for personal renewal and to show appreciation to mothers everywhere with their life-giving power. Take a moment out of your day to call your mom and say thanks—thanks for giving you life, for nurturing you, for passing on family traditions, for the important lessons she taught. Also take a moment to thank Eguski for her blessings in some way that suits your vision and path. Pray, chant, sing, meditate, light a candle. Ask her for another year filled with goddess magic and miracles!

To encourage Eguski's renewal and warmth every day, rise early this morning and wait for sunrise. As the first beams of light caress the horizon, open your arms and hug the goddess. Feel the energy and power in those rays to transform and overcome anything you may face. Gather the goddess into your heart for now and always.

December 25

🕎

Christmas/Yule (*Various Locations*)

HERTHA

Themes: Rebirth; Kinship; Health; Longevity; Tradition

Symbols: Dormant Trees; Snow

About Hertha: In ancient times, on this day people venerated Hertha, the Teutonic goddess of fertility, domesticated animals, magic, and nature. In Germanic tradition, Hertha descended through the smoke of any fire today and brought gifts, much like an early Santa Claus figure (giving her solar associations, too). Her connection to nature has survived in the name for our planet: earth.

To Do Today: Yule takes its designation from a Gaelic word meaning "wheel," representing the turning of time's wheel back toward the sun. In early times, this festival included parties for various sun gods and goddesses; it eventually was translated into the celebration of Christ's birth. Any light source or burning incense can symbolize Hertha's presence today. Besides this, look to the world's traditions for magical ways of making your celebration special. For example, Swedes eat a rice pudding with one lucky almond; whoever gets the nut receives good fortune. Russians toss grain into people's homes for providence as they carol. Armenians make a wish on the Yule log when it's ignited and sometimes make divinations by the cinder patterns made afterward. Bohemians cut apples in half. If there's a perfect star in the center and it has plump seeds, it portends joy and good health. Finally, kiss someone under the mistletoe for a long, happy relationship.

December 26

⚕

Boxing Day (*Various Locations*)

PANDORA

Themes: Hope; Prosperity; Wishes

Symbols: Boxes

About Pandora: Unlike the later associations with Pandora, this goddess's name means "all-giver" or "sender of gifts." And even when the evils of the world threaten, let us not forget that Pandora's box still, and always, holds hope.

To Do Today: Unlike modern connotations of putting away boxes, the name for this holiday came from the old custom of tradespeople and servants carrying boxes today to receive gratuities. This is how we come by the tradition of Christmas bonuses!

In keeping with this tradition, with a uniquely magical twist, make a special wish box for yourself or your family today. Begin with any box that has a good lid. Fill it with special cloth and trinkets that represent your goal(s). Also place therein one object, herb, or stone to represent hope (basil and amethyst are two good choices). Decorate the exterior lavishly and leave it in a special place with a candle that you can light briefly each day. When a wish is fulfilled, carry the corresponding token to keep that energy with you or give it to someone who needs that specific vibration in their life.

The token for hope, however, in the tradition of Pandora, never leaves the box, so that hope will always be part of your home.

December 27

☷

Kwanza (African-American)

ODUDUA

Themes: Kinship; Unity; Devotion; Creativity; Community; Love; Fertility

Symbols: Black Items

About Odudua: In the beginning, Odudua created the earth and its people. In Yoruban tradition, she presides over all matters of fertility, love, and community. Her sacred color is black.

To Do Today: This African American festival celebrates family unity and the black culture. It is also a harvest festival whose name means "first fruits." Every day of the celebration focuses on important themes, including Odudua's harmony, determination, community responsibility, purpose, creativity, and faith.

One lovely tradition easily adapted is that of candle lighting. Each day of the festival, light one red, green, or black candle (the colors of Africa). Name the candle after one of Odudua's attributes you wish to develop (try to choose the color that most closely corresponds to your goal). Igniting it gives energy and visual manifestation to that principle. Also try to keep one black candle lit (in a safe container) to honor the goddess's presence during this time.

To inspire Odudua's peaceful love in your heart and life today, wear something black. This will absorb the negativity around you and put it to rest.

December 28

Feast of Fools (Europe)

THALIA

Themes: Humor; Festivity; Recreation

Symbols: Party Decorations

About Thalia: Among the Greek muses, Thalia is the goddess of festivity and humor. She inspires today's celebration with unbridled revelry and joyfulness to round out year on an upbeat, playful note.

To Do Today: During the Middle Ages, around this time of year, a mock religious ritual took place, much like the impious Saturnalia. Normal roles were often reversed, and reverence went by the wayside, replaced by fun and pleasure. I see no reason not to follow the example of our ancestors and give ourselves time to frolic a bit today. Do something that energizes you, inspires you, or makes you laugh out loud. For example, throw yourself a party complete with silly decorations and hats. Watch your favorite comedy flicks with a friend. Or, go out dancing, play video games, socialize with folks who make you feel good, and generally let Thalia live through (and in) your pleasure.

To keep Thalia's playful, enthusiastic energy with you, bless an amethyst (for joy and luck), saying,

> *Thalia, inspire my humor and muse;*
> *throughout my life, joy diffuse.*

Carry this with you anytime you feel your sense of humor waning.

December 29

♆

Ginem (Malay)

TAKEL

Themes: Banishing; Health; Protection; Harvest; Thankfulness; Kinship

Symbols: Root Crops

About Takel: In Malay, this goddess supports the heavens with a pillar from the center of her creation, the earth. Takel is the supreme goddess of agriculture and its abundance. She comes to us at the end of the old year to keep us healthy and well provided for in the new.

To Do Today: Each December, people in Malay give thanks to the spirits for Takel's abundance and the success of families, and they pray for ongoing health, protection, and victory over any evils they may face. It is an example worth considering. Follow Malaysian custom and consume Takel's bounty today through luscious feasts. As you take the first slice or serving of any entrée, set it aside for the goddess. Don't forget to include root crops, especially yams or sweet potatoes, in your feast today. These are some of Takel's sacred foods, and they will fill your heart with an abundance of love.

Later, after dinner has settled, dance in a joyful manner, being thankful for what you have instead of worrying about what you don't. Takel will join you in that dance, and the energy it generates will empower the next year with health, prosperity, and unity.

December 30

✡

Halcyon Days (Greece)

IRIS

Themes: Winter; Peace; Protection; Air; Mediation; Promises; Beginnings

Symbols: Rainbow; Water

About Iris: This Greek messenger to the gods traverses between the earth and heavens, appearing as a winged maiden on a shining, hopeful rainbow. In this form she represents the calm after the storm—the end of the year's activities and the advent of a new beginning. Traditional offerings to her include figs, cakes, wheat, and honey. In some stories it was Iris's job to gather water from the underworld for use in taking sacred oaths.

To Do Today: The word *halcyon* comes from a legendary bird that builds its nest on the ocean in the winter, sedating the winds with its song to safeguard its young. Thus, the week before and after the winter solstice are said to bear both the halcyon's and Iris's calm ambiance and hopeful demeanor.

To inspire an improved outlook, find a rainbow sun catcher and put it in a window today so that Iris's radiance can fill your home. Get an extra one for your car (or maybe a rainbow-colored air freshener), so you can keep that energy with you throughout the day.

For another aromatic approach, open a window briefly today and let Iris fly in on wings of change and refreshment. Burn some violet or lavender incense as you do. These two aromatics accentuate this goddess's vibrations.

December 31

Hekate's Day (Greece/Rome)

HEKATE

Themes: Moon; Beginnings; Magic

Symbols: Serpent, Horse or Dog (her sacred animals); Light (specifically a torch); Myrrh; Silver; Moonstone

About Hekate: This Greco-Roman goddess rules the moon and opportunities. Tonight she opens the path through which the old year departs and the new enters. People customarily worship Hekate at crossroads, where worlds meet, which may be why she became a witch's goddess. On this, her festival day, she bears a torch, lighting the way to the future.

To Do Today: At the eve of a new year, take a moment and pat yourself on the back for a full year of goddess-centered thinking and action. Note your achievements, and thank Hekate for helping you find the way when your vision seemed clouded. An additional benefit here is that speaking this goddess's name today banishes unwanted ghosts, including those figurative ghosts of past negative experiences. Let Hekate take those burdens so your new year will begin without anything holding you back.

To accent this goddess's powers in your life throughout your celebrations today, wear white or silver items, and light a white candle in her honor. For a token that will emphasize Hekate's magic and lunar energies whenever you need them, bless a moonstone, saying,

> *Hekate, fill this silver stone;*
> *keep your magic with me where'er I roam.*

Carry this, keeping the goddess close to your heart and spirit. Happy New Year!

Last Words

Every attempt has been made to put the holidays and celebrations throughout these pages into their proper cultural context and to honor them in that setting. Each civilization has special customs and traditions that we cannot fully understand, because we were not, or are not, there. Nonetheless, if we approach each tradition with the same respect we have for our own, our understanding of the world and of its diversity and similarities will be enriched. It is my hope that by this point in the book you've found your global vision broadened and the Goddess's energy growing steadily within. Bright Blessings.

—Trish

Selected Bibliography

For those readers who would like to learn more about the world's festivals, holidays, and/or goddesses, these reference books will get you started. Hundreds of resources were used in assembling these pages, but these twenty-three represent the most informative core texts.

Ann, Martha, and Dorothy Myers Imel. *Goddesses in World Mythology.* New York: Oxford University Press, 1995.

Bonheim, Jalaja, ed. *Goddess.* New York: Stewart, Tabori, & Chang, 1997.

Bruce-Mitford, Miranda. *The Illustrated Book of Signs and Symbols.* London: DK Publishing, 1996.

Budapest, Z. *The Grandmother of Time.* San Francisco: Harper & Row, 1989.

Conway, D. J. *Ancient Shining Ones.* St. Paul, MN: Llewellyn Publications, 1993.

Farrar, Janet, and Stewart Farrar. *The Witch's Goddess.* Custer, WA: Phoenix, 1987.

Flaherty, Thomas, ed. *The Mystic Year.* Richmond, VA: Time-Life Books, 1992.

Gregory, Ruth. *Anniversaries and Holidays.* Chicago: American Library Association, 1983.

Henderson, Helene, and Sue Ellen Thompson, eds. *Holidays, Festivals, and Celebrations of the World Dictionary.* Detroit: Omnigraphics, 1997.

Hutchison, Ruth, and Ruth Adams. *Every Day's a Holiday.* New York: Harper & Brothers, 1951.

Jordan, Michael. *Encyclopedia of Gods*. New York: Facts on File, 1993.

Leach, Maria, ed. *Standard Dictionary of Folklore, Mythology, and Legend*. San Francisco: Harper & Row, 1984.

Leach, Marjorie. *Guide to the Gods*. Santa Barbara, CA: ABC-Clio, 1992.

Lurker, Manfred. *Dictionary of Gods and Goddesses, Devils and Demons*. New York: Routledge & Kegan Paul, 1995.

Monaghan, Patricia. *Goddesses & Heroines*. St. Paul, MN: Llewellyn Publications, 1993.

Motz, Lotte. *Faces of the Goddess*. New York: Oxford University Press, 1997.

Rufus, Anneli. *The World Holiday Book*. San Francisco: HarperSanFrancisco, 1994.

Spicer, Dorothy. *Book of Festivals*. Detroit: Gale Research Co., 1969.

Stone, Merlin. *Ancient Mirrors of Womanhood*. Boston: Beacon Press, 1979.

Telesco, Patricia. *Victorian Grimoire*. St. Paul, MN: Llewellyn Publications, 1995.

——. *Futuretelling*. Freedom, CA: Crossing Press, 1998.

——. *Language of Dreams*. Freedom, CA: Crossing Press, 1997.

Walker, Barbara. *Woman's Dictionary of Symbols and Sacred Objects*. San Francisco: Harper & Row, 1988.

Goddess Index

Author's note: The inclusion or exclusion of specific goddesses in this book is no indication that one is "better" than another. There are literally thousands of profound, life-changing goddesses from which to choose. This book represents but a small variety from around the world whose attributes accented a day's or seasons's energies. For more insight into world gods and goddesses, and their specific histories and characteristics, refer to the selected bibliography.

GODDESS INDEX	DATE	GODDESS INDEX	DATE
Maid Marian (England)	September 4	Nemetona (Great Britain/Germany)	July 11
Makara Sankranti (India)	December 19	Nephthys (Egypt)	November 2
		Nepthys (Egypt)	September 13
Mala Laith (Scotland)	July 5	Nerthus (Germany)	March 13
Malkuth (Israel)	September 16	Nicneven (Scotland)	October 31
Mama Kilya (Peru)	September 20	Nina (Mesopotamia)	December 2
Mary (Various)	May 13	Ningal (Mesopotamia)	September 21
Marzenna (Poland)	March 23	Nisaba (Mesopotamia)	November 1
Matariki (Polynesia)	November 18	Niskai (W. Europe)	September 29
Mati-Syra-Zemlya (Russia)	April 27	Nokomis (Algonquin)	January 24
		Nossa Senhora dos Milagres (Calif.)	September 8
Matrona (Germany)	September 10		
Mawu (Africa)	April 26	Nugua (China)	June 8
Meditrina (Rome)	July 16	Nu Kwa (China)	February 13
Meme (Uganda)	October 21	Nungeena (Australia)	January 18
Meng Jiangnu (China)	September 12	Nut (Egypt)	March 27
Mielikki (Finland)	January 13	Nuvak'chin'mana (Native American)	July 27
Mina Koya (Native American)	November 27	Oba (Santaria/Nigeria)	February 26
Minerva (Rome)	February 23	Odudua (Nigeria)	December 27
Minne (Germany)	July 14	Okame (Japan)	November 21
Mnemosyne (Greece)	June 14	Oki Tsu Hime (Japan)	November 8
Mother of All Eagles (Native American)	June 20	Old Woman of the Sea (Native American)	July 28
Mother of 10,000 Things (Indo-China)	January 25	Olwen (Wales)	August 19
		Oniata (Iroquois)	February 20
Mujaji (Africa)	March 29	Oonagh (Ireland)	November 11
Nakisawame-no-Mikoto (Japan)	August 6	Ops (Italy)	August 25
		oShion (Europe)	July 12
Nantosuelta (Gaul)	February 11	Oshun (Nigeria)	January 21
Narucnici (Bulgaria)	July 31	Ostara (Germany)	March 17
Naru Kami (Japan)	December 8	Oya (Nigeria)	January 20
Nat (Scandinavia)	October 17	Pandora (Greece)	December 26
Nejma (Morocco)	May 17	Papa (Polynesia)	September 19

Topical Index

As mentioned in the introduction, this list can help you find entries that pertain to personal needs and goals. Review the spells, activities, and goddesses for empowering that aim, then decide which approach and goddess is most meaningful to you. After that, the magic's up to you!

ABUNDANCE: 1/28; 2/2; 2/3; 2/11; 2/13; 3/1; 4/11; 4/26; 5/12; 6/26; 6/29; 7/12; 8/2; 8/5; 8/17; 8/21; 8/29; 9/4; 9/10; 9/19; 9/21; 9/22; 10/1; 10/6; 10/15; 10/26; 11/6; 11/9; 11/13; 11/15; 11/16; 11/24; 11/26; 12/19

AIR: 3/24; 3/27; 4/29; 6/20; 10/8; 12/30

ANIMALS: 1/15; 5/11; 6/13; 8/24; 10/4; 11/12

ART: 2/8; 2/19; 2/27; 3/7; 3/21; 4/17; 4/23; 5/19; 5/21; 6/14; 6/25; 7/7; 7/13; 7/28; 8/19; 9/17; 9/24; 11/23; 11/25; 12/5; 12/8

AUTUMN: 8/29; 9/10; 9/22; 9/30; 11/5

BALANCE: 3/4; 3/22; 3/29; 6/8; 7/4; 8/23; 9/16; 9/22; 9/23; 10/24; 11/7; 11/19; 11/22; 12/22

BANISHING: 2/15; 3/4; 6/15; 7/8; 8/4; 9/6; 10/7; 10/18; 10/29; 11/3; 12/7; 12/11; 12/12; 12/13; 12/16; 12/18; 12/29

BEAUTY: 1/2; 1/8; 3/16; 3/22; 4/8; 4/17; 4/28; 5/2; 5/26; 6/4; 6/17; 7/17; 7/18; 8/11; 9/4; 9/17; 10/5; 10/28; 10/29; 11/8; 11/28

BEGINNINGS: 1/1; 2/10; 2/28; 3/24; 6/19; 6/29; 9/11; 11/16; 11/29; 12/30; 12/31

BIRTH: 1/8; 1/14; 3/26; 4/26; 7/30; 10/8; 12/24

BLESSING: 1/22; 3/1; 3/5; 4/3; 5/2; 5/3; 5/14; 5/18; 5/25; 5/26; 5/27; 6/12; 7/19; 7/27; 10/7; 11/15; 11/27; 12/9; 12/19

CHANGE: 1/4; 1/13; 2/24; 3/9; 3/23; 4/2; 5/25; 6/1; 6/11; 7/30; 8/27; 10/3; 11/22

CHARITY: 4/8; 4/13; 6/7; 7/18; 8/27; 10/16; 10/25; 11/6; 11/14; 12/13

SPIRITUALITY: 2/22; 3/3; 3/12; 3/20; 4/2; 6/17; 7/8; 7/30; 7/31; 8/26; 9/3; 10/1; 12/1

SPORTS: 2/20; 6/28; 7/13; 7/15; 7/24; 10/20; 11/13

SPRING: 2/3; 2/7; 3/11; 3/13; 3/16; 3/19; 3/23; 4/2; 4/25; 4/28; 4/30; 9/20

STRENGTH: 2/25; 3/25; 4/21; 5/23; 7/2; 7/13; 7/23; 7/24; 10/6; 12/6

SUCCESS: 2/16; 3/12; 4/11; 5/22; 9/29; 10/12; 10/25; 12/17; 12/21

SUMMER: 5/2; 5/23; 7/1; 8/29; 11/3

SUN: 4/23; 4/30; 5/3; 5/13; 5/14; 5/15; 5/27; 6/16; 6/22; 6/27; 7/23; 8/19; 9/20; 12/19

THANKFULNESS: 4/19; 6/26; 7/18; 8/31; 9/19; 9/22; 10/13; 10/15; 11/6; 11/14; 11/24; 12/6; 12/19; 12/29

THEFT: 4/20; 6/27

TIME: 3/9; 5/2; 5/30; 6/2; 7/1; 7/21; 7/29; 8/7; 8/11; 8/13; 9/1; 9/20; 9/29

TRADITION: 1/20; 1/26; 2/19; 2/27; 2/28; 3/7; 5/3; 6/10; 6/11; 6/25; 7/6; 7/13; 7/24; 8/17; 9/27; 10/5; 12/25

TRAVEL: 3/31; 5/14; 6/28; 7/12; 10/12

TRUTH: 4/15; 5/25; 6/6; 6/27; 9/3; 9/28

UNITY: 2/22; 3/3; 3/5; 5/6; 5/7; 5/28; 6/11; 7/5; 7/14; 7/19; 8/9; 8/17; 8/20; 9/1; 9/12; 10/1; 10/4; 10/24; 11/29; 12/20; 12/27

UNIVERSAL LAW: 4/26; 5/25; 6/19; 7/4; 7/8; 8/20; 10/1; 10/14; 10/20; 11/1; 12/1

VICTORY: 2/16; 3/25; 4/4; 5/22; 5/23; 5/29; 6/15; 7/10; 7/13; 11/5; 11/8; 12/12; 12/17

WATER: 3/31; 4/7; 4/9; 4/18; 5/27; 6/7; 7/25; 7/28; 8/5; 8/21; 8/23; 9/1; 9/21; 10/13; 11/9; 11/26; 11/28

WEALTH: 4/11; 4/14; 7/12; 7/17; 8/2; 8/25; 8/26; 8/28; 9/30; 10/19; 10/28; 11/9; 11/16

WEATHER: 2/2; 2/7; 2/12; 2/27; 3/11; 3/23; 3/29; 4/9; 5/2; 5/5; 5/7; 5/10; 6/17; 6/23; 7/27; 8/12; 9/19; 9/26; 11/3; 11/27; 12/20

WINTER: 3/23; 4/30; 7/27; 10/31; 11/3; 12/3; 12/11; 12/22; 12/30

WISDOM: 1/5; 1/17; 1/26; 1/31; 7/5; 7/8; 9/14; 9/22; 10/9

WISHES: 3/16; 3/24; 4/3; 4/6; 4/29; 5/1; 5/26; 5/27; 7/11; 7/26; 8/11; 9/8; 10/13; 11/9; 11/29; 12/26

WORK: 1/7; 4/21; 7/12; 9/5

YOUTHFULNESS: 1/6; 3/2; 3/16; 4/1; 4/6; 8/30; 9/4; 10/10